A Murder in West Covina

Chronicle of the Finch-Tregoff Case

by

James L. Jones, M.D.

Edited by
Lillian Biermann Wehmeyer, Ph.D.

Library of Congress Cataloging in Publication Data
Jones, James A Murder in West Covina
1. Title

Library of Congress Catalog Card Number: 93-72153

ISBN: 978-0-615-48100-5

Printed in the United States of America

1 2 3 4 5 6 7 8 9 10

First Paperback Edition

Visit AMurderinWestCovina.com

FOREWORD

Reading the book *A Murder in West Covina* was not easy for me. When I came to the part of Dr. Finch's testimony, I had to pause to the next day. But this time I am not alone as I relive this story; I have James L. Jones, M.D., by my side, a fellow human being.

In a way, I almost knew that someday someone was going to put all the material together and write a documentary of the Finch-Tregoff murder trials. I am glad that it was James L. Jones who did become the author to link the events together and make us understand a little better. He has succeeded in putting all material together with a tasteful mix of facts and interviews with people that remembered the event from thirty-five years ago. He has managed to recreate the atmosphere that surrounded the three trials. It makes me feel like he was there with us.

He has done the difficult part, to pull out the most vital parts of the trials. I would add that he has given the case a "soul."

Today we know a lot more about the effects that experiences like this event have on people like myself, and we deal with the effects of the trauma more effectively. For example, I know that victims are not separated from the crime scene at such an early stage, as I was, and are given time to adjust.

You need each other very much when you experience death and lose someone you love. We all have experiences, bad and good, that form our lives. This event is part of my life, and it is hard to say in what way it affected me. I will never forget this experience, maybe because violence cannot be rationalized.

This documentary also shows how many human lives can be affected by one single person. There is always a reason or explanation to why we act the way we do. We should never give up searching for the truth, the whole truth.

But if one eventually does tell the truth, that must not mean that he is excused from taking the responsibility for his actions. Will Dr. Finch take the truth with him when he one day leaves this earth, or will he tell it before? For me, this case is not finished until I know.

Marie Anne Lidholm
March 8, 1993

ACKNOWLEDGMENTS

Many thanks to the journalists and other observers who witnessed and memorialized the events dramatized in this chronicle, and to the librarians and custodians who tended their records over the years.

Thanks to Callie Linder and the rest of my reading committee and to Tony and Gina Capobianco, for haunting libraries with notable dedication.

Mostly, thanks to the people of West Covina for sharing their story.

DISCLAIMER

This chronicle of the Finch-Tregoff case is a dramatization based on facts obtained from personal interviews, news media records, and court documents. The only name changed is that of the family later purchasing the Finch residence; all other characters are real and were famous persons, elected or appointed public employees, persons who knowingly made statements of public record, those explicitly releasing their names for use, or those allowing interviews under generally accepted rules of investigative journalism.

This portrayal of facts is for strictly literary purposes and is not intended to defame, libel, or otherwise injure any person's character. Persons made famous by the events studied herein are considered to have possibly regained their legal right to privacy and no reference is made to their current lives.

A Murder
in West Covina

Chronicle of the Finch-Tregoff Case

TABLE OF CONTENTS

To those victims of domestic violence unable to tell their story. May the past whisper for them.

prologue:

The Cardinal

EVA REED SETTLED comfortably on the grass in front of her school, leaning back onto a young elm tree and looking through her yearbook, *The Cardinal*. She was seventeen years old and had just finished her junior year. Covina High School had less than one hundred fifty students. Most had signed, usually adding a message hinting at hopes for Eva or dreams for themselves.

Were her closer friends included? "Missing a couple," she noted. Eva thought herself a plain girl whose important interests did not include boys. Her father, Tom Reed, was presiding judge at the local Citrus Municipal Court; he asked his children to be serious students. Eva was earning excellent grades and planned to be a teacher.

Her friend Lyle Daugherty plopped beside her.

"He was a good kid," Eva would later tell me, "just the nicest kid in the world."

"Eva," Lyle said, "I haven't signed your yearbook. Don't you like me?"

"Stop being silly. Here. Write something here." Her young, quick fingers moved to an opening on the page and tapped quickly. Eva was a year older than Lyle. She knew his family well; they had one of the larger farms in the area.

"Oh," Lyle moaned knowingly, "look where Bernie signed." He was looking at a page titled "Characteristics."

"You know, I wouldn't say anything bad, myself, but that's one person a lot of people are glad to see graduate," he continued. "I've heard them say so." He started writing his note. "Even though he's leaving for college, well, I wonder if he's really gone. You know what I mean?"

Almost sixty years later, Eva's fingers moved across that same page as she showed me her *Cardinal*. The book was carefully tended, without a single tear. The pulp was yellowed, but the pictures were still clear, as were the messages from the past.

We met to talk of one of her schoolmates, one more memorable than others, R. Bernard Finch.

On the "Characteristics" page, the signer was to choose a trait best describing him, then put his name in the blank next to it. Next to "Spotlight" were H. Schulte and T. Finch. Nita Kennedy had filled in "Kissable." And next to "Stupendous" was just one name, Bernie Finch.

Eva chose not to answer any questions about people she knew in 1934. Instead, she talked of life in the San Gabriel valley during those times. And, as she talked, I listened to the *Cardinal*.

Other informants told me Bernard had announced he was planning to be the richest man in the valley and was choosing medicine as the way to do it. He was the only kid in school to have his own car, not a bad feat in 1934, and the "spoiled" oldest child and only son in his wealthy family. Good-looking, with big, brown eyes and dark, curly hair, he was known as a "charmer" and usually had his way.

I searched Eva's book for any hint of the future. There he was in the varsity tennis photograph. "Best high school tennis player in the valley" many had said. Then on page nineteen I saw his name under "Exclusive Organizations, Heckler's Club." I read on.

"Qualifications for membership: the prospective member of this organization must possess an uncanny ability to bother people."

Part I

The Death of Barbara Jean Finch,
the Preliminary Hearings, and
Grand Jury Indictments

one

The Death of Barbara Jean Finch

SATURDAY, JULY 18, 1959
LARKHILL DRIVE
WEST COVINA, CALIFORNIA
11:30 P.M.

A NINETEEN-YEAR-OLD SWEDISH girl took off her robe and laid it on the foot of her bed. She had just checked on the children she watched. The six-year-old boy was asleep. The eleven-year-old girl, Patti, had gone to bed. They had all watched the Miss Universe Pageant, held in nearby Long Beach, and then the news before turning off the television.

The Swede walked into the bathroom, running her fingers through her long, blonde hair. Picking up her hairbrush, she studied her image in the mirror.

Everyone says I'm attractive, she thought to herself. *But am I really?* Leaning forward, she poked at an early blemish that seemed to be exploding on her cheek.

She had come from Sweden the previous September to work as a governess for a wealthy physician and his wife, tending their six-year-old son and the wife's daughter by a previous marriage. It had been obvious for some time the couple was not getting along. The doctor had moved out three weeks earlier after his wife announced she was filing for divorce. This saddened the young girl. Her own parents

3

had divorced when she was fourteen. She knew how the children would suffer.

Brushing her hair, she contemplated her future. *It would be nice if I could keep my position long enough to finish my art studies.* Art was her first love; she had been studying since age five. Teachers always praised her talent for observing things and transferring them to paper or canvas.

Her ability to see and remember was soon to be tested in one of the most publicized crimes of the century.

She heard a car arriving in the garage. There was a familiar squeak of a brake—it was the doctor's wife. The motor stopped. She waited, expecting to hear footsteps and the sound of the door opening into the house. Nothing. Then: Angry voices, a woman screaming for help.

She put on her robe and glasses, then ran to the hall. There she met Patti, who had also heard the noise. "Come quickly!" she commanded. The two went to the sliding door that led across a patio to the garage.

They opened the patio door and began running to the smaller door of the garage, forty feet away. From inside a woman's voice screamed, "Marie, help!" and a dull thud echoed out—the sound of a body being slammed against something hard.

The two stopped; the older grabbed the other by the shoulders, instructing her in a thick Swedish accent. "You go back to the house and wait for me there." Patti ran back and locked the patio door behind her; she stood watching.

The light in the garage was out. The governess flipped the switch on the wall. There, lying on the garage floor, was her mistress. She was next to the driver's side of her car, a Chrysler convertible. The woman seemed dazed and was trying to sit up, holding the right side of her head. Blood was coming from wounds on her cheek and temple.

The governess ran toward her mistress. But someone grabbed her, lifting her trim, five-foot, one-inch frame up and over to the garage wall, and without saying a word began pounding her head against it.

Once.

She could feel the plaster of the wall crumbling beneath her head. Her glasses clattered onto the concrete floor.

Twice.

Pieces of plaster rattled inside the wall.

Then nothing.

She woke not knowing where she was; then remembering, she tried to get up. The garage was dark again.

"Get into the car or I'll kill you," he was yelling. It was the man she worked for, the physician. And she was sure he was going to kill her.

"Please don't kill me." She was sobbing. "Don't kill me!"

The garage seemed to explode. It was a gunshot. Sparks flashed from a gun muzzle. She could see the man's outline against the dim night sky as he stood between her and the garage door. And she could see the revolver in his hand.

"Get in the car!" the man again commanded.

She staggered to the driver's door of the convertible, passing her dazed mistress, who still lay on the garage floor. Once in the car, the young woman leaned toward the left corner of the seat, keeping her head just high enough to see.

The man lifted the semi-conscious older woman; she wobbled, unable to stand on her own. He pulled her around the back of the car, then up to the passenger door. Her bloodied left hand was on top of the car, trying to hold back, leaving wavy streaks of red, but the man was too strong. He opened the door and pushed her down onto the front seat. She was sitting sideways now, her feet on the garage floor. Her right hand was at the side of her head. Blood from her ear ran between her fingers, dribbling down her forearm, then dripping onto her white cotton dress.

He slid behind the steering wheel.

"Give me the keys or I'll kill you, I mean it!" he said to his wife. He held the gun with his left hand and took the woman's small white purse, rummaging through it with his right, seeking the keys. Then he noticed the keys were still in the ignition. He started the car, racing the motor three times. The lights came on. The radio was playing.

He reached to pull the woman in. She was gone.

She was running for her life, down a steep irregular slope that led to the house next door. Her father-in-law, the father of the man who had just attacked her, lived there. She was a few feet from safety.

The long heel of her right shoe came off. She moved slowly, hobbling, nearly stumbling.

The governess left the car and ran to the house when the man chased his wife. Patti was opening the sliding-glass door.

"What happened?" Patti was crying.

The two went to the telephone, and the older girl dialed the number for the police. As she dialed, there was another gunshot. She turned to look outside, listening to the shot reverberate through the dark hills surrounding the house—each echo rumbled from farther and farther away.

She was on the phone to the West Covina police station. It was 11:47 P.M.

"Police," the voice said.

She spoke slowly, telling what had happened. "He's going to kill her. He has a gun and he shot at me, too."

She hung up and turned to Patti. "We must go outside and look for your mama." They walked onto the home's asphalt driveway, looking into the night. The Chrysler's motor was still running. On the car's radio: Connie Francis singing "Everybody's Somebody's Fool." They never saw the woman.

Soon, two police cruisers were winding up the long black driveway.

The man, the physician, was running wildly down the hill, past his father's house. He had just watched his wife of six years die. His arms were raised out to the sides for balance as he fought the Boston ivy grabbing at his shoes. He weaved through the many eucalyptus trees standing around the homes. In one hand was his wife's purse and some of her jewelry; in the other, the gun that had killed her.

He did not go back to his house where his twenty-two-year-old, red-haired lover was waiting behind a thick bougainvillea plant. He ran the opposite way, not knowing what he was going to do.

Hours later, the woman who had waited for him was driving east, up the Cajon Pass, to an apartment in Las Vegas, two hundred miles ahead. The pass was the traditional eastern "end" of the Los Angeles basin. Through it, fifteen miles of highway rose four thousand feet, winding through the San Bernardino mountains to the high Mojave desert. Once through it, the traveler was free of the metropolis.

Stars faded quickly in the sky before her as a blanch spread from the horizon. Soon, she would be in the desert. There would be few cars and no radio stations for the next four hours.

She turned on the radio; the last sounds of Los Angeles poked through the crackle and fizzle.

It was then that she heard the first reports of the death of Barbara Jean Finch. And the bulletins said police were looking for the man she loved, Dr. R. Bernard Finch. The radio fizzed.

Barbara Jean Finch. *Getty.*

Valley Tribune.

two
The Library

A RARE RAIN was beginning as I parked my car near the West Covina Library. Large pellets of water stung at my face and kicked up small circles of dust on the sidewalk, leaving small damp circles. As it turned out, this rain signalled an end to California's longest drought in recent memory.

Desert dust and smog had long been settling onto our buildings, sidewalks, trees, and mountains. Soon, everything would be scrubbed clean by a storm that would last for days. Tomorrow the air would be clear enough to see the San Gabriel Mountains to the north and even the more distant buildings of Pasadena, twenty miles to the west.

I was about to look into the past, to a time when a tidal wave of world attention washed onto West Covina. In 1959 one of the most publicized crimes of the century took place in this then-rural community.

The eastern part of the San Gabriel Valley had changed many times. With the introduction of irrigation water and refrigerated railroad cars in the early part of the century, the valley had been converted from desert to farmland, supplying citrus fruits and some vegetables to markets "back east."

9

During the '60s, a ripple of blue- and white-collar workers settled into the many housing tracts that replaced the groves. Many who moved here worked in the area's booming aerospace industry.

In the '70s large numbers of Hispanics migrated into the area, and in the '80s a wave of Asians. West Covina had evolved into a multicultural suburb, home to over one hundred thousand people.

But in 1959, West Covina was a farming community of less than eight thousand people. Everyone was known, especially if they were rich and beautiful. And no one could imagine a murder in the town.

Anyone who has lived here long has something to say about the Finch murder, and usually knew someone close to it.

This is the story of that murder—told as often as possible by the people who lived and worked here and by those whose lives were affected and whose perceptions of human nature were sharpened.

It is also a study of the dark side of the mind, of intrigue, infidelity, betrayal, deceit, and manipulation. It is also a story of naive courage and the faith of uncomplicated innocence.

As I reached the library entrance, the damp circles on the sidewalk had joined into one long, clear, shimmering film, pushing to the walkway's edges. I shuffled my shoes on a mat and entered. After checking out some microfilm at the reference desk, I studied the machine to project the past. The reel whirled to Monday, July 20, 1959. The Sunday papers had been printed on Saturday, before the murder took place, so the first print news was published on Monday. I fine-tuned the focus knob just enough to take out the blur. There it was: "West Covina Medic Faces Murder Quiz."

three

Crime Scene Investigation
Freeway Pursuit
Prior Fame

THE SWEDISH GOVERNESS' name was Marie Anne Lidholm. After calling the police, she went outside with Patti Daugherty, hoping to find Patti's mother. The second police cruiser winding up the long asphalt drive was driven by rookie patrolman James Keith.

INTERVIEW WITH JIMMY KEITH
WEST COVINA POLICE DEPARTMENT
MAY 19, 1992

"I retired twice, but I always got bored just sitting around. So I was glad when they kept finding things for me to do," he told me.

Jimmy was in his late sixties and about five feet, eight inches tall. He was large for his height, weighing about two hundred twenty pounds. When he stood, the roundness at his middle pushed his arms noticably to the sides. He had a full head of hair, half gray; it was combed straight back on the sides with a little '50s wave Vitalised in front. His voice drawled, hinting of a Southern childhood.

11

As I laid some newspaper articles out on the table in front of us, he hooked bifocaled, wire-rimmed glasses behind each ear and leaned down closer.

I asked him what he remembered of the night of Saturday, July 18, 1959, when he was still a rookie patrolman. He would remember with clarity and detail.

"I showed up for my shift about 11:30 that night," he began. "My shift went from midnight to 8:00 the next morning. We would get briefed when the afternoon shift got back, then go out on patrol."

The San Bernardino Freeway, completed the year before, made it necessary for at least two cars to patrol the city.

"Because of the freeway we would have one guy patrol north of the freeway and one guy south; there just wasn't enough places to cross under it."

In the station waiting for the afternoon watch cruisers to return had been Jimmy; Donald (Pappy) Rund, a veteran officer; Ron Evans, a volunteer "reserve" who answered the phones; and Rob Laughlin, who was the watch commander going off duty.

"Sergeant Bill Handrahan was supposed to be here, but he was late. He was late a lot, so none of us was wondering where he was, particularly."

At 11:47 P.M. Ron Evans answered the phone.

Jimmy continued. "We got the call that there had been a shooting at the Finch residence. Everybody knew where Finch lived. He was a well-known doctor in the area, and we had been out to his house before on disturbance calls. We must have had five cars up there within five minutes of getting the call. Lieutenant Laughlin rode with me, Pappy took his car, and Ron put out a call to the shift coming off to go to the house.

"I immediately went to the garage where I observed a late model, red Chrysler convertible. The engine was running on the car and the radio was playing real loud. You could see that the stainless steel frames, just above the windshield on each side, were matted with blood and hair. The side of the wall in the garage, which was finished like the inside of the house with plaster, had a large hole in it.

"We observed that Barbara Jean Finch was lying, I believe face up, at the bottom of a stairway that leads from Bernard Finch's house down to his father's house. His dad lived next door, you know."

Jimmy asked me for a piece of paper, then began drawing a diagram of the scene. He advised, "You know, *Life* magazine had a big layout of this when they did their story on it, which, as I recall, was pretty much as I remembered it.

"Going from Dr. Finch's house to his dad's is this steep staircase of about, I believe, seven steps, just carved out of the dirt. Standing at the top of the steps we shined our lights down and saw her body. Then one of the guys went down to make sure she was dead, and we left everything alone and waited for the coroner to show up. That was my job. I went to the Citrus exit on the freeway and waited for the coroner and showed him the way up to the house."

The coroner arrived at 2:00 A.M. There were about twenty people at the scene: Allen Sill, the Chief of Police; Captain William Ryan, who would be the lead investigator; a dozen reporters from local newspapers and broadcast media; and a few other officers.

It was Jimmy Keith's first homicide. Although he had been a butcher for four years before joining the police force, he was unprepared for what he saw.

JIMMY KEITH

"I remember when the coroner got there he turned her over and put one finger in her back and the other in her front. He told me the bullet had gone right through her and could have hit her right in the heart. As soon as he put his fingers in the holes, I went over to some bushes and got sick." He looked up from his diagram, directly at me. "We had all seen her or pictures of her. She was such a beautiful woman. To see her like that just made me sick.

"Anyway, after our preliminary search of the grounds and the house, I was assigned to stand watch on the north side of the property."

INTERVIEW WITH ALLEN SILL
FORMER CHIEF OF POLICE
WEST COVINA POLICE DEPARTMENT
MAY 25, 1992

In July of 1959, Allen Sill had been Chief of Police for two years. I met him at the South Hills Country Club, next to the crime scene.

"William Ryan was an excellent investigator who never left a stone unturned. He was in charge of the entire operation," Sill was telling me. Chief Sill was at the Finch residence the entire night, looking for physical evidence and talking with Marie Anne Lidholm and Patti Daugherty.

"As I remember, somebody found pieces of rubber gloves, the kind that doctors put on before an operation, on the driveway. I guess my big contribution that night was finding the electric cord that had been unplugged. It was on the south side of the garage."

As Sill searched the area on the south side of the garage, he noticed something out of place. Rocking with the gentle night breeze was a line of shadow, hanging from the roof. Raising his flashlight, he recognized the end of an extension cord. He looked to the left, seeing the male part of another cord. He thought for a moment, then went into the garage and returned with a chair. Standing on the chair, he plugged the two cords together.

"Hey! Who turned on the lights!" someone shouted from the driveway. Floodlights now illuminated the entire driveway. With the lights on, everything and everybody on that side of the house could be easily seen.

JIMMY KEITH

"My car had the best radio, and since the Finch house was up on the hill, I would get calls from the station and radio to the other cars that was searching for Finch. We thought he might still be in the area. I was also looking down in the valley for anybody that might be driving around. In those days, there weren't that many cars out at night, so if I saw any movement, I would radio down to Pappy and he would go and check it out."

Jimmy could possibly have been the arresting officer for both Dr. Finch and Carole Tregoff had it not been for two chance incidents. The first was an unpleasant encounter with a police dog six weeks earlier.

He was pointing at a spot on his diagram, a corner on the north side of the house.

"I learned later that Carole Tregoff was hiding in some thick bushes, here, for three or four hours. Well, I was standing over here the whole time, less than twenty feet away from her. All night long, the Finch dog, a white Samoyed—I heard later his name was Frosty—would go into those bushes. Then he kept coming out to me. He would stay just a few feet away from me for a couple of minutes, then go back into those bushes.

"I was afraid of this dog. I normally am not afraid of dogs, but I was afraid of this one because just a few weeks before somebody had brought a police dog to the station. They asked me to bring the dog inside. I asked the guy if the dog would bite and he said, 'No, he won't bite you 'cause you're in uniform.' Well, he tore up my right leg pretty bad, and I needed some stitches.

"Anyway, I found out later that Tregoff was sitting right there in those bushes. The dog was running over to her, then back over to me."

"How did you find that out?" I asked.

"She told Handrahan." Handrahan was the late-for-duty watch commander the night of the murder. "He was her next-door neighbor in La Puente. They'd known each other a long time. Anyway, later she told Handrahan that she had hid in the bushes till almost daybreak."

And because Jimmy Keith had been attacked by a dog six weeks earlier, Carole Tregoff would be seen by no one. Her story of hiding in the bushes for hours would later be discounted by the police. Jimmy Keith will always know it was true.

Police did, however, see her car.

Jimmy was pointing at his diagram again. "Her car was down here, parked next to the tennis courts at the Country Club. It was a De Soto convertible. Pappy took down the license plate number, and I remember he told me later that there was a tear on the driver's seat."

The car would be gone by morning.

"Somehow she got down to that car and got away without anybody noticing. I don't know how, but I was there most of the night and I know she didn't get past me."

Some speculate that Carole went to her car when the high speed freeway chase began.

FINCH HOUSE

DRIVEWAY

MRS. FINCH'S
OTHER SHOE

A KILLING RE-CREATED, AS THE PROSECUTION CLAIMS IT HAPPENED

In this re-creation of the state's version of the killing, lines show the movements of Mrs. Finch (white line), Dr. Finch (dark line) and the maid (dotted line). That night Dr. Finch and Carole waited near the garage, and when Mrs. Finch drove in, the doctor attacked her. The maid, Marie Anne Lidholm (A) and Mrs. Finch's daughter

(B) heard screams and ran to the door. Marie Anne rushed to the garage and saw Mrs. Finch lying near the car (C). Marie Anne was set upon by Dr. Finch who banged her head against the wall (D), and then he ordered her to the car. She noticed Mrs. Finch was in the car (E). Suddenly Mrs. Finch jumped out followed by her husband.

Marie Anne raced back to the house (F) to call police. Mrs. Finch (G) ran down driveway, losing a shoe, with the doctor in pursuit. Carole meanwhile had hidden in the bushes (H) after dropping the "murder kit." Dr. Finch caught up with his wife near the earthen steps (I). He fired down at her. She fell, rolled over and died (J).

Lyle Daughtery was notified and came to take his daughter, Patti, to his home in nearby Baldwin Park. Soon after, Jane Wagner, Bernard Finch's sister, arrived to take Raymond, Jr. As she was taking him to her car, the young boy pulled away and ran into the house. Once in his room, he walked slowly to the kitten curled on his bed.

Marie Anne would tell me that a few weeks before, Barbara Jean had allowed Raymond, Jr. to have a long-begged-for kitten.

He took the cat into his mother's bedroom. There, lying on the bed, was Marie Anne.

MARIE ANNE LIDHOLM
TELEPHONE INTERVIEW
JUNE 22, 1992

"I laid down in Mrs. Finch's room because it was closer to the living room where all the officers were. I just felt safer," Marie would explain to me later. "You know they hadn't caught Dr. Finch yet.

"I had just hung up the phone when the little boy came in. My father had called from Sweden to tell me they had read about the murder in the morning paper already. It wasn't even morning! I couldn't believe they found out so soon.

"I'll never forget when Raymond Junior came to me with his kitten. He was such a bright little boy, and he loved his kitten very much. He was so sad, he had just lost his mama."

The boy walked to Marie Anne and carefully placed his sleeping pet in her lap. "I want you to take care of Kitty for me, Marie Anne. My daddy wants to kill everybody. Keep Kitty safe."

As the boy walked to his aunt's car, the night breeze freshened, swaying the chorus of adolescent eucalyptus trunks that surrounded the house.

JIMMY KEITH

"About the next thing that happened was that, just before dawn, we got a call that a fella, just down Citrus Street from the Finch house, had his car stolen and that it had been found somewhere in La Puente by a Los Angeles police officer who was trying to get to work that morning."

Carl Mossberg of 1849 South Citrus, directly across the street from the Finch residence, would later tell police he heard his automatic bell sound just after midnight, indicating that a car was entering or leaving his property. Thinking a family member was coming home late, he did not look to see who it was. The keys had been in the car.

He learned his late model, Ford station wagon had been stolen when he received an early morning phone call from Officer William D. Booth of the Los Angeles Police Department. Booth, of 1659 North Malo Street, La Puente, found the certificate of ownership in the car that was blocking his driveway. Booth called West Covina Police, and Officer Don Goddard was sent to take a report and search the car.

Within minutes of Officer Booth's call, West Covina Police received a call from Mr. Leon Serruys of 15418 East Alwood, also in the city of La Puente. His car was missing as well. He, too, had left the keys in the ignition.

Esker Oxley and her neighbor, Ann Reynolds, lived across the street from Serruys. Don Goddard put their statements in his report. Both were awake, watching television, at 12:30 A.M., when they noticed the Serruys's Cadillac leaving. Thinking that Mr. Serruys was the driver, they did nothing.

They would also each recall hearing, just before the car left, someone running down East Alwood Street; looking, they had seen it was a man in a sports coat wearing no hat and running to the east. Each woman told Goddard the man was carrying nothing.

FREEWAY PURSUIT
SUNDAY, JULY 19, 1959
JUST BEFORE DAWN

Jimmy Keith and Pappy Rund were perched on an overpass of the San Bernardino Freeway.

JIMMY KEITH

"We knew that this white Cadillac had been stolen in La Puente and thought he might try to use the freeway. We had people staked out all over the place looking for him. We come to find out that he had three or four apartments all over the valley—I guess for his girlfriends. There was one in West Covina, near the hospital, and a couple in Monterey Park. We was watching them all. In those days you didn't need a warrant, you just walked in and sat down and waited for somebody to show up.

"Anyway, a little after 5:00 A.M. Pappy spotted the Cadillac going westbound, towards L. A. We turned on the lights and sirens and began our pursuit."

Sirens and lights were activated by a "Unitrol" switch on the dash. Once the switch was turned on, the red "gumball" on the top of the cruiser would light and turn and the horn ring in the steering wheel would control the "growler" siren. The arrangement was temperamental.

"You'd push on the horn ring and the siren would start. It took forever, maybe five or six seconds, for the siren to get up as high as it would go, then you'd have to let it wind down or else you'd burn it up. You tried not to leave it on for long. They used so much juice that the engine would slow down whenever you would wind them up."

Pappy took the lead in the chase.

"Pappy knew Finch. He had lived in the area for a few years and had actually met him a few times, so he went first. The freeway didn't have much traffic on it in those days, especially that time of morning, on a Sunday."

There was no traffic on the freeway except the three cars, moving at over a hundred miles per hour. As the chase began, the white Cadillac was less than a quarter of a mile ahead of the two cruisers.

"He must have had it floored, 'cause we was going almost flat out. We had brand new '59 Chevys with the interceptor engines, and our four barrel quadra-jet carburetors. You know, the more I talk about this, the more I can actually visualize it happening." Jimmy looked up and off to the side. He was silent for a moment.

It is known that memory of high stress events is more vivid; the adrenaline pumping through the brain causes recent memory to transfer into long-term memory moment by moment, so every sound, sight, smell, and emotion is remembered with real-time clarity. It seemed Jimmy was remembering his pursuit of Finch "frame by frame." He turned back to me. "Anyway, we radioed ahead and asked the sheriffs to set up a roadblock at Soto Street, near the County Hospital."

Twenty miles away, three sheriffs' cars lined across the westbound San Bernardino Freeway near downtown Los Angeles; a sharp curve was just to the east. A approaching motorist would see the units too late to exit. The headlights and "gumballs" were left on. The three deputies had been told the suspect would reach them in about ten minutes; each leaned back onto his car, eyes focused on the curve of freeway in front of him.

Coming to them from the east, the three cars were reaching speeds of one hundred twenty miles per hour. Keith and Rund had closed to within a hundred yards of the Cadillac.

But it was not to be. Jimmy was to miss making another arrest in the case.

JIMMY KEITH

"What that old woman was doing coming onto the freeway at that time of morning, I'll never know," Jimmy still wonders today. Two vertical lines appeared between his eyebrows.

"It's all different in there now, but back then, as you go westbound on the freeway, just before you got to Rosemead, there was an area fifteen to twenty feet wide that was all gravel and rocks. It was between the inside traffic lane and the railroad tracks. That was the only spot like that; the rest of the freeway had a concrete wall to protect the railroad tracks.

"She come onto the freeway and she didn't come onto the number one lane, she just come right across the whole freeway and run Pappy off the road. He had no choice. He could have run into her or gone onto the gravel. Anyway, I got run off with him."

Both cruisers hit the gravel, fishtailed briefly, then spun widely, kicking up gravel and dust. The engines stalled; the sirens whined down and stopped. The rays from the two red lights on top of the cars sliced through the dust and gravel settling about them. Pappy and Jimmy looked to see if the other was okay.

The woman slowly drove on, apparently not knowing what she had done.

JIMMY KEITH

"If it hadn't have been for that little open spot of gravel, we would have hit the wall or that woman there. And I know it was a woman 'cause I seen the hat she was wearing.

"We never stopped to bother with her or anything. She just kept on going. We started our cars up and kept on going into L. A."

They reached the Soto Street roadblock a few minutes later and learned Finch had not arrived.

"They told us that nobody had come through there. That's when we figured he got off on Del Mar Street and started back eastbound.

"The only other thing I remember about that night was that the reporters was all wondering how much the Finch house was worth. They needed to know for their story. None of them could agree on a figure so they asked me. Heck, I had no idea, so I just guessed. 'Oh, I figure about $80,000, you know, give or take,' I told them. From then on, whenever they wrote about it, the house was worth $80,000."

SUNDAY, JULY 19, 8:00 A.M.
CITRUS STREET, WEST COVINA

A lanky thirteen-year-old boy's legs were pumping hard on his almost-new Columbia Beach Cruiser. Going south, the street was a tiring uphill grade; he stood on the circling pedals for more speed. Ahead of him he saw dozens of parked cars and hundreds of people slowly moving on the hills. Legs aching, he pumped harder.

The boy was Dan Leonard, and his adolescent world had been excited minutes before as he watched a televised news account of the Finch murder.

INTERVIEW WITH CAPTAIN DAN LEONARD
WEST COVINA POLICE DEPARTMENT
MARCH 12, 1992

Dan is now a captain in the West Covina Police Department. I met him at the station. He spoke proudly of his bike.

"It was a Columbia Beach Cruiser with chrome fenders, a chrome horn, and those optional mud flaps you could get. It even had whitewalls. I was really proud of it. My dad had given it to me the Christmas before. Nobody in town had a better one." As he spoke of his bicycle, he leaned back in his chair, looking up and off to the right.

I asked him to talk about the Dan Leonard of 1959. I had been told that Dan was an intelligent man, with sharp insights into human nature honed by almost thirty years' service as a peace officer.

"I was working on my star rank in Boy Scouts with plans to continue on to Eagle Scout," Dan told me. "I guess two of the more important things in my life at that time were the Boy Scouts and police work. I wanted to be a policeman."

Dan was now six feet, two inches tall, and weighed about two hundred twenty pounds. His short and curly hair was about half gone; what remained was rust-colored, just beginning to gray. His mind was quick, his memory acute.

"I saw on television the news reports of the Finch murder. It was early Sunday morning. Dr. Finch had been identified as a suspect in the murder of his wife, Barbara Jean. I rode my bicycle up to the site, which was blocked off by police officers.

"I was pretty excited. There were at least a hundred officers and reporters walking around that hill. Because of my interest in police work, I kept asking questions."

Dan was to learn that tragedy offers its own opportunities. In these first hours following the death of Barbara Jean Finch, Dan would unexpectedly meet his chance for fame.

A policeman in plain clothes had been standing at the entrance to the Finch driveway, across the road from Dan. He looked again at the red-headed kid who had been asking questions of anyone and everyone. Soon, the kid's eyes met his. The man slid his thumbs behind his belt and walked slowly across Larkhill Drive.

Dan's stomach stirred as the officer neared. He thought he was going to be asked to leave. The older man bent his knees until the two were at the same height.

27

A long moment passed as the officer studied Dan. "Hey, kid."

"Yeah?" The young man's voice broke to a higher pitch.

"You want to help us out?" The officer raised his eyebrows.

"Me? Sure! You know, I'm interested in police work, you know. I'd like to be a policeman some day. In fact, I wrote Chief Sill last year, asking if I could wash the patrol cars or—"

"We're looking for a gun." The man stood up, looked away, then back at Dan Leonard. "Hmm, you see, it's like this. We're looking for," he watched Dan's eyes widen, "a murder weapon."

Dan's mouth was open. "A search, you're searching the scene for a gun! I understand."

"Yeah," the policeman nodded, talking faster. "You can look for it, too, you know. And I tell you what. You find that gun and we'll make you a policeman. All you got to do is search the sides of the road from here to all the way down to Cameron, then over to Mt. SAC Road and up to the College. You find that gun, kid, and we'll make you a policeman."

The kid was speeding down Citrus Street. If the gun was there, he would find it, no matter how long it took.

DAN LEONARD

Dan still gets excited when he talks about the search for the gun. "I rode my bicycle all over the place. I walked up and down ravines looking for that gun for days. You know, school was just out and I had the time. If I just could have found that gun! Well, I really thought they would make me a policeman."

He never found the murder weapon. In the thirty years since, neither has anyone else.

"You know," he continued, "this town has never seen so much excitement. We had reporters from virtually all over the world."

"Why was that so?" I asked.

"Well, Dr. Finch was a famous person. His family had lived in the area since 1908 or 1909, I believe, and they were quite wealthy. His dad owned land and was an optometrist. Also, his dad was part owner in the town's only jewelry store, on Citrus Street in Covina."

Bernard and Barbara Jean Finch were "socialites" as well. They were members of South Hills Country Club. Dr. Finch was an A-rated tennis player and the couple were members of the exclusive Los Angeles Tennis Club and regularly mingled with Hollywood's rich and famous.

"I'm sure there were at least two hundred people there that Sunday," Dan was telling me. "Cars were parked all the way down Citrus."

INTERVIEW WITH BILL
SOUTH HILLS COUNTRY CLUB MEMBER

I heard another account from a country club member who played golf that Sunday. Bill had been a friend for years.

"It interfered with play for days. There were people all over the course, especially number nine and ten. Some of them had the metal detectors, back then they called them mine sweepers. We were worried they might get hit by a ball."

Play continued, nonetheless.

SUNDAY, JULY 19, EARLY AFTERNOON
NEAR LARKHILL DRIVE AND CITRUS STREET
WEST COVINA

Officers searched through the thick Boston ivy surrounding much of the golf course and all of the adjacent hill below the two Finch residences. Occasionally, a sliced second shot from the first hole's fairway would threaten them, but they continued, undaunted in their search for anything out of the ordinary. About two dozen officers had been searching since dawn for evidence; quite often one would reach down, then rise, white globe in hand. After a quick inspection, the find would be pocketed.

Raymond Finch, Dr. Finch's father and next-door neighbor, was talking to some of the officers and a few reporters. They stood in front of the garage of his son's home.

"My son hasn't been himself lately," he said. He looked over toward his own home. "Barbara Jean fell just a few feet from my home, right over there." He pointed. "Ten more feet and she would have made it to the safety of my home. Oh my God, what a tragedy!"

He looked back at the group. "My son is sick; he's been off the beam for three or four months. He's been in therapy for about three months now, you know, trying to get himself under control. You just can't work thirteen or fourteen hours at surgery every day without cracking up. He just blows up easily."

Ten feet away Chief Allen Sill was talking with another group.

"Where are the children now?" someone asked.

"The people who were in the house have all been taken to other locations. The governess, Miss Lidholm, is now at the house of some friends in Pasadena."

"What about the kids, Chief?"

"Dr. Finch's sister, Jane Wagner, took the six-year-old boy, Bernard, Jr., to her home in West Covina. Patti Daugherty, Mrs. Finch's daughter by a prior marriage, was taken to her father's home."

"She's Lyle Daugherty's girl, isn't she, Chief?" one of the reporters asked.

"Yes, she is," he answered. He spoke and turned quickly, hoping to walk away from the next question.

"When did that 'wife swap' actually take place, Chief? Do you have the year for us?" The group was swarming behind him as he walked.

"I'm not going to get into that," Chief Sill said. "I've got a murder investigation to conduct here."

As Chief Sill entered the house, he learned Dr. Finch had been arrested in Las Vegas by deputies of the Clark County Sheriff's Office.

A teletype had been sent to Las Vegas asking for assistance in locating the suspect. In it was a description of Carole Tregoff's De Soto and its California license plate number. On duty in Las Vegas when the teletype was received was Deputy Conrad Simmons, who—some thought remarkably—remembered the plate number. In May he had ticketed the De Soto for expired tags. The car had been parked at the Fairview Apartments; the address was 419 Desert Inn Road.

Finch had given a preliminary statement to Clark County sheriffs and was being held pending arrival of West Covina officers. Sill and Ryan would fly to Las Vegas. The next plane left at 6:00 P.M.

As the two made plans, reporters outside exchanged stories of "The Wife Swap."

PRIOR FAME

The death of his wife in 1959 was not the first event to bring attention to Dr. Finch. There was also the popularized "wife swapping," said to have taken place in the early '50s. The story is dutifully included in most narratives.

It was 1951. Dr. Finch was married to his first wife, a former classmate at Covina High School, the former Frances Simpson. They lived on Rockway Street in Baldwin Park, a city next to West Covina, with their three children. Next door: Mr. and Mrs. Lyle Daugherty.

Lyle was married to the beautiful Barbara Jean. Their only child, Patti, was three years old. Their family physician, conveniently, was their next-door neighbor. Finch, who practiced at the prestigious Magan Clinic in Covina, attended Barbara Jean during her pregnancy and delivered Patti by caesarean section in 1947.

Eventually, each man would marry the other's wife.

A friend of mine, David Graves, lived near Rockway Street.

INTERVIEW WITH DAVID GRAVES
WEST COVINA RESIDENT
MARCH 28, 1992

"Well I was a young man at the time." He spoke from behind the menu of our Marie Calendar's restaurant in West Covina. "I remember the incident very well. It caused quite a stir in the neighborhood.

"My family moved to town in 1945, from San Francisco. Dr. Finch and Dr. Frank Gordon were our family doctors; they were in partnership, you know." Doctors Gordon and Finch had started a practice together on West Garvey Avenue shortly after Finch had left the Magan Clinic. Gordon was married to Bernard's sister, Marion.

"Dr. Finch was a well-respected physician in our community, although he was beginning to lose credibility due to his improprieties. It was a small community in those days, and news like that travels fast, you know.

"Of course, when the rumor started that he had switched wives with his neighbor, this became the talk of the town. My closest friend in grammar school, Norman Crabbe, lived on Rockway, and I lived two blocks from him on Willow Street, just around the corner. Yeah, it was quite a scandal. I heard my parents talking about it often. They were quite upset, and it was about then we started using Dr. Gordon exclusively as our doctor.

"Moral standards in those days were stricter than they are now. Well, even for today it would be bizarre for two couples to switch like that. And in those days it was looked down upon to get divorced in general. I know Finch and Barbara Jean moved away soon after, and the other couple stayed for quite a while.

"Doctor Gordon would come to our house on calls, and being a friendly sort of a guy, he would usually stay and visit. Doctors in those days were different. He didn't just make a house call. He would stay for dinner and talk with my parents for hours. Doctors were different.

"Anyway, I remember him telling my parents that he wanted to end his partnership with Finch, that he thought the publicity of his improprieties was hurting the reputation of his practice.

"Today, news of a 'switch' would be back page news if it made the newspapers at all, but in those days, it was big news. I remember my parents being shocked. We had reporters from all over asking questions. They would go to my friend Norman's house and ask his parents about it."

The rumor fires were fanned more when Barbara Jean's father spoke to the press after the murder and said he, too, thought there had been some "swapping" on Rockway Street.

Other informants told me they are certain Lyle Daugherty did not become involved with Frances Finch until quite some time later, after the doctor and Barbara Jean married and moved to an apartment in Covina.

Eva Reed told me, "That came later, after the divorces were all final."

Another source told me, "Lyle and Frances had known and liked each other in high school, you know. Frances was a cheerleader and a very popular girl. She and Lyle started their romance after Barbara Jean moved away."

Allen Sill added, "It was two or three years after Finch and Barbara Jean moved away that they became interested in each other."

For the newsmen at the murder scene that day, "wife swapping" was the perfect spice for a murder story that would have other intriguing twists.

Raymond Finch finished talking to the officers. Walking carefully down the hill that led to his house, he noticed something unusual in the Boston ivy. It was a square shadow, not blended with the curving lines of the ivy. He walked over.

It was a brown leather attaché case.

"Fellas, I think I might have something here," he said.

A dozen officers ran over immediately, one carrying his "mine sweeper."

Another officer held a leash attaching him to a German Shepherd. "I musta been by here a dozen times," he said, looking down at the case. The dog was lunging to the side, barking, seeming to have noticed something in the yard of a neighboring house.

"Don't open it," Officer Frank Meehan of West Covina was bending down to pick up the case. "I'll take it inside. Not a word of this to the press, Mr. Finch—if you don't mind, sir."

four
Finch Arrest in Las Vegas
Statement of Carole Tregoff Pappa

SUNDAY, JULY 19, 1959
LAS VEGAS, NEVADA
10:30 A.M.

HIRAM POWELL, CLARK County Deputy Sheriff, was driving his car around the gravel parking lot to the side of the Sands Hotel. He guided the unmarked cruiser alongside a two-door De Soto convertible. As he walked closer to his find, small nuggets of white rattled and popped under his feet, and the dust his car had kicked up swirled lazily around him in the warm, late morning desert breeze. At the top of the driver's seat he noticed a three-inch tear in the cloth fabric, as though one might have torn it putting something into the back.

Circling to the rear of the car, he took a small notebook from his pocket and opened it. He held the pad in front of him at arm's length, glancing from it to the license plate, then back.

Inside the casino he showed his badge to a change girl and asked her something; she turned and pointed to Carole Tregoff.

Carole was at the bar in her waitress uniform waiting for the next round of drinks to be dealt to the late morning gamblers, just a few of whom were scattered about. The sounds of any gambling hall bounced around the large room. Slot machine arms were slamming. Coins clanked and rattled into metal bins. The occasional, unmistakable shouts of people winning at craps could be heard.

He showed her his badge.

"Yes, I'm Carole Tregoff," she said.

"Miss Tregoff do you know where Dr. Bernard Finch is?"

"Yes, he's at my apartment on Desert Inn Drive," she answered.

The veteran officer studied the pretty redhead. She looked quite tired and, he thought, too thin. Her eyes met his for only brief moments, quickly returning to her waitress tray. He waited to make eye contact with her again.

The pause made her nervous. She spoke, still looking down. "He's been with me since Friday; I picked him up at the airport."

He waited longer than usual before his next question. She continued to avoid his eyes. Her mouth was drawn tight and pulled down at the sides; the muscles and veins in her neck stood out like cords.

"That's 419 Desert Inn Drive, isn't it, ma'am? You see, we'd like to ask him a few questions." He spoke slowly, watching her react.

"Is it about his wife?" She didn't look up.

"Yes," Powell waited and watched, "it's about his wife. You, uh, heard about her," he paused some more, "did you?"

She answered quickly, "Of course, we've all heard about it. It's been on the radio all morning."

11:15 A.M.

Hiram Powell and Ray Gubser, Jr., had been knocking on the door to Carole Tregoff's apartment for fifteen minutes. No one answered. They were accompanied by two uniformed officers.

"Go find the manager and get the key," Gubser told one of the men. "You can tell 'em we got a murder suspect in here."

He kept knocking.

The key arrived and the men entered, looking carefully around the apartment. In the sole bedroom they found a middle-aged man, soundly sleeping.

"Dr. Bernard Finch?" Gubser spoke loudly, then kicked the bed with his foot twice. "Dr. Bernard Finch!" He was yelling.

The man rolled over and sat up. He appeared confused, but not surprised to see the officers.

"Dr. Finch," Gubser continued, "you are under arrest for the murder of Barbara Jean Finch last night in West Covina, California." He began scanning the room. "Is there a gun in the room?"

"No, there's no gun," he answered. "Hey, where are you guys from?"

"We're from the Clark County Sheriff's Department. Now get dressed," Gubser ordered. "We're going to go down to the station."

As Dr. Finch was being booked, Gubser and Powell were handed a message. Carole Tregoff had called. She had left work early and was back at her apartment, requesting to talk with the officers who had arrested Dr. Finch.

They returned to the Fairview apartments shortly after 1:00 P.M. Gubser would later testify about this second visit. "Same thing the second time. We banged on the door for about fifteen minutes and nobody answered. So we asked the manager to let us in again." Carole was also found sleeping. "We waited in the living room until she was dressed."

Carole came out of the bedroom. She stood next to a small dining room table. Both officers noted she seemed tired and nervous.

"You had some questions for us, ma'am?" Powell started.

"Yes," she said. "Why did you take Dr. Finch to the police station?"

"He's been arrested for the murder of his wife," said Powell.

Squeezing the edge of the table, she took a breath. "He's been with me since Friday."

The detectives quickly glanced at each other, then back at the girl.

"Then you wouldn't mind coming back with us and making a statement to that effect, would you?" Gubser spoke slowly and carefully. Both men were searching her face.

She looked from them, to the floor, nodding as she spoke. "Of course, of course I will."

"But before we go back," Gubser said quickly, "uh, you don't mind if we check around a bit, do you? I mean for any of the doctor's things he might need while he's with us."

She kept nodding and they began their search. They found a few personal articles: a shaving kit, some luggage, and a ring of keys. They didn't find the pistol that killed Barbara Jean Finch.

Once at the station, Carole was shown to a small waiting area near the room where Dr. Finch was being interrogated. With her at all times was a uniformed officer, Sergeant Richard D. Butcher. She was shown the way to the ladies' room; Butcher was standing nearby when she came out.

It was about 2:30 P.M.

The door to the interrogation room opened. Ray Gubser and Hiram Powell came through.

"We're going out for a bite to eat," Gubser announced. "Would you like to come along?"

"No," she answered, "I just want to see Dr. Finch."

"Well," Powell started, in a matter-of-fact tone, "You might have to wait until the officers from West Covina get here. We don't expect them till after supper."

"I'll wait." She shifted in her chair. She had not eaten since the night before.

Gubser and Powell looked at each other, then back to Carole. Officer Butcher crossed his arms and widened his stance.

Gubser spoke. "Now Carole, there's something we need to talk to you about. You see, you are going to have to wait here until these boys from West Covina get here. You know, they want to talk to you, too. Now if you agree to stay here, that's fine—but if you don't, we'll have to put you under arrest. I guess you might say that technically you're under arrest as a material witness."

"I understand." She stood and took a deep breath. "Can I have a cup of coffee?"

As the three were leaving the station, a small group of reporters approached and began asking questions about statements Finch may have made. Alan Jarlson of the *Las Vegas Sun* had been asked to cover the story for the *Los Angeles Times*. Gene Tuttle worked for the Las *Vegas Review-Journal*; he asked about Carole Tregoff.

"She's being held in technical custody, boys," Gubser answered. "That's all." He took Carole by the arm, and the three walked away from the group.

Jarlson and Tuttle looked at each other. Each spoke: "What's technical custody?"

Gubser and Powell questioned Bernard Finch some more when they returned. Neither policeman took notes, and there was no stenographer present. The doctor told them he had been

STATEMENT OF CAROLE TREGOFF PAPPA TO CLARK COUNTY SHERIFFS

It was 4:30 P.M. when Carole was led to an interrogation room. The room was small, ten feet on a side. There were no windows. A small rectangular table was in the center of the room. Around it were four straight-backed chairs. Carole sat on one side; Gubser and Powell on the other. To Carole's right, stenographer Delia Andrews took shorthand notes.

The officers knew Carole Tregoff had spoken to Bernard Finch that morning, before leaving for her shift at the Sands. It took forty-five minutes to prepare her statement. She would give a narrative of her activities since the Friday before and answer direct questions. Carole was aware of radio and print media reports that Marie Anne Lidholm had seen Dr. Finch at the house. She would tell of driving back to West Covina on Saturday.

She was finishing her statement. "When I got back to Las Vegas, I found Dr. Finch asleep on my sofa. I told him I had heard on the radio that his wife had been killed and that they were looking for him. He said, 'Well, if they are looking for me, then I guess they'll find me.' Then," she continued, "I got dressed for my shift at the Sands. I had to be there by 10:00 this morning."

Carole, in this statement, was the first person to say she was at the murder scene.

Delia Andrews had started her job as stenographer for the Clark County Sheriff's Department two weeks before. She went to the Records Division to type Carole's statement. Returning fifteen minutes later, she handed a stack of six sheets of paper to Carole.

"I'd be happy to re-type it," Carole offered after a few minutes of reading. "There's a few things that need to be changed."

"Well, I'm afraid that's not allowed, ma'am." The stenographer looked at the officers.

"Well," Powell helped, "why don't you both go over and work on it. You can tell her what to type, Carole."

Both women went to the Records Division. After a few minutes they returned, and Carole was asked to read her statement aloud before signing.

Up to this point, she had not been advised of any rights pertaining to her.

"Now you know," Powell told her before she began reading, "Before you sign I want you to know that you don't have to give us a statement."

Carole nodded.

"And," he continued, "if you read the little printed statement at the top of each page you'll see, you know, that what you sign can be used as evidence."

The statement was printed at the top of each page: "I have been advised that anything I say may be used as evidence in a court of law." She was not asked if she read or understood this statement.

The men leaned forward, listening intently as she began reading aloud. First, she recounted the arrival of Dr. Finch on Friday.

"Dr. Finch has been with me since Friday, June 17. I did drive him back to West Covina last night. On Friday evening, while working at the Sands hotel, I received a long distance call from Dr. Finch, who was in West Covina, California. He advised me he did not have to work Saturday, July 18, and that I was to meet him at McCarron Airport at 11:30 Friday night."

She said the two went to the Sands for a late dinner, then back to her apartment, arriving about 2:00 A.M.

Her shift at the Sands, Saturday, was from 10:00 A.M. to 6:00 P.M.

"After I got off from work, we immediately left for Los Angeles and arrived in West Covina at approximately 11:00 or 11:30 P.M. We went up to the lawn of Mrs. Finch's house and waited for her to come home."

Then she painted her picture of the minutes before the death of Barbara Jean Finch:

The convertible came up the driveway, past Bernard Finch and Carole Tregoff, and stopped in the two-car garage. Barbara Jean was getting out of the car as the two approached. Carole was a few feet behind Bernard.

"We want to talk to you about a couple of things," he said casually.

Mrs. Finch was standing by her car. She was angry. "Well, I sure don't want to talk to you!" She screamed.

Barbara Jean reached back inside the car and came out with a pistol in her hand. She pointed the gun at Carole, who screamed and backed away. Bernard jumped to grab the gun. Carole ran down the driveway.

"I was frightened and I ran into some shrubbery that surrounds the house. Later, I went to my car and drove back to Las Vegas," she finished.

The officers asked some questions.

"Where was Mrs. Finch when you left the garage?" Gubser asked.

"I don't know," Carole answered.

"Where was Dr. Finch?"

"He was standing near my left side, about four feet away from Mrs. Finch."

"Why did you go to West Covina that night?"

"Dr. Finch had previously asked me to go with him so we could both talk to her and get things straightened out with their divorce. This time I had agreed to go. In going through the divorce, she was making things as hard for him as she could. She was interfering with his work."

"Had you seen Mrs. Finch before last night?"

"Yes, at social occasions, at her home, and at my previous employment."

"Does Dr. Finch help support you?"

"He has given me money when I needed it, but he has never supported me."

"After you ran from the garage last night, did you hear anything, like a gun being fired?"

"Once, maybe twice."

"Did you see Dr. Finch or Mrs. Finch running from the garage?"

"No."

"Did you see Mrs. Finch's housekeeper at any time?"

"No."

"How long did you stay in the shrubbery surrounding the house?"

"About six hours."

"Six hours?"

"Yes."

"Where do you go after you left?"

"I returned to Las Vegas in my car. I arrived about 9:00 A.M. this morning."

"Did Dr. Finch tell you how he returned from West Covina?"

"He said he had driven. However, he wasn't sure how he had obtained the car, but he said that he had probably stolen it—didn't know from whom or where."

"Were you and Dr. Finch planning on getting married after the divorce?"

"Yes."

"Did you leave Los Angeles and come to Las Vegas because of trouble with Mrs. Finch, or for other reasons?"

"Dr. Finch thought perhaps I might be subpoenaed as a respondent at her divorce action."

"Have you ever seen Dr. Finch in possession of a firearm?"

"Yes."

Carole was finished reading. She signed the statement.

She asked to see Dr. Finch and was told she would have to wait until the West Covina officers arrived.

It was 7:00 P.M. The DC-3 carrying William Ryan and Allen Sill was on final approach to McCarron Airport. Sill waved vainly at the burnt cloud drifting from Ryan; he had been relieved when all were asked to put out their cigarettes. Ryan was a chain-smoker and his habit was a continuing irritant to the Chief, who prided himself in not smoking or drinking.

Before leaving, they had been told Finch was saying he had been in Las Vegas since Friday night. Each was wondering what he might say when told Marie Anne Lidholm's head injuries did not impair her memory. And that she remembered seeing him in West Covina.

ALLEN SILL

"That's A-L-L-E-N, Jones, not A-N." Allen Sill was making sure his name was spelled correctly. We were in the parking lot next to the South Hills tennis courts—less than a hundred yards from where Barbara Jean Finch's body had been found, thirty-three years before.

"Guess who was in charge of getting these tennis courts built," he told me. "None other than Raymond Bernard Finch."

He talked about his first days in West Covina. He had been thirty-six years old when asked to be Chief of Police. The previous chief had been Bum Stanford, a likeable pig farmer from nearby El Monte.

Bum kept the pig farm going while he was chief, I had been told. Chief Sill lives in the same house as in 1959, when he got the late night call from Ron Evans telling there had been a homicide at the Finch residence.

To help take his mind back to July, 1959, I showed Allen Sill some reproductions of newspaper photographs. He looked at one longer than the others. It showed two West Covina officers standing over the body. One was holding a large box of a camera up to his eye as though he were framing a picture of the body; the other was shining a flashlight down onto it. I had not identified the men and asked the Chief who they might be.

"The guy with the camera is Frank Meehan. He was more or less our official photographer." He was holding the picture in his hands, looking closely at the man with the flashlight. "I don't recognize the other guy."

"Is it Jimmy Keith?" I asked, hoping I might have a photographic record of Jimmy that night.

"Oh no," Sill laughed out loud. "That's not Keith; he was like a ball even back then." He raised his arms out to his sides at forty-five degree angles, elbows straight. "No, that's not Jimmy."

Chief Sill was six feet tall and appeared to be in his early seventies. He weighed about one hundred seventy pounds. He wore no glasses and his hair was black; just the slightest gray was creeping in above his ears. His memory was quite clear.

"I had talked with Finch on the phone a couple of times prior to July 18. He called me once, I remember, just to give me his side of the story. It was common knowledge that there were problems in the house, that they weren't getting along, and there had been several disturbance calls.

"He was a prominent member of the community, his family was quite wealthy, and he was part-owner of his own hospital and all. But he was not too highly regarded."

Sill talked fondly of William Ryan, who had died just a few months before from pancreatic cancer. Then he talked about the case in general.

"You know, the Finch case wasn't that difficult. We had a suspect and an eyewitness. The difficult part was handling all the press and media attention it attracted. Every day dozens of reporters would be at the station asking us for the latest developments.

"The other problem I had was that there was no clerical support for us. If you can believe that—when I came on board here we had not one secretary. And no records department, either; each guy would kind of keep his own records in his desk. It was that kind of a town. That's the main reason I asked the sheriff's office to send us some help. We didn't need help investigating the case; I needed secretaries who could type and file.

"So the Monday following the murder they sent us Ray Hopkinson. We called him 'Hoppi.' He was a great guy! Loved to gamble—he was always going to Las Vegas," Sill reminisced.

I tried to focus him on July 18, 1959. "What do you remember about that night?"

"Oh, mostly," he began, "being a new Chief of Police, I was worried mostly about flubbing up and making any mistakes. If I had flubbed that case, no telling where I would have ended up.

"Ryan took charge right away. If it hadn't have been for the maid, Lidholm, it would have been a much more difficult case. She was quite upset that night. She had just had her head smashed into that wall, and the lady she worked for had been found dead. I would say she was distraught. But she was a good witness for us that night. She remembered things quite well. As far I know, none of the attorneys ever shook her story."

The chief remembered in detail how it was known to search for Finch in Las Vegas.

"It was common knowledge that he was shacking up with Tregoff in Las Vegas, and we knew that he had stolen that red Cadillac in La Puente. So we teletyped Clark County sheriffs and told them to look for this car. We also gave them the license plate number of the car we found down the hill, near the tennis courts.

"I guess you know somehow Tregoff made it down there and took off in her car."

Sergeant Raymond D. Butcher, the same deputy who would watch Carole Tregoff at the Las Vegas Sheriff's station, had found the stolen Cadillac parked at an automobile repair shop a few blocks from the Fairview Apartments on Desert Inn Road.

"I got a phone call the next day, Sunday, that they had him in custody. Ryan and I flew out on the next plane. It was a DC-3, as I recall. We got to the sheriff's office at about 8:00 P.M. You see, in those days there was no municipal police for Las Vegas. The city was patrolled by the sheriff's department. A fella named Lamb was sheriff of Clark County at that time. I think they named a street after him. We met Hiram Powell and Ray Gubser, and they provided us with a room in which to interrogate Finch. They recorded it for us and gave us a tape. We came back on Monday.

"Now, that was the first time I met Carole Tregoff. She was waiting for Finch in the waiting room as we went in. I introduced myself to her, and then we went in to question Finch."

"How did he appear? What was his demeanor?" I prompted.

"Cool, he was very cool. I was surprised that a man of his intelligence and training would talk to us. You know these were the pre-Miranda days, but all the same he could have refused to talk to us at all. I remember he waived extradition; he could have fought that for weeks if he'd wanted to.

"But I remember he was friendly and would talk to us about anything; except when we would ask him about anything connected with the murder, he would say 'I don't think my lawyer would want me to answer any of those kinds of questions.' We didn't push it; we kind of bounced around the whole subject, moving in closer and closer.

"We had a rather long interrogation, which we were told later was invaluable to the prosecution.

"As I recall, he never admitted at being in West Covina that night."

The questioning ended at 10:30 P.M. Carole Tregoff had been waiting almost twelve hours to see Bernard Finch. She was allowed into the small room; officers and reporters were present the entire time.

Las Vegas papers would report that as the two embraced she told Finch, "I'm coming back to West Covina so I can be with you. I want to be with you."

Finch was quoted: "It will only be a few days. It will be all over and we will be together again."

Carole was asked to return to West Covina and make another statement. She agreed, saying she would drive back the following day. Officers gave her a ride to the Fairview Apartments at 11:00 P.M.

ALLEN SILL

I asked Allen Sill about Monday's flight back to West Covina.

"Oh he was a very affable guy. He made himself to be a very likeable guy. If you had any preconceived idea of what a murderer would be like, he didn't fit it. I remember being struck with how he could smile and look around and engage people. People would seem to be attracted to him. He was a good-looking man, a charmer-sort-of-guy. Looked like Paul Newman, I thought.

Ryan and Finch return from Las Vegas.
Valley Tribune.

"I guess my contribution at the scene was finding that cord dangling down. You never know when something like that is going to be important. Turned out when they talked to some lady who lived up the hill there, they learned the light was on every night, that she had never seen it turned off. So it made a good case for someone unplugging the wires so they wouldn't be seen. You know, for purposes of showing premeditation."

Chief Sill talked about the hordes that came to West Covina.

"Mostly I was trying to manage the reporters. There were dozens of them every morning, at the station and out at the crime scene. Every morning we would have a sort of press conference. Some of the reporters actually were quite helpful.

"I remember a guy from the *Herald-Express* named Howard Hurtel. He had been a crime reporter for years and had covered the Black Dahlia case. He was always coming up to me saying 'Hey Chief, did you ever think of this angle?'" Sill was chuckling. "I'd always pass his ideas onto Ryan; some of them were actually quite good.

"And most of the reporters knew that we had to preserve the evidence. That was another problem. You know if we found some evidence, we didn't want the defense lawyers to know about it. It was before the days of Discovery. Now all they got to do is ask and you got to tell them everything."

five

Dr. Finch Booked for Murder
Second Statement of Carole Pappa
Visit to Crime Scene

MONDAY, JULY 20, 1959
WEST COVINA POLICE STATION

BY MID-MORNING CHIEF Sill, Bill Ryan, and Bernard
Finch were in West Covina, and the doctor had been booked
for murder.

West Covina had no jail facilities at the time. Dr. Raymond Bernard Finch, like other suspects, was placed in
manacles and chained to a wall.

The large crowd of reporters and curious spectators
was not controlled. Many would wander up to Finch and
have their picture taken with him. Policemen would pose
as though unlocking the manacles.

CONVERSATION WITH RON EVANS
WEST COVINA POLICE DEPARTMENT
APRIL, 1992

Ron Evans, the reserve officer who had answered
the first call from the Finch residence on the night of

the murder, was there much of the time. I met him at the new West Covina Station.

"It was at the old station, you know, Doc, where the Chamber of Commerce is now. On Sunset and Cameron. It was nothing more than a converted small house. We had this small counter like about here," he drew a counter in the air with his hands," and a swinging half-door over here," he pointed to his right, "that everybody was trying to get through at the same time. There must have been a couple a hundred people here, all of them wanting a picture of Finch or Pappa."

He referred to Carole Tregoff as "Pappa."

Carole Tregoff Pappa had received her interlocutory judgment from her marriage to James Pappa. Her legal name would not change for a few months. She would often be called "Mrs. Pappa."

JIMMY KEITH

Jimmy Keith was there on Monday, too. "Everybody wanted to get a picture of Finch, and a lot of people wanted to get their picture taken with Finch— you know, putting on or taking off the handcuffs. It was like a circus."

This crowd of people from all over the world was Jimmy's first indication of the enormous amount of attention the crime was attracting.

"It was big," Keith remembered. "People still ask me what I know about the Finch murder. Everywhere I go, they ask me if I was there. It kind of makes you feel like you are a celebrity. This thing was in all the TVs and all of the newspapers by then. Why, it was all over the world."

Hoppi Hopkinson, of the Los Angeles Sheriff's Department, moved in with his secretaries.

Carole Tregoff's arrival, in a low-cut sundress and dark glasses, caused a stir of excitement. Photographs show her usually wiping away tears with a handkerchief.

Finch was allowed a phone call to his personal attorney, Glenn B. Martineau. Martineau advised him to say nothing and recommended a criminal lawyer be retained. His suggestion: Grant B. Cooper.

Grant B. Cooper was one of the most respected and famous defense attorneys of the time. A former prosecutor, he had gone into private practice years before, specializing in criminal law. He represented the rich and famous and was the best money could buy. He was also known as a brutally effective cross-examiner.

Carole had found a quiet place at the station; she was waiting see Bernard Finch. Hoppi Hopkinson eased into the chair next to her with something to say. The two were alone.

"Carole," he began, "we want you to make an additional statement. Before you do, I want to tell you something. It's important. If you and Dr. Finch sat in your apartment and planned this whole thing and then drove over and killed his wife, well, you better not make this statement. You might as well tell me now you're not going to say anything."

"I'm telling the truth and will make the statement," Carole responded quickly. "And I want to see him, I want to see Dr. Finch. Can I see him?"

"I think so," Hopkinson responded. "First we need to get that statement."

Her statement and answers were the same as those she had made in Las Vegas the day before. Toward the end of the session, Ryan paused and looked at Hopkinson.

"Well," Carole asked, "Is that all? Can I see Dr. Finch now?"

Ryan rose, saying nothing, then left the room. Hopkinson stayed, studying some notes. His eyes avoided Carole's.

Ryan returned carrying a small brown-leather attaché case. Sitting slowly, he placed the case on the desk, studying her face. She looked from the case to Ryan. He was lighting a cigarette, still watching.

"Carole," he asked, "have you ever seen this bag before?"

She answered, "No."

"You've never seen it before, and you have no idea what's in it. Is that right?"

"That's right." She was studying her wrists, crossed in front of her. "Now, when can I see Dr. Finch?"

Later, she was allowed to visit Finch in a private office. Hopkinson stood nearby, watching the two through the glass in the door. He heard nothing until at one point Carole reached over and grabbed Finch's wrists with both her hands. She began crying and said loudly, "But I want to be in here with you!" For the rest of the conversation the two talked quietly, often embracing.

TUESDAY, JULY 21, 1959
VISIT TO CRIME SCENE

Grant B. Cooper was driving on Citrus Street. Ahead of him, guiding him to the Finch residence, were two police cruisers. In one was his client and William Ryan; the other carried Carole Tregoff and Hoppi Hopkinson. Earlier he had met his client, then requested a visit to the crime scene before the arraignment in Municipal Court, scheduled for 11:00 A.M.

Southern California's famous Santa Ana wind was blowing dry, dusty, hot desert air around the south hills of West Covina when the group arrived at Larkhill Drive. It would be the first of many visits to the property for all. Carole wore her sundress and sunglasses.

Cooper kept his suit jacket on and also wore sunglasses. Having learned of the visit, a small group of reporters had arrived earlier. This was their first chance to photograph Cooper. He was usually described as "ruggedly handsome, with a resemblance to John Wayne." The flamboyant attorney was fifty-six years old.

William Ryan conducted the tour. They were standing midway between the homes of Dr. Bernard Finch and his father.

"It appears as though the deceased was running to this house here," Ryan pointed to the residence of Raymond Finch, "down these steps, when somebody shot her."

"She suffered a gunshot wound. We don't know for sure that anyone shot her you know." Cooper played with the policeman.

The group walked up the hill, stopping on the asphalt driveway, in front of the garage.

"And here is about where Mrs. Pappa says she saw Mrs. Finch produce a weapon. Is that right, Mrs. Pappa?" Ryan studied her closely, waiting for her reply.

"Yes," Carole said, her voice tense. She spoke rapidly. "Just about here—I was standing here and she pulled a gun on me."

There was a pause; Ryan said nothing. Cooper was the first to speak.

"Ryan, I want a complete search made of this area for a murder weapon."

"We've been looking for three days, Mr. Cooper. I hope we find it also." As soon as Cooper asked for the search, Ryan felt his men would never find it.

The group returned to the West Covina station and after another conference with Cooper, Finch agreed to make a statement. He knew both Carole and Marie Anne had by now said he was at the residence on Saturday night.

Finch told officers he remembered being at the house; however, details would be fuzzy. "My mind is in a fog, boys. Things are just too hazy," he said. He said little more.

six

Preliminary Hearing
of R. Bernard Finch
Arrest of Carole Tregoff Pappa

TUESDAY, JULY 21, 1959
CITRUS MUNICIPAL COURT
WEST COVINA, CALIFORNIA
11:30 A.M.

"All rise," the bailiff ordered. "Court is now in session, Judge Albert K. Miller presiding."

Judge Albert K. Miller, San Gabriel Valley's most colorful jurist, was in his mid-seventies, a rotund five feet, eight inches tall, had mostly gray hair, and was usually smoking a pipe.

Dan Leonard rode his bike to the courthouse. Nothing was to keep him from these hearings, not even school.

DAN LEONARD

"I hate to tell you, I skipped school most of that week and rode my bike over to see the proceedings," he was confessing to me. The Citrus Court had been built to serve a rural, east San Gabriel Valley. Miller's courtroom, the largest of three, could seat only twenty people, and there were two hundred wanting in.

"There were two clerks of the court," Dan continued, "and they recorded their transcripts by writing with those old-fashioned, long feather pens.

"I can still see those long feathers coming up from their desks, moving all around as they wrote down everything."

Known as unorthodox and unpredictable, Judge Miller was a delight for the press. I knew his judicial style and temperment had been a focus of controversy; I listened to the anecdotes.

ALLEN SILL

"He was a character, all right. Once he told a lady shoplifter that if she promised never to steal again, he would pay her fine. Well, she promised, he took some money out of his wallet and gave it to the clerk, and the woman walked out. He was always doing something that had us talking at the station."

JIMMY KEITH

"You never fooled with Judge Miller," Keith explained. "You couldn't chew gum or talk in his courtroom. Women had to wear proper attire. If they didn't, he would ask them to leave, saying 'You women don't wear enough clothes these days. What makes you think you can come into my courtroom dressed like that!'"

Men had to wear suit coats, unless it was too hot.

DAN LEONARD

"I saw this kid was sitting in the courtroom with this little black box held up to his ear. I knew he was going to get kicked out; he was sitting in the front row.

"Judge Miller, after watching him awhile, said, 'Young man, what is that box near your ear?' 'Why it's a transistor radio, Your Honor.' 'A radio,' Miller said. 'Well, what are you listening to?'

"It turned out the kid was listening to the World Series game, so Judge Miller came out from around the bench, cleared people from the front row of spectator seats, had the defense and prosecution counsel tables turned around, and then he sat next to the kid and they both listened to the game as he conducted court from the front row."

It was clear to me: Judge Albert Miller had his own ideas on running a courtroom.

Miller arraigned Finch on the charge of murder and accepted his plea of innocent.

"Your Honor, we request bail," Cooper announced.

"Request for bail is denied. The District Attorney has recommended no bail and I don't tinker with the D. A.'s recommendation until after the preliminary hearing."

Miller spoke quietly with his clerk, then announced the preliminary hearing would begin the next Monday.

WEDNESDAY, JULY 22, 1959

Grant Cooper's assistant petitioned Judge Lewis Drucker of Los Angeles Superior Court. Finch wanted to attend his wife's funeral, scheduled for Friday.

Drucker refused, saying, "His attendance at the funeral services would be improper under the circumstances." Planning to attend were Finch's business partner, Dr. Gordon, and the latter's wife. Mrs. Gordon was the former Marion Finch, younger sister of the accused.

At about the same time the divorce attorney for Barbara Jean Finch, Joseph T. Forno of Los Angeles, gave telephone interviews to several newspapers.

"Dr. Finch threatened a number of times to take Mrs. Finch to the desert and kill her," he was quoted. When asked about the status of the divorce action, he noted that the Finches had been scheduled to appear in conciliation court the next day to discuss their differences. "Dr. Finch had expressed a desire to reconcile with his wife. The divorce action was postponed. In the meantime, we asked for all of the community property and estimated it was worth $500,000 to $1,000,000."

"No-fault divorce" was not to come for many years. A wife who could prove "fault," especially adultery, had a very good chance of getting virtually all of the community property.

Forno also spoke of a restraining order on Dr. Finch. "We filed an order to show cause after he violently assaulted his wife on June 25 of this year, trying to force her into his automobile. Dr. Finch had threatened his wife with a gun in the past, also. She was in constant fear for her life. This was preceded by an attempt on May 16 to strangle her at her home in West Covina." Forno continued, "It was after this first assault Mrs. Finch decided to file for divorce."

Mrs. Finch had filed divorce papers, and, at a June 11 hearing before Superior Court Judge Roger A. Pfaff, had requested and been granted $1,650 a month in alimony and child support. She was also given complete control of Dr. Finch's revenues from the clinic. All the revenues were deposited into her personal checking account. Barbara Jean paid the clinic's bills with her personal checks. She also signed her husband's salary checks.

Pfaff had issued a temporary restraining order directing each party not to harass the other.

Also reported widely at the time was a series of stories dealing with the quality of Dr. Finch's practice. Reporters had been searching the records of the county's civil courts.

There were at least ten outstanding malpractice suits against Finch. Two involved the deaths of children: one by aspiration of vomitus during an operation and the other by post-operative tetanus.

Interestingly, the most recent suit had been filed by James. T. Pappa, former husband of Carole Tregoff Pappa. Mr. Pappa filed his suit the Tuesday before the murder, claiming Finch had negligently repaired a knee abnormality.

Other stories described how Dr. Finch had changed office addresses many times. In July, 1951, he had resigned from the medical staff of Inter-Community Hospital, about the same time his relationship with the prestigious Magan Clinic was terminated. It was then he and Dr. Gordon opened their joint practice on West Garvey Avenue. Finch practiced out of Monrovia Hospital until 1956, when he resigned from that staff as well. His practice was primarily out of Lark Ellen Hospital until 1958, when he and Doctor Gordon opened their own West Covina Hospital.

Most physician sources advised that West Covina Hospital did not have the best of reputations within the medical community. Rumors constantly circulated about unnecessary surgeries.

**FORMER MEMBER OF MEDICAL STAFF
INTER-COMMUNITY HOSPITAL**

"What did him in at Inter-Community Hospital, primarily, was those nephropexys," a member of the medical staff at the time told me. A Nephropexy was a rarely performed operation in which a sagging kidney, an alleged cause of back pain, was raised up and secured with sutures. "He did dozens a month. After the surgery committee got on his case, he resigned from staff."

And there were suspicions of alcohol abuse.

**INTERVIEWS WITH
WEST COVINA POLICE DEPARTMENT OFFICERS
JIMMY KEITH AND DAN MARTIN
MAY 20, 1992**

Jimmy Keith told of traffic stops for erratic driving. "We all thought he was an alcoholic; he had been stopped several times for driving too fast or recklessly. We would always let him go with a warning. You know, in those days you took care of people, being that he was a person of status and all."

Another source, Dan Martin of the West Covina Police, remembered stopping Finch on Azusa Avenue. "I saw him going down Azusa avenue doing about seventy.

"I pulled him over. He was in his doctor's coat and had his stethoscope in his pocket. He said he was going to the hospital on an emergency, so I let him go. The smell of alcohol almost knocked me over."

2:00 P.M.
WEST COVINA POLICE STATION

Allen Sill talked to about fifty reporters, announcing autopsy findings. As he spoke, he read from notes taken during a phone report from Coroner Gerald K. Ridge.

"The dead woman had received two head wounds. Each caused minor fractures. Blood from the wounds had flowed down her shoulders, indicating she was standing after they were received. A bullet entered her back near the tip of the scapula and exited near her left breast, severing an artery and causing death within minutes."

The reporters asked about Carole Tregoff's statements; this was their first news of her story.

Sill's account was interrupted several times by questions. "Mrs. Carole Tregoff Pappa, girl friend to the suspect Finch, revealed under questioning that Mrs. Finch aimed a revolver at her Saturday night. According to her, she and Finch went to the residence Saturday night in order to talk to Mrs. Finch about getting an amicable divorce. Mrs. Pappa says that Mrs. Finch refused to talk to them and reached into the car and produced a revolver. She saw Dr. Finch lunge for the gun, then she ran into some nearby bushes."

The Chief announced investigators would today be questioning those who last saw Barbara Jean Finch alive, her friends at the Los Angeles Tennis Club.

THURSDAY, JULY 23, 1959

The funeral for Barbara Jean Finch was held in the early afternoon at Means Funeral Home in West Covina. Internment was at Oakdale Cemetery. Barbara Jean's brother, Jack Reynolds of Lancaster, California, made the arrangements.

Doctor and Mrs. Gordon attended as promised.

At the Finch residence William Ryan and Coroner Gerald K. Ridge had been studying the grounds for hours, trying to match autopsy findings to the physical evidence.

Also present at the Finch home was the assistant district attorney just assigned to the case, Fred N. Whichello. A twenty-five-year veteran of the District Attorney's office, the slim, lanky Whichello had been assigned by his new boss, District Attorney, William B. McKesson.

Whichello, known as thorough, methodical, and sometimes pedantic, never hesitated to speak with the press. And after studying the crime scene and talking with Ryan and Ridge, he announced his first major decision.

"Based on the evidence I have seen so far, I think I will file first-degree murder charges."

"Fred, you have no murder weapon or bullet," commented one of the reporters.

"I don't think the missing murder weapon or fatal bullet is enough to keep me from getting a conviction for first-degree murder. I've got enough other evidence, maybe even something you haven't read about in the papers yet," he teased them. It was obvious he was enjoying the excitement of interacting with so many newsmen. "I've also got two skull fractures and a bullet that was fired from more than three feet away—no way it could have been an accident."

Fred was well regarded as a prosecutor. He had been at the Pomona Division of the Los Angeles Superior Court for many years and had a good record with felony cases. Dan Leonard saw him during the preliminary hearings at Citrus Court.

DAN LEONARD

"He was about five feet and eight or nine inches tall. Had a balding head that was mostly of gray hair, and he wore horn-rimmed glasses. When examining a witness he would be polite, but persistent and deliberate, never raising his voice."

Whichello did not like the idea of married men and women having affairs; this was obvious.

Dan remembered. "Whenever he addressed Carole Tregoff he would always say Mrs. Pappa, with the emphasis on the 'Mrs.' And there would always be a little pause after he said it, just so the fact that she still had her married name would be obvious to everyone."

Carole and James Pappa were granted their interlocutory decree in January of 1959. According to the agreement, she would use her married name for one year, then legally become Carole Tregoff. Fred Whichello would always call her "Mrs. Pappa."

The press lined up in front of the investigators as they started to leave. They pried at Whichello for the "other evidence" at which he had hinted.

"What other evidence?" one asked. "You said you had enough *other* evidence."

Ryan took a step toward Whichello; the prosecutor was already speaking.

"We have an attaché case," he started. "It's a brown courier-type case containing very significant evidence. It was found within throwing distance of where Mrs. Pappa said she was hiding, and its contents," he paused, "well, its contents are not at all typical of what a doctor would carry."

The reporters had heard rumors about the attaché case; now there was confirmation. They would, in their next editions, talk of the "mystery bag" and the "murder kit."

2:00 P.M.
LOS ANGELES COUNTY JAIL

It was custom for prisoners to come to the visitor's area and give interviews. There were about twenty reporters waiting for Finch when he gave this, his first, interview. He was calmer now, more relaxed. He would be described as "boyishly friendly." Remembering reporters by their first names, he would often ask about their families.

With confidence he announced he had been trying to reconcile with Barbara Jean for months, but that she would have nothing of it.

"I had been trying for almost two months to effect a reconciliation with my wife before this horrible thing happened. I'd send Barbara presents and flowers. I invited her out to dinner many times to discuss the matter. All failed. She just wouldn't discuss it with me."

"Did you murder her, Dr. Finch?" one asked.

"Please," he smiled, showing his palms and waving them from side to side, "just call me Bernie. I have attorneys I have complete confidence in who have advised me not to discuss the case, I'm sure they know what they are doing."

4:00 P.M.
WEST COVINA POLICE DEPARTMENT

Fred Whichello was interviewing Marie Anne Lidholm for the first time. Assessing his witness, he knew she would be questioned by Grant Cooper, a respectable cross-examiner. He listened to her story, trying to evaluate how she would hold up on the stand.

As they were saying their final words, he took a half-step back and leaned against an office doorway. The young girl would be walking out alone. She shook his hand and started to leave.

He watched intently as she went toward the half-door that kept visitors from the inner workings of the station. The press quickly encircled her.

The pretty blonde was wearing a plain white sweater and her horn-rimmed glasses. She held a small purse in front of her. The reporters were all talking, some within inches of her face. Flashbulbs were popping; their light made her wince and blink.

"Miss Lidholm," one of them asked first, "are you aware that your story differs significantly from that of Dr. Finch and Miss Tregoff?"

Whichello watched. She showed no nervousness, no apprehension. After a pause she spoke slowly, with a thick, Swedish accent. "I am telling the truth. If their story is different from mine, then they are lying." Her chin rose slightly higher. "I will not change one word from what I have told the police."

Then she was asked, "Was Dr. Finch kind to you?"

"He was very kind to me." She paused, looking down. "I don't know what came over him; I guess he must have been mad."

MONDAY, JULY 27
WEST COVINA POLICE STATION

It was preliminary hearing day, but first, investigators had a treat for the reporters who came to the usual morning press conference.

Measuring three feet on a side, an enlarged photograph of the contents of the "mystery bag" was on display. Chief Sill and Hoppi Hopkinson stood behind William Ryan as he detailed the contents, pointing with his fountain pen.

As Ryan spoke, reporters recorded the "murder kit" contents in their notepads.

Inside the brown leather attaché case:

- two pieces of rope, each two feet in length
- an eight-inch kitchen knife
- a plastic sheet about two feet on a side
- a half empty box of .38 caliber ammunition
- an elastic bandage roll, or "ace" wrap
- a small bottle of Seconal tablets
- two sets of surgeon's gloves
- a vial of injectable Seconal
- a syringe and needle
- a flashlight
- a brown shaving-kit bag

Ryan with Murder Kit.
Valley Tribune.

"We also found fragments of the rubber gloves about twenty six feet from the body," Ryan advised the press, "and the torn-off end of a finger of the glove inside the victim's car."

9:30 A.M.
CITRUS MUNICIPAL COURTROOM OF
JUDGE ALBERT K. MILLER

DAN LEONARD

"It was standing room only. There was maybe forty or fifty people in this room made to hold, at most, twenty-five.

"Dr. Finch was very distinguished-looking, very well-groomed. Whichello was mild and quiet and businesslike. I knew one of the court reporters, Red. He and Tommy Williams, the other recorder, would never look up; once things got going those feathers on the quill pens never stopped moving."

"Just call me Bernie, boys," Finch told the group of newsmen surrounding the defense table. "You know, I haven't felt this good in years. It's good to get some rest."

"We are not presenting any evidence at this time," he continued to the group. "The prosecutor is not producing anything damaging, but he is presenting facts fairly. The witnesses, I am sure, will vindicate me."

"I realize that I'm tired," he admitted. "I am heartened by the many letters of support I am receiving, particularly from my old friends at the College of the Medical Evangelist."

Bernard Finch had graduated from the school, now known as Loma Linda University College of Medicine, in 1943.

One reporter said, "Your dad claimed that you were off the beam."

"My dad is sick; a lot of the time he doesn't know what he's saying. He has diabetes you know," Bernard explained.

I wondered how a teenager, even one as resourceful as Dan Leonard, could manage to obtain a seat for this preliminary hearing.

DAN LEONARD

"I knew Joe Taburdi," he explained. "He was the sheriff's liaison officer and was there every day of the hearing. I always got a seat next to the court reporters.

"One day—I can't remember which one—Judge Miller came in and sat down and looked directly at me. He leaned over to Red and said, 'That darn kid's here again.' I thought he was going to kick me out, but he didn't."

"What was Finch like?" I asked.

"Dr. Finch was stoic; he appeared to be in control. He was cool, very cool. Sometimes he would smile and wave to a newspaperman or photographer. But for the most part he was very cool."

The purpose of the preliminary hearing: To determine whether or not, in Judge Miller's opinion, Dr. Finch should be held for trial.

Fred Whichello was at the prosecutor's table to the right of the courtroom. Grant Cooper was not present at the preliminary hearing; Finch, sitting to the far left of the defense table, was represented by Ned Nelson.

Whichello's first witness was Gerald K. Ridge, who detailed his autopsy findings. He was followed by Captain Ryan, who described the evidence. Ryan testified that a key ring found in Finch's belongings in Las Vegas had two keys that fit the attaché case, the so-called "murder kit."

TUESDAY, JULY 28

Hollywood made an appearance at the hearing this second day. The producer of the Perry Mason television show, L. Patrick Gray, had her picture taken with Judge Miller. She was quoted as saying she was looking for ideas for a show. She was introduced to Marie Anne Lidholm.

Eric Ambler with L. Patrick Gray. *Getty Images.*

MARIE ANNE LIDHOLM

"I later would work for them in their household," Marie told me. "I remember meeting a lot of famous people and going out to a lot of fancy restaurants. I wonder now if they were just showing me off to their friends."

Marie Anne wore a schoolgirl plaid dress and a simple white pullover sweater, buttoned tight at the neck. As she was sworn as a witness, Bernie, seated at the defense table, examined the contents of the "murder kit." Once her testimony began, he leaned forward, resting his chin on interlocked fingers, watching intently.

"When I came to, Dr. Finch had a small gun in his hand; he told me to get in the car," she was telling the court.

Whichello: "What happened after you got into the car?"

Daily Tribune.

Lidholm at Preliminary
Hearing. *Valley Tribune.*

Lidholm: "Dr. Finch ordered Mrs. Finch to get into the car. When she sat down on the passenger seat, I think one foot was still out of the car. He said she should give him the keys or he would kill her."

Whichello: "Then what happened?"

Lidholm: "Mrs. Finch ran out of the car. Dr. Finch ran after her."

Judge Miller: "Miss Lidholm, did Dr. Finch have the gun in his hand at this point?"

Lidholm: "I don't know. I can't remember if he had the gun in his hand at this point."

Ned Nelson cross-examined Lidholm and asked her to demonstrate how Dr. Finch had grabbed her in the garage.

...AN EYEWITNESS WITH A SOUVENIR

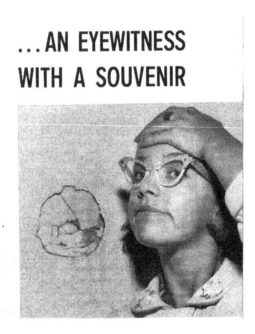

"He had one hand over each side of my head, like this." She stood and put her hands on Nelson's head in order to demonstrate. She covered his ears with her palms, then grabbed at the back of his head with her fingers. "Then he slammed me against the wall, several times." She sat back down, pulling her dress forward from the back so it would not wrinkle.

Nelson: "What are your feelings toward Dr. Finch now?"

Lidholm: "He didn't treat me very nice that night, I think." She looked down, took a deep breath, then looked back up. "I just can't believe he would do a thing like that to me. I have been trying to help him with so many things."

Nelson then asked about discrepancies between her original statements to police and prosecutors, and her testimony this day. She had first said Finch had the gun in his hand when she entered the garage. Today, Marie Anne said she saw the gun after the first gunshot, as she regained consciousness. She also talked of how Finch had once "stolen" one of the family cars from Barbara Jean.

During this questioning she broke down and Miller called an early recess for lunch.

Lidholm. *Getty Images.*

As the crowd returned for the afternoon session, Carole Tregoff arrived with her stepmother, Gladys Tregoff. Excitement spread through the crowd as dozens of flashbulbs popped. Carole wore a black sheath dress with a broad, white collar, white gloves and sunglasses with pointed outside tips. The front row on the right of the courtroom had been roped off for witnesses, and Carole Tregoff Pappa had been asked to be one.

Dan Leonard watched his friend, Joe Taburdi, show the women where to sit.

DAN LEONARD

"How can I describe Carole Tregoff?" Dan asked himself.

"Well, I was an adolescent young man and she was very attractive to me. That's for sure. She was attractive to most everyone, I suppose. She had a classy look about her—red hair and fair skin and dark, dark, eyes. If you were casting a movie and needed a murderess, she would be the last one to choose. I would call her 'classically beautiful.'

"She had done some modeling, you know. She was tall, about five feet, eight inches, and stood very straight."

Early Modeling Photo. *Getty.*

Life Photo of Carole
Tregoff. *Getty.*

The courtroom buzz droned until Judge Miller gaveled it to silence.

Whichello: "We call Mrs. Carole Pappa, Your Honor."

Gladys Tregoff squeezed her stepdaughter's hand, then let go as Carole went to the witness box. This was her first sworn court testimony. She had no legal advice or representation and had not been told she might be a suspect. No one would tell her that what she was about to say could be used as evidence against her.

"Mr. Whichello was very calm and deliberate," Dan Leonard said. "He was never rude and never raised his voice."

Whichello was also aware that only one person had made statements that placed Carole Tregoff at the crime scene. That person: Carole Tregoff. The prosecutor began by asking her to talk about circumstances preceding her move to Las Vegas.

Tregoff: "I moved to Las Vegas in May of this year to avoid being subpoenaed in Dr. Finch's divorce action."

Whichello: "Who paid the rent on your apartment there?"

Carole: "My mother helped out. I paid some myself. Dr. Finch paid the deposit for the apartment."

She repeated her story that Finch had phoned her asking that she meet him at the airport. Then, in response to questions, she took the courtroom back to July 18, 1959.

Tregoff: "Dr. Finch convinced me to drive back to West Covina with him in order to help him talk Mrs. Finch into an amicable divorce and an out-of-court settlement. We left Las Vegas after my shift at the Sands was over. Dr. Finch picked me up at the Sands in my car. He brought some clothes I changed into and we left directly from there. We alternated driving, and when we got to West Covina, Dr. Finch was driving. We parked the car in the parking lot of South Hills Country Club. We knew that if she saw my car, she would not come out of the house."

Whichello: "Who went up the hill first?"

Tregoff: "Dr. Finch went ahead, then he turned and waved for me to come up. He waited for me on the driveway of his father's house, which is about half-way up the hill to his own house. He asked me to bring the flashlight, as I was wearing soft-soled shoes. The flashlight was in a case, so I reached into the car and grabbed the whole case and brought it with me."

Whichello, holding up the mystery case: "Is this that case?"

Tregoff: "Yes, that's it. It contained the flashlight. It also contained some sleeping tablets for me. I had been having some trouble sleeping lately and had asked Dr. Finch to get me some sleeping pills."

Whichello: "When did you first see this bag, Mrs. Pappa?"

Tregoff: "Dr. Finch had it with him when he arrived at the airport Friday night."

Whichello: "And when did you see it next, after Dr. Finch arrived?"

Tregoff: "On the way to Los Angeles, the next night. He asked me if I needed anything for the apartment. I told him I needed a few things, including a can opener. So on the way down he bought me a little kit with a hammer and a screwdriver and a knife, and put it in." Carole seemed calm. As she spoke she looked mostly at the wooden rail in front of her.

Whichello walked over to the witness; a slight smile seemed to have eased into his face.

He rested both arms on the rail to Carole's left, leaning toward Carole. She looked away, down to the right.

Whichello: "Did you ask him to buy you some .38 caliber bullets?"

Carole's control seemed to fade. Mouth drawn down at the sides. Her stepmother leaned forward from her seat. All in the room were still. The prosecutor waited, then asked another question.

Whichello: "Did he have another bag, the other little smaller case?" He was referring to the shaving-kit containing .38 caliber bullets.

Carole answered quickly. "No, the smaller bag was not in the case then. The first time I saw that, it was under the front seat of Mrs. Finch's Chrysler. I put it in the larger attache case later."

Whichello raised himself from the rail. He was silent. This was new, unexpected information.

Whichello: "So, you put it in there later?"

Tregoff: "Yes."

Whichello: "Very well." He walked back to his table. Then turned back to face Carole. "Continue on with what happened, Mrs. Pappa. What happened next, after you went back to get the flashlight?"

Tregoff: "We went on up to the lawn and played with the dog for a little while. We waited outside. Dr. Finch went inside the garage and found some rope. He said he wanted the rope to tie bumpers on the boat he kept at Lido Shores, near Newport. He asked me to put the rope in my purse but it was too big so I put it in the attaché case instead.

"We wanted to play with the Finch dog, Frosty, so we took some gloves out of the case and blew them up and played with them like they were balloons. Then after awhile Mrs. Finch came home."

In response to Whichello's questions, Carole told how Barbara Jean Finch had pointed a gun at her.

Tregoff: "She reached into the car and came back out with a gun that was pointed directly at me. Dr. Finch reached behind Mrs. Finch and grabbed something out of the car and threw it at me. It hit me in the stomach. He said 'Get out of here!' Then I ran down the driveway and to the right. I tripped on a sprinkler head, and the small bag he had thrown at me went flying. After that I heard some more scuffling sounds like more than one person was involved, and then the lights went on all around the house.

"Then I heard a sound—Dr. Finch shouting like he was surprised or in trouble or something. I could not make out the exact words. I thought I should go back in there because I did not know what was happening. I came back into the entrance of the garage. I saw his hat on the floor of the garage."

Whichello's right thumb and forefinger rubbed his chin as he paused for a moment. This was the first Carole had spoken of going to the garage a second time.

Whichello: "Now that was the second time you were in the garage? You're telling us you went a second time? Is that correct?"

Tregoff: "Yes. I looked up and saw Barbara. She was on the right side of the car with her left side towards me. She turned around and looked over. I could see she had a gun in her hand. Then she ran across the driveway toward Dr. Finch's father's house. I picked up the hat and went back down the driveway to the grape-stake hedge near the house. I took the hat with me and threw it down. Then I hid in the bushes till about 5:00 A.M."

Whichello: "Why were you hiding behind the hedge?"

Tregoff: "I was scared."

Whichello: "Were you afraid of being shot?"

Tregoff: "I imagine I was."

Whichello: "So when the police came you felt protected then, I suppose, so that you could come out from the bushes?"

Tregoff: "It seems I was too scared to move."

Whichello: "So you stayed there until about 5:00 A.M., then you left, without being observed?"

Tregoff: "I am not sure. Something like that."

Before court adjourned, Carole told of returning to her apartment and finding Finch. She testified he appeared "shocked" when she told him that his wife had been killed and that he was a suspect.

Whichello questions Tregoff minutes before her arrest.
Valley Tribune.

WEDNESDAY, JULY 29, 1959

Judge Miller arrived at Citrus Municipal Court at 9:00 A.M., earlier than usual. He found Herbert "Red" Hennes, his court's bailiff, inside, and the two returned to the judge's station wagon. Before leaving home, Miller had loaded forty five folding chairs into his car. He directed Hennes to set them in the vacant areas around the courtroom. Some were in the center aisle, others next to the judge's bench in front of the attorneys' tables.

Later, a packed room watched Carole weaving through the extra chairs, sometimes shuffling sideways, pelted, as usual, with flashes of light. As she lowered herself into the witness chair, Judge Miller reminded her she was still under oath.

Whichello: "Did Dr. Finch ever agree to marry you when his divorce was final?"

Tregoff: "Well, it was never as direct as that."

Whichello: "I have here," he was standing at his desk holding a slim stack of paper, "the statement you made to the Clark County sheriffs. In it you say that you two were planning on getting married. Do you wish to change that statement at this time?"

Most thought Carole seemed calmer as she began her testimony, more self-confident. She looked directly at the prosecutor as she spoke.

Tregoff: "A lot of things were said that were not in that statement."

Whichello walked toward his witness, hands behind his back. His voice slightly raised.

Whichello: "Well, did he ever say that he loved you?"

Tregoff: "More or less." Her left fingers were at her temple.

Whichello: "And had you ever told him that you loved him?"

Tregoff: "More or less." She was looking away from him.

Whichello: "And," he was within inches, his eyes fixed on her, "prior to this tragic incident did you have sexual intercourse with Dr. Finch?"

The room filled with gasps and the garble of hushed, short sentences.

Tregoff: "No!" She turned and looked at Whichello. "This was not a cheap relationship."

Whichello: "You must answer the question." His left palm slapped the wooden rail. "Did you ever have sexual intercourse with Dr. Finch?"

Attitudes toward premarital sex were still quite Victorian.

Her confidence drained, Carole started sobbing, burying her eyes in a white handkerchief. "I prefer not to answer that," she managed, "other than what I said."

Whichello walked to the front of the bench and faced Judge Miller. "Your Honor, I must ask that you direct the witness to answer my questions."

For a few moments, Miller watched the sobbing girl in the witness chair. "Let's take an adjournment." He waited for the girl's sobbing to wane. "Mrs. Pappa, as there is no privacy in this courtroom, I would suggest that you use my chambers as a place to gather yourself. I would suggest that you bring your mother along."

Carole's stepmother met her at the witness stand and helped her down. Red Hennes showed the two women to a single door to the right of the courtroom leading to Judge Miller's chambers. He stood back, holding the door open for them. After they had passed, he looked at Miller. The judge nodded, and Hennes went inside with the women, closing the door.

Miller stayed on the bench for a few moments, packing his pipe. Reporters gathered below his perch, most asking if he would require Carole to answer. He lit up and launched balls of smoke, avoiding a response.

After a few minutes, the judge stepped down and walked toward his chambers. As he did, he looked out to the courtroom and made eye contact with a man who was sitting in the front row of spectator seats. The man had dark, short hair and was wearing a lightweight, dark suit; he stood as the judge neared. Miller went into his chambers, closing the door behind him.

The man in the suit had been following. After the door closed, he turned and stood in front of it. He was facing the courtroom, hands crossed in front at the beltline.

Inside his chambers Miller talked with the witness.

After fifteen minutes, Carole Tregoff was once again walking to the witness stand. Fifty people watched, wondering if she would be told to answer Whichello's question. She settled into the chair, looking toward her stepmother. The only sounds were the occasional pops and fizzes of flashbulbs.

Whichello: "I ask you again, Mrs. Pappa," he spoke slowly, "Have you had sexual intercourse with Dr. Finch?"

Her fingers were at her left temple, her hand hiding the side of her face.

Tregoff: "Yes." She spoke in a whisper.

The courtroom stayed quiet, except for the scratching noises of the two quill pens.

Whichello asked her to tell what happened after she returned to her apartment and found Dr. Finch asleep on her sofa. She repeated the story she first gave to Clark County deputies.

"I have no further questions, Your Honor." He was through.

Carole breathed deeply.

"I have no cross-examination for this witness," Ned Nelson announced.

Miller said nothing as he watched Whichello straightening a stack of papers on the prosecutor's table. Carole looked up, then over to the judge.

"May the witness leave, Mr. Whichello?" Miller finally asked.

Carole looked at the prosecutor, then at the two men rising behind him. William Ryan and Hoppi Hopkinson were both squaring the lapels of their coats.

"No, Your Honor," Whichello announced. "She may not, because she is going to be arrested."

The room filled with gasps and excited mumbling.

Carole Tregoff's eyes widened as the two officers approached her. As Ryan leaned forward, there was a flurry of flashed light. He spoke to her, then reached for her left elbow. The two officers led her out of the courtroom, past spectators and reporters. She was not handcuffed as they directed her to the back seat of an unmarked car.

Within an hour Carole Tregoff had been booked for first-degree murder. Her preliminary hearing was set for the following week.

As Whichello left Citrus Court that day, he was besieged by the press.

"When you look at all the evidence," he told them, "the relationship of the parties, the type of wound, and the murder kit—why, her own testimony showed an active participation.

"We are confident that the two of them planned this thing together. We think they planned to tie up Mrs. Finch, inject her with a lethal dose of Seconal, and run her car over a cliff." He started walking to his car, then stopped and turned back to face the group. "Oh, there was another thing. We've discovered a new will, made up by Barbara Jean Finch just three months ago, and it left Dr. Finch the bulk of the estate."

FRIDAY, JULY 31, 1959

It was a few minutes before Judge Miller was to announce whether Bernard Finch would be tried for murder. Ned Nelson was being questioned by reporters in the hall outside the courtroom.

"Do you represent both parties, Mr. Nelson?"

"I will be trying to get bail for both parties today. There are precedents for this kind of thing."

Bail was not mandatory. It was granted at the discretion of the judge, never for murder defendants if premeditation was suspected.

"Has Mrs. Pappa asked for a lie detector test?" One of the reporters followed up on a rumor.

"Mrs. Pappa has asked for a lie detector test, but I have advised her not to do so. It would serve no useful purpose at this time."

Instead of a brief announcement of his findings, as was the custom, Miller made an extraordinary twenty-minute statement in which he analyzed all the evidence heard in his court the last three days. He also made remarks about Carole Tregoff, who had not yet had her own preliminary hearing.

He first acknowledged his long friendship with the Finch family.

"I have known the Finches, father and son, for years and years, and they have been admired friends of mine. I cannot consider my friendship with the litigants in any court case. If that were so, there would be no law at all."

Everyone waited.

"I don't think that any reasonable person would have thought Barbara Jean Finch was in the frame of mind to want to talk about a divorce at all, let alone at midnight. And it doesn't make sense to me that anyone would bring along his paramour to talk to his wife about a divorce, either."

Miller said he had concluded the two were lying in wait. "Otherwise they would have invited themselves into the house or stayed at the house of the father next door.

"Now about this satchel they found the next day: All the articles have been discussed at length here, and every single one can be reconciled with the intention of being used to kill someone.

"It would seem to me that Dr. Finch first went up the hill to check to see if the coast was clear, then he signalled for Carole to come and join him.

"What happened was something they had not expected. The young Swedish exchange student spoiled the whole affair when she heard a call for help."

He reviewed Marie Anne's testimony, noting that the last time the doctor was seen by her, he appeared to be in hot pursuit.

"Later, the deceased was found lying on the wet grass, with death her only companion. I think this was exactly the result he wanted, else he would have been sorry, sobbing his heart out, crying, 'Why did I do it! My God, what have I done?'"

Miller looked directly at Finch now. "This was no sudden, accidental event; it was a planned occurrence. It was intended that the deceased end up lying on the cold lawn there, the woman he had sworn to love and cherish.

"The defendant will be held over for arraignment in Superior Court for the crime of murder."

Ned Nelson rose to make a motion for bail. As he spoke the noise behind him quieted. "Your Honor, there is inadequate evidence for premeditation in this case. There are precedents that would allow us to get bail if there is no premeditation."

The judge was quick to respond, his voice louder. "They were lying in wait, and the first time the gun was seen, it was in the defendant's hand. That sounds like premeditation to me."

Miller rose, gavel in hand. "And you have the coroner's testimony that the gun was fired from six feet away. You'll have to convince me the deceased held the gun six feet behind her back and pulled the trigger and killed herself. That's too preposterous for belief!" He raised the gavel, ready to adjourn. The crowd stirred, squeezing itself to the door.

Ryan taking Carole Tregoff to West Covina Jail. *Valley Tribune.*

Tregoff Booked. *Valley Tribune.*

Nelson persisted, talking quickly now. "I submit the evidence shows that the victim herself produced a weapon and that this negates any premeditation of willful desire on the part of the defendant to take a life. If my client had had a premeditated desire to kill his wife, he would have shot her in the car!"

The room quickly quieted; the spectators turned, looking at Nelson.

Miller asked, "Well, where did he get the gun, then? The maid saw *him* with the gun, counselor."

"I don't know," Nelson answered. "Probably he got it from the victim."

The gavel fell and Bernard Finch's preliminary hearing was over. His date for arraignment in Pomona Superior Court: August 17.

seven
Booking and Preliminary Hearing
of Carole Tregoff Pappa

FRIDAY, JULY 31

Carole Tregoff was persuaded by her parents to hire her own attorney. She would be represented, for only a few days, by Milo V. Olson.

She was booked for murder at the West Covina police station on Thursday. Newspapers showed photographs of her manacled to the wall; the headlines read "Scarlet-haired Beauty Languishes in Chains." Today she would be moved to Los Angeles County jail. Carole did not speak to the press. Her stepmother Gladys, however, gave an interview at her home in South Pasadena. She defended her stepdaughter and spoke highly of Dr. Finch.

"My daughter is not a tramp," she said to the group of reporters gathered at her comfortable home on Oak Hill Drive. "She's not."

"Most everything Carole attempted to do, she did well," she continued. "She used to ice skate, is a good swimmer, and she took piano for awhile when she was a kid. But like all kids she didn't want to practice, so we stopped the lessons."

She held up a book, pointing to its title, *The New Dictionary of Thoughts*. "She is fascinated quite a bit with words.

She would always cut out poems and things from papers. Carole has a wonderful mind and she remembers things so well. That's why she did so well in her job with Dr. Finch."

MONDAY, AUGUST 2, 1959
10:15 A.M.

Bernard Finch was conducting one of his interviews at the visitor's room of County Jail. He had, at this point, seen Marie Anne Lidholm and Carole Tregoff testify. He had an announcement for the press.

"Everything will be explained at the trial, boys. Carole was telling the truth about what she saw, and so was Marie Anne. They just didn't see everything. They weren't in the garage at the same time, that's all."

"Bernie," one of the senior reporters asked, "what about the fact that Clark County sheriffs have located the clerk you bought some of the items in the 'murder kit' from? How can you explain that?"

"Sure I bought those items; I'll explain all of that when my attorneys let me, don't worry. And as far as Marie Anne and Carole are concerned, there is a missing ingredient that will explain what happened. Something that happened when Barbara Jean and I were alone in the garage."

There was a brief pause. Most reporters had their heads down, writing. "Missing Ingredient" would figure into most of their next headlines.

Then Finch talked of "jail life." "You know, you go from forty years as a respected citizen to a 'thug.'"

"What's it like being in jail, Bernie?"

"I live in a 'tank' with sixty-two other men. There are about five men to each of the twelve cells in the tank. A cell is about eight feet long and six or seven feet wide. There are two bunks to a cell. The rest of the inmates sleep on the floor." He lowered his voice and looked directly at each reporter, one at a time. "The place is full of bedbugs, cockroaches, and mosquitoes. I've probably got four dozen bites on me now as we sit talking." He was pointing to spots on his left forearm.

"Look at these other men here," he motioned to the other inmates who were visiting with their families and attorneys. "Most of these guys want to get out of here so that they can commit more crimes." His eyes grew big. "I'm anxious to get out to take care of my little boy and to resume my practice. And I definitely will return to my practice when I get out."

"Did you shoot your wife, Dr. Finch?" one asked.

He smiled and looked down, then directly back at the reporter. "You know, I can only say so much—my attorneys, you know." He looked away again, then back at the man. "But I will say this." He jabbed the desk top with his index finger. "Anybody who is attacked with a gun has two alternatives: he can get killed or he can kill the one pointing the gun at him."

They scrawled faster, most speculating they would see a self-defense strategy at the trial.

Nearby in the District Attorney's office, it was being announced Carole Tregoff would change lawyers. She would be represented by the firm of none other than Jerry Giesler, acclaimed "lawyer of the stars," and his associates.

Giesler was famous for having represented Clarence Darrow, Charles Chaplin, Robert Mitchum, and others. He was a passionate defense attorney, having once broken his hand banging on the jury rail during a closing argument. He routinely tutored his junior partners in strategy. "The best defense is a good offense," he would say. "Always attack the prosecution, using his own case against him, like the Oriental art of jujitsu."

Giesler was ill and assigned the case to his associate, Robert Adam Neeb, Jr. While a member of Giesler's firm, Neeb had prepared and presented the defenses of Errol Flynn and "Bugsy" Siegle.

Shortly after noon, in the women's section of County Jail, Carole gave her first interview.

She appeared to be in good spirits, not as thin and distraught as at the Finch preliminary hearing. She laughed and joked with newsmen, but turned quite serious when asked about Finch.

"What are your feelings toward Dr. Finch, Carole?"

Her face darkened. She looked directly at the questioner, an unmistakable sneer slowly appearing on her face. She said nothing.

"Does the sneer mean you no longer love him?" the reporter continued.

"I guess so." She replied matter-of-factly, her voice quieter; she was looking down.

"Does it or not, Carole?"

She looked up. "Yes."

"What kind of strategy have you and Mr. Neeb discussed about your case?" someone shouted from the back.

"My civil rights were violated." She was speaking louder. "I was asked to testify against myself and that's not right."

Fred Whichello was leaving his office when he learned of Carole's comments. The press wanted his reaction.

"Well, our case," he told the small group, "rests on the glaring inconsistencies between her statements to the police and her testimony at the preliminary hearing."

"That's all her own testimony, Fred," one reporter said. "Shouldn't she have been advised of her rights?"

"Well," he paused, "she wasn't a suspect. We never thought of her as a suspect until she gave her testimony. Only after she gave her testimony was she considered a suspect. We're still confident for a convication."

Whichello would later reveal he had decided, after consulting with District Attorney McKesson, to drop the case against Carole if her testimony and police statements were ever ruled inadmissible.

TUESDAY, AUGUST 11, 1959
CITRUS MUNICIPAL COURT
9:00 A.M.

The bailiff stood in the empty courtroom of Judge William Micajah Miller, looking at the locked double-doors. The doors were jerking and there were dull thuds of something bumping from the other side.

He was wondered how to open the doors without getting hurt. An estimated 300 people were waiting outside to get a seat for the preliminary hearing of Carole Anne Tregoff.

A local reporter was memorializing the reasons some had for coming.

Doris Ware was eight months pregnant. "I squeezed in through the front door of the courthouse anyway," she explained. "I wanted to see if Carole Tregoff looked like her pictures in the paper. I just saw her go by; she's prettier."

"I just wanted to see what Carole looked like," said another.

A psychology professor from Utah State College said, "I came hoping to learn about the interactions of people, from the people in the crowd right up to the judge."

Many older would-be spectators were observed being elbowed and pushed from their places in line.

Some had not come so far. "I just live around the corner anyway," said Florence Carpenter.

"I just came here to pay a traffic citation and decided to get in line when I learned this was the place where the Tregoff trial was," said Dick Harthon.

And one of Carole's co-workers from the medical clinic was present. Dorothy Kateley said, "I have known Carole since she started working at the hospital. She's a fine person, and I still think Dr. Finch is a fine doctor."

The bailiff pushed against the left door as he turned the keys in the other. The knob turned. Both doors pushed opened. A wall of squeezed people pushed through, throwing the bailiff to the side.

Within minutes all seats were filled. Many standing complained they had lost their places in line unfairly.

"I got here way before you did this morning," one complained to a seated spectator. "How'd you get that seat!"

"All stand for His Honor Judge William Micajah Miller." The bailiff yelled, hoping to quiet the crowd.

Judge Miller stood at his bench; he had never seen such a commotion in his courtroom. The seated were determined to keep their prize.

He made his first decision of the hearing. "You can all stay if you keep quiet and behave yourselves." The room quieted. "If anyone behaves in a manner not fitting for these proceedings, I will instruct the bailiff to remove you immediately.

"Court will come to order," he commanded. Then, after looking around, he noticed that the defendant and her counsel were not present. "Does anybody know where the defendant is?"

"They were unable to get in, Your Honor," the bailiff yelled from the back of the room. "I told them to go around and come in through the press entrance."

Walter Reynolds, Barbara Jean's father, was given a seat in the section reserved for witnesses and press. He was talking to William Ryan, who was leaning forward, listening intently.

Reynolds was sixty-three years old and despite his heavy drinking habits was able to keep a job as the manager of a men's clothing store in Sherman Oaks. His face was flushed and he had a W. C. Fields nose. He spoke slowly, gesturing with his right hand often.

"She knew they were going to try to kill her," he was saying. "Two weeks before they killed her I stayed at the house and she asked me to put new locks on the doors."

A few weeks earlier, just before his admission to a rest home for treatment of his alcoholism, Reynolds had given his daughter a diamond ring for safekeeping. The ring and some other articles had been stolen two weeks before the murder.

"I'd sure like to find that ring," he leaned closer to Ryan, his eyebrows raised, "and the clothes and perfume that was stolen, too. And I bet you I know just where they are, too."

The two then talked of Reynolds's observations as a patient at Finch's West Covina Hospital for a hernia repair. "It was a year and a half ago and," he hesitated, "I don't know, there just seemed to be something going on between Finch and Carole. Just the way they would look at each other and talk."

The small door to the right of the courtroom opened. The excitement in the courtroom crescendoed as Robert Adam Neeb, Carole's new attorney, entered. His client, not far behind, held her hand up to block the sputtering fizzes of light from the photographers. Behind Carole was a young Minnesotan: Donald Bringgold was Mr. Neeb's junior associate.

Judge Miller pounded his gavel.

Carole's appearance had changed. She was dressed more conservatively in a high-collared dress and wore no sunglasses. Neeb led her past Whichello and Ryan, now seated at the prosecutor's table.

The crowd was roaring.

"This will be my last warning," Miller admonished. "Any more outbursts like that and I'll clear everybody out of here."

After announcing he would call fourteen witnesses and need three days to present his case, Fred Whichello asked his first witness, Dr. Gerald K. Ridge, to take the stand.

The testimony of the deputy coroner and William Ryan took up the entire day. There were no surprises for the defense team.

During an afternoon recess, Whichello consulted with the D. A.'s office by telephone. Thursday, Miller would decide if Carole's statements and testimony could be admitted as evidence. After the conversation with his boss, Whichello made an important decision. He would announce it to the press before the next court session.

THURSDAY, AUGUST 13, 1959

The hearing had been postponed until Thursday because of a busy court calendar. Before the proceedings, Whichello was talking with the small group gathered around his desk. The accused and her counsel were not present.

"Well, I guess you might call it a 'love nest,'" he told the group.

Whichello was born in 1903 in England; Queen Victoria had died less than two years before. His legacy from the Victorian age: there are many things men and women simply do not do.

"Of course we all know that Mrs. Pappa was having sexual relations with Dr. Finch while they were both still legally married. She admitted this in open court under oath at Dr. Finch's preliminary hearing, just before we arrested her as she stepped down from the witness stand." He raised both eyebrows and held his hands out in front of him, palms up.

The case was bringing him attention. Today he was to address the prestigious group of Service Club and Chamber of Commerce past presidents. He was featured as an expert in preparation of capital cases.

"We have," he continued, "determined the existence of this love nest in Monterey Park shared by the couple. We think this proves that the doctor had no thoughts of reconciling with his wife, as he had told the reconciliation court, and that a divorce was imminent."

The reporters were all scrawling in their small notebooks, composing their "LOVE NEST" headlines for the next day.

Whichello waited. When they looked up, he went on.

"It is a possibility that our case against Mrs. Pappa will be dismissed on the basis that she may have incriminated herself, without having been properly warned, during the preliminary hearing for Dr. Finch."

Then he outlined his strategy. "If this is the case, I feel we can go to a grand jury, get an indictment for murder, and then get her tried that way. We would be able to enter into evidence the existence of this love nest and, I think, could maybe even still use her testimony to get an indictment."

He went on, lecturing on the rules of evidence for grand juries. "They're more relaxed than for trials. They let you enter things like that. You see, she gave that information freely, before she was a suspect."

FRIDAY, AUGUST 14, 1959

Whichello would finish his case today. It consisted, so far, of the dry, technical testimony of investigators, coroners, and ballistics experts. William Ryan outlined the physical evidence.

Marie Anne Lidholm told her story once more. During her cross-examination, Neeb highlighted that she did not see Carole Tregoff on the night of the murder.

Before court convened, Judge Miller told all attorneys that he would rule that day on the admissibility of Carole's statements and testimony.

"If I rule against you, Fred," he told the prosecutor, "I don't think you have a case, and the defendant will be released."

Whichello returned to his desk. He had to convince Miller that Carole's statements were innocently obtained during an investigation of another suspect, and therefore should be allowed.

"Your Honor, I call myself to the stand." He walked to the witness box and was sworn in.

It was a "made for Hollywood" move that filled the court with chuckles.

Whichello made a statement maintaining that Carole was not a suspect until she testified.

"It was only then, when she made statements that were glaring discrepancies with her statements made to Las Vegas and West Covina police, that we decided she was an accomplice."

"Her testimony," he concluded with a complex sentence, "included an active aid of the other defendant by abetting in the sense that a knowledge of the purpose of the other defendant in proceeding to the premises in question was present."

It was Robert Neeb's turn to cross-examine. Fifty-three years old, the six-foot, four-inch, gregarious defense attorney had striking facial features, a prominent nose framed by blue eyes, and bushy, expressive eyebrows. Although his quick sense of humor was well-known, only one of hundreds of photographs show him smiling; the rest suggest him pensive, morose, sometimes brooding.

Neeb rose, saying briskly, "I'd like to go on record, Your Honor, as saying that this is the first time I have had the opportunity to cross-examine a Deputy District Attorney." He and the prosecutor had been good friends for years.

To the crowd's delight Whichello interjected, "He's been waiting for this for years, Your Honor."

Neeb: "Then what you have testified to is your state of mind after you became involved with the case."

Whichello: "Yes, and thereafter."

Neeb: "You have stated it was along the latter part of her testimony at Dr. Finch's preliminary hearing that you decided to arrest Carole Tregoff."

Whichello: "That is correct."

Neeb: "So *after* that decision, after you decided she was a suspect, you continued to ask her questions?"

Whichello: "Yes, I believe there were basically two questions asked after that decision was made, after recess, during the end of her testimony."

Neeb: "Before or after the question about her intimacy with the doctor?"

Whichello: "Before she answered the second time, when she said 'yes.'"

Neeb: "Now at any time during these proceedings, did you or presiding Judge Miller advise Miss Tregoff of her possible arrest, or that anything she might say could be used as evidence against her?"

Whichello: "No."

Both sides would have the weekend and Monday to prepare their final arguments.

MONDAY, AUGUST 17, 1959
POMONA SUPERIOR COURTROOM
OF JUDGE JAMES G. WHYTE

Ned Nelson appeared with his client, Dr. Bernard Finch, and asked for a continuance of his arraignment. Grant

101

Cooper was to be involved in another case for at least two weeks. Fred Whichello did not oppose the request.

Many speculated, all wanted to see if Carole Tregoff's case would be dismissed. Whichello had decided his case would be stronger if Tregoff and Finch were tried together; If Carole Tregoff were released, he would need time to prepare his grand jury presentation seeking indictments of both suspects.

TUESDAY, AUGUST 18, 1959

It was late morning. Fred Whichello and Robert Neeb had finished their arguments to Judge Miller. All waited as he returned to the bench after a brief recess.

Neeb told Carole he thought there was a good chance her case would be dismissed. After all, the deputy D. A. and the judge had themselves said there was no case against her without her own testimony. And since she had been under subpoena to testify, she had in essence been compelled to testify against herself.

Whichello had prepared for an adverse ruling from Miller by quietly checking with the clerk of the county grand jury about the group's schedule. He had made an appointment with their smaller Criminal Complaints Committee, which made preliminary decisions as to which cases would be heard.

In his earlier address to Miller, the prosecutor had explained his delimma:

"What is a prosecutor supposed to do when a witness voluntarily turns from witness against a defendant to witness against herself? Jump up, shout her down, and advise her of her constitutional rights?"

After lunch, the court clerk began passing out copies of the judge's ruling. Copies went to the attorneys first, then the press. Whichello got his copy first and began reading; his left thumb and forefinger were rubbing his chin.

Carole was seated between Don Bringgold and Robert Neeb. Neeb, closest to Whichello, got the group's first copy. He skimmed the first page, then looked away, lips pursed. He leaned over and whispered to Tregoff and Bringgold. The defendant lowered her head. She kept it lowered for the rest of the hearing.

"Defendant will rise," the judge instructed. Carole rose, as did her attorneys. The men looked grim and disappointed. Her head was still lowered; she was visibly sobbing.

Miller spoke quickly.

"There appears to me to be reasonable cause to believe or strongly suspect that the crime of murder has been committed, and there are reasonable grounds to believe or strongly suspect that Mrs. Pappa may be guilty thereof. She will be held to answer the charge of murder."

Neeb's request for bail was turned down.

The room echoed with Carole's sobs, heard over the buzz and chatter of people starting to leave. Photographers circled around Neeb and Carole and captured her distorted face as she cried for minutes afterward.

Whichello had dodged a legal bullet today. His plans to take the case to the grand jury for an indictment were on hold, but he still was uneasy about having to use Carole's own testimony against her. He had great respect for Carole's legal team, and knew they would file more challenges and appeals.

This would be Judge Miller's first brush with fame. His second would follow a few years later. He was to be convicted of taking bribes in traffic cases and would serve eighteen months in California's Chino facility for men.

The next few weeks saw legal maneuvering by the prosecution and the defense teams. Whichello wanted the two defendants tried together, as did, it seemed to many, Grant

B. Cooper. Neeb and Bringgold tried desperately to obtain separate trials.

Arguing that an impartial jury could not be impaneled. Cooper submitted a motion that the trial be moved out of Los Angeles County.

eight
Superior Court Arraignments
Securing of Assets

MONDAY, AUGUST 31, 1959

Carole Tregoff and Bernard Finch appeared for arraignment in the Pomona division of Los Angeles County Superior Court. Judge James G. Whyte accepted Finch's plea of innocent. Neeb was granted a continuance.

Grant B. Cooper asked Judge Whyte to instruct all counsel to stop making remarks to the press about the case. Neeb agreed, but Whichello objected violently.

"I've never heard of such an instruction!" he proclaimed. "The public has a right to know what goes on in here."

Whyte denied the motion.

A few days later, Whichello gave an exclusive television interview, with newscaster Baxter Ward, in which he said, matter-of-factly, that both defendants were guilty of murder. He indicated he would seek the death penalty for both.

FRIDAY, SEPTEMBER 4, 1959

Meanwhile, a race for the Finch assets was on. Lyle Daughtery had been granted custody of his daughter. He had quietly determined that his former wife, Barbara Jean, signed her will three months before her death, but had never properly filed it, making it, therefore, invalid. The document appointed Bernard Finch executor.

Edward M. Raskin, appeared before Judge Kenneth Chantry in an effort to protect the assets for Patti Daugherty.

"We seek protection of the assets and of the child's, Patti's, right to them." Raskin argued. "We think that Dr. Finch might try to dissipate the assets and encumber them to the child's disadvantage."

To avoid the appearance of impropriety, Lyle asked the court to appoint trustees at his former wife's bank, The Citizens National Trust and Savings Bank, to be special executors of the estate. The bank had agreed to do so; it had already filed a lawsuit against Finch, alleging he forged Barbara Jean's signature to a $3,000 check a few weeks before her death. They were seeking restitution.

Representing Dr. Finch at the hearing was Gerald R. Knudson, Jr. He opposed the motion and advised the court of certain facts: Just hours before, Barbara Jean's will had been formally filed filed in Probate Court. Bernard Finch was now the executor of his wife's estate.

Grant B. Cooper had also filed with the court papers making himself the assignee of Finch's entire interests in the family home, in the West Covina Clinic and Hospital, and in various cars and boats. The entire estate was estimated at $750,000. The defense of Bernard Finch would be well financed.

INTERVIEW WITH STEVE AND NADINE HAYS MARCH 22, 1992

"About this time we were all feeling sorry for Carole," Nadine Hays, long a resident of the area, told me. She had been plugged into the gossip circles of West Covina.

I had invited the couple, long-time friends, to my home. Nadine was seldom at a loss for words; Steve, as was his custom, seemed always to be patiently waiting for the right moment to say something.

"At first, a lot of us thought she didn't know as much as the prosecutors thought she did," Nadine continued. "At least, that was the opinion of most of us women in the neighborhood at the time.

"I thought she just happened to fall in love with him, or whatever, and then was taken in and used by him.

"This was the talk of the town for years and years and years," Nadine went on. "We knew the Kearths, who had bought the house after the murder and moved in, and we used to go to many functions there, usually having to do with little league or something. Seems like whenever there was a party there, someone—and the Kearths hated this—would start talking about the murder.

"And it made this town famous. My husband Steve and I were traveling in London once and somebody that saw we were from West Covina asked us about the Finch case. You know, they wanted to know who we knew, what we knew. Remember that, Steve?"

"Oh, yeah," Steve was nodding. "I remember that."

Like Nadine and the rest of the neighborhood women, the press was generally sympathetic to Carole.

nine
Information from
Minnesota and Las Vegas
Bail for Carole Tregoff

FRIDAY, SEPTEMBER 4, 1959

THE BAILIFF IN the Minneapolis city jail eased a full coffee cup toward the desk in front of him, resting it next to his newspaper. He was reading about the murder case in Los Angeles.

He looked up. Three men were walking toward him. Two wore suits. Between them was a short, slightly built, pale man; his hands were behind him, his head held down.

"Must be them," the bailiff thought to himself. He was expecting the delivery of a prisoner, a fugitive who had escaped from a Minnesota work farm and been arrested eighteen months later, in Milwaukee, for writing bad checks.

This latest guest-to-be of the Minneapolis municipal jail was a well known local pimp and confidence man who earned his living measuring the dark side of human nature, sometimes venturing to Las Vegas to ply his trades.

"Well," said the bailiff, "back to see us again, heh, Jack?" The two knew each other. "Okay, you know what to do."

The prisoner emptied his pockets and put his watch and jewelry on the desk.

"I heard you had walked off the farm, Jack. Just decided to walk off. You got to be crazy. You could do some real time, now." The bailiff was counting the cash in the man's wallet when he noticed a collection of pictures, most of them of prostitutes that worked for his prisoner.

Curious, he scanned through the photos, studying the faces. Most of the women were not attractive. Few were smiling, most appearring rough and used. He sifted, then stopped, eyebrows raised. One seemed more professional than the others.

His instincts stirred; this picture did not fit with the others. And something about it seemed familiar. He moved it slightly closer.

He had it! After taking the photograph out of the plastic holder, he held it down next to the picture on the front page of his newspaper. It was the same person, he was sure. The differences in dress and expression did not fool him.

He looked up at the prisoner. "What's a guy like you doing with a picture of Carole Tregoff in your wallet, Jack?"

The man was nervous. "We were friends in Las Vegas." His voice was a monotone, measured for the situation.

The bailiff was already on the phone to his detective bureau. Others were soon on their way to interrogate Jack, more officially known as James Patrick Cody.

SATURDAY, SEPTEMBER 5, 1959
CLARK COUNTY SHERIFFS STATION
11:30 P.M.

Hiram Powell had been called from his home to speak with two nineteen-year-old women arrested earlier for solicitation to prostitution. The girls had made statements to the arresting officers before being booked and now were waiting to talk with Powell.

As Powell walked toward them, they giggled.

"Hi ya, Hiram," said one, a thin dishwater-blonde. She seemed to have a cold, occasionally sniffing and snorting. As she spoke, it was obvious her nose was plugged. "Your mommy's going to be mad 'cause you're up past your bedtime." The two giggled louder.

Powell was unamused. But he tolerated the two women. He knew they had information about the Finch case.

"Anything you two want to tell me, you know, before you are booked for solicitation to prostitution?" He spoke to them firmly, leaning forward. He also spoke slowly.

"Now Hirie," the other girl spoke now, singing his name, teasing, "we didn't do anything *that* bad. You'll tell them to let us go, won't you? Especially if we tell you something?" The chubby brunette was smoking an unfiltered cigarette. Powell noted her face was pitted and her hair matted, in need of a wash.

The two wanted to return to their homes in Minnesota, but their pimp, a man named Richard Albert "Richie" Keachie, was keeping them in Las Vegas with threats. Their arrest was putting a damper on their plans to make the money for their escape.

Powell leaned forward. "Well, you're going to have to tell me first."

The two were serious now, looking at each other. Without a word their decision was made.

The blonde spoke. "Okay," her face was emotionless now. "You know that doctor guy in California who killed his wife. Well, we know somebody who knows him and his pretty little girl friend."

Powell did not move. He said nothing. She studied him, then leaned forward as far as she could.

"Turns out the doctor's girl friend has been looking for somebody to 'take care of the doctor's wife." She stopped, looking at Powell some more. She glanced at her friend quickly, then back at Powell. "We both heard Richie talking with a friend of his from when he worked at the Sahara. Didn't we?" She looked at her companion, nodding her into speaking.

"It's true," the other added, after a pause.

"Hmm." Powell said. His eyebrows rose up; he smiled just slightly.

The girl knew they had a deal. She leaned back in her chair, crossing her arms. Her words came more quickly, her voice hardened. "And we'll tell you who she hired to do it, Hirie."

WEDNESDAY, SEPTEMBER 16, 1959

Carole Tregoff and Robert Neeb walked out of the Pomona Superior Courthouse. A half inch of rain had fallen in the early morning. The sidewalks were still wet, and the air smelled clean of smog. Judge Lewis Drucker had just allowed Carole bail of $25,000. It had been forty-eight days since her arrest.

The District Attorney's office had strongly opposed the judge's decision. Granting bail was more arbitrary in these days before mandatory bail legislation. Now granted, it carried a message.

"The proof of presumption of guilt is not so strong as to make me deny bail," Drucker had said.

Just before the afternoon paper deadlines, a bulletin from the D. A.'s office was issued.

"BULLETIN: The District Attorney's office here announced at 12:45 P.M. today that a Nevada State University student, Donald Sanford Williams, has given a statement to Las Vegas police saying that he had arranged with Carole Tregoff Pappa and Dr. R. Bernard Finch, early in 1959, to hire two men to kill Mrs. Barbara Jean Finch.

"The D. A.'s office said a nationwide bulletin had been put out for the two men, named Richie Keachie and James Patrick Cody. One of them is believed to be in Minnesota."

THURSDAY, SEPTEMBER 17, 1959

Donald Sanford Williams walked up the steps to the Clark County sheriff's station. He would be meeting with Captain William Ryan. He was approached by three local reporters."

"What will you be talking about today, Don?" one of them asked.

Carole Tregoff had been one of his good friends in high school, and they had been neighbors in South Pasadena. He was reticent to say anything that might harm her. Earlier, at his home, police had advised he might be considered an accessory to murder if he introduced Carole to anyone willing to murder Mrs. Finch.

"Oh, not much," he mumbled and looked down, hoping they would let him pass. "I won't say much. I just knew Carole from when I lived in California, and she had asked me to help her out with some problems she was having."

They were standing in front of him now. He continued. "She asked if I knew any gangsters in this town or anyone engaged in that activity. She said, 'One of these days why don't you introduce me to somebody?'"

Williams had introduced her to his friend Keachie.

"Keachie said he didn't want the job, so he asked a fellow named Cody if he wanted to do it." Williams was walking sideways on the steps, trying to outflank the men; they shuffled, pacing him.

All three asked, "Do what?"

Quickly he said, "She probably wanted to get some dirt of some sort on Mrs. Finch."

Williams was never quoted by the press as saying he had been approached about a "murder."

He made a verbal statement to Ryan and left the station. Within minutes Ryan was briefing Fred Whichello by phone. Fred soon met with several reporters who had been waiting in Pomona for some news of Williams's statement.

Fred was brief. "Carole Pappa asked her lifelong friend, Mr. Williams, to find two tough guys who could kill Mrs. Finch. Mrs. Pappa and Dr. Finch were hiring a killer."

Contacted by phone at his office, Robert Neeb said, "It does seem odd to me that Mr. Whichello would make such statements so soon after Mrs. Pappa had been released on bail. It all sounds ridiculous to me."

Neeb made other remarks that would start a fierce rivalry between the two men and strain their friendship. "But I will not comment further except to say that there seems to be a question of ethics involved here. Evidence, if there is any, should be tried in the courtroom and not be publicly aired, as Mr. Whichello continues to do."

Williams would later deny he had ever said Carole wanted to hire anyone to commit a murder.

WEDNESDAY, SEPTEMBER 23, 1959

Fred Whichello and William Ryan were on the late night plane from Minneapolis to Los Angeles. Whichello had taken the window seat in hope that Ryan's cigarette smoke might somehow be drawn to the aisle.

They had spent two days interrogating Cody. Again and again they had questioned him to see if his story would change; both were confident he would give convincing testimony that Carole Tregoff and Bernard Finch had hired him to murder Barbara Jean Finch.

"How much time is he looking at up there?" Ryan asked.

"The rest of his sentence for the bad checks, plus whatever he gets for walking off the prison farm," Whichello replied. He was tired and wanted to sleep; his mind mulled legal strategy. Before leaving, he had called District Attorney McKesson and given him his plan.

"We could have this thing before the grand jury by next Tuesday. I think we would have no problem getting murder one indictments and conspiracy to murder."

"Murder one?" Ryan asked. Taking a drag off his cigarette, he looked straight ahead, knowing what Fred would say next.

"And I would ask for the death penalty, Bill." Whichello was looking out the window now, his eyes closed. "If anybody deserves it, these two do."

"You would have to get immunity for all three of these guys. They're not going to say much without it," Ryan speculated.

"Shouldn't be a problem," the veteran prosecutor mumbled, dozing.

McKesson had expressed concern over the plan: The grand jury might not be able to grant immunity for a crime committed outside their jurisdiction, Los Angeles County. Though the murder had been committed inside the county, the conspiracy was hatched entirely in Las Vegas.

"The job of the grand jury is to determine the facts, whether a crime may have been committed. They're supposed to get at the truth," Whichello had pleaded with his boss. "And besides, they can do anything they want to; they're the grand jury." He had saved his pragmatic points for last. "I'm afraid Neeb is going to get our current case dismissed on appeal. He's been calling everybody. Best guess now is he'll go to district appeals first. With an indictment by the grand jury, I'd have a case that didn't use her own testimony."

McKesson agreed.

Neeb, Bringghold, Tregoff in court.
Valley Tribune.

THURSDAY, SEPTEMBER 24, 1959

Jerry Giesler, Robert Neeb, Jr., and Donald Bringgold, as attorneys of record for Carole Tregoff, filed a brief with the California District Court of Appeals asking that her case be dismissed. The brief reasoned she was being held and prosecuted on the basis of her own testimony, which had been obtained without advising her about self-incrimination. The brief named Whichello, saying he had asked grossly incriminating and degrading questions.

WEDNESDAY, SEPTEMBER 30, 1959

District Attorney McKesson told reporters Carole was under twenty-four hour watch at her home in La Puente. In two days a hearing in Pomona Superior Court would determine whether her bail should be raised in light of the "murder for hire" evidence.

"When Friday comes," said McKesson, "I don't want Carole to be across the Mexican border or somewhere. Police are watching her twenty-four hours a day."

Jimmy Keith helped watch Carole's home.

JIMMY KEITH

"One day, all of a sudden, she surprised the heck out of us by bringing out some cookies to eat. I guess she just made them or something. Shook the guys up at first. We weren't sure she knew we was there." He was chuckling. "But she just walked right on over and asked if anybody wanted some of those cookies.

"She seemed like a nice person to me. You know, if she had just kept her mouth shut, she might never have seen the inside of a jail."

FRIDAY, OCTOBER 2, 1959

Carole walked out of court, still on the same bail of $25,000.

"If Mrs. Pappa had wanted to flee prosecution, she would most likely have done it after learning that her bail might be revoked in today's hearing," Judge James G. Whyte said.

Whichello had requested the bail be revoked or at least raised to $100,000 based on the new "murder for hire" evidence.

"I have statements from three men who say Mrs. Pappa was trying to find somebody to kill Barbara Jean Finch, Your Honor. One of them says she paid him $1,400 to do it," he had pleaded.

Before Carole left, Whichello personally served her with a notice that a grand jury hearing was scheduled for the following Tuesday. He boldly subpoenaed her as a witness.

Donald Bringgold obtained, the same day, a dismissal of the supoena. In granting the dismissal, Judge Lewis Drucker agreed that a person accused of a crime cannot be made to testify against herself during criminal proceedings.

ten
Grand Jury Indictments
Motions to Separate and Move Trial

TUESDAY, OCTOBER 6, 1959

PUBLIC ATTENTION WAS focused on Sandy Koufax, who was to pitch against Bob Shaw of the White Sox in the fifth game of the World Series. The Dodgers were up three games to one. It was one of the few stories ever to have larger headlines than the Finch-Tregoff affair.

The grand jury saw and heard Whichello's parade of usual witnesses: the coroner, the investigating officers, and Marie Anne Lidholm. And there was the new witness, James Patrick Cody. Described by the press as "dapper," he was, according to other witnesses, anything but.

He was twenty-six years old, dressed at all times in a cheap suit with a silk handkerchief in the pockets. His hair was dark, curly, and greasy, combed straight back.

"He sort of looked like a short Eddie Haskel from the old *Leave it to Beaver* show," one person would say later. "He was an habitual criminal," said others, "with no honor, no morals, no remorse, and no loyalty except to himself."

Popular mystery author Eric Ambler, writing for Life magazine, described Cody. "Cody belongs to that rare and remarkable subdivision of the human species, the amoral realists with no illusions about their own frailties and no

117

sense of guilt. The odd thing about such men is that, having no pretensions to being any less odious than they are, they sometimes achieve a kind of honesty. Such a man is a defense attorney's nightmare. He can admit to the basest behavior without the least trace of embarrassment."

Pictures of him show a pale, small, and thin man, always with a blank and expressionless face. Cody was on loan from the Minnesota prison system. For having walked off the prison farm, his term had already been extended a year.

Cody refused to testify until his request for immunity was signed by Judge Lewis Drucker. The order for immunity was rushed to the grand jury room within minutes of his arrival, and Cody took the stand to tell his story.

Looking directly at the grand jurors, he responded to Whichello's questions regarding his status as hired killer.

"I never really intended to do it," he explained. "I was just stringing them along for the cash, you know.

"I remember Carole told me, 'If you don't kill her, the doctor will; and if he doesn't, then I will.'"

And asked about Carole, "I thought she was a very nice person, but I guess even nice people have bad thoughts sometimes."

WEDNESDAY, OCTOBER 7, 1959

Hoppi Hopkinson read the statement Carole had made to police in Las Vegas. Her sworn testimony from Dr. Finch's preliminary hearing that had led to her arrest was not offered by Whichello as evidence.

The last witness was Donald Williams, who told of introducing Carole to his friend, Keachie.

"She never said anything to me about a murder or anything like that," he said. "I never had any idea there would be a job like that. Carole told me she was afraid Mrs. Finch had some damaging evidence on her and her boy friend that would hurt them at the divorce hearings."

Jury Foreman C. F. Van de Water later told reporters that the members of the grand jury were skeptical about Cody's testimony, not finding him credible.

"The testimony of Mr. Williams, however," he said, "was a straightforward testimony that tended to corroborate the testimony of Cody."

Whichello got what he wanted. Shortly after noon both Carole Tregoff Pappa and R. Bernard Finch were indicted for murder and conspiracy to commit murder. The two original cases, A 218160 for Finch and A 218806 for Pappa, were consolidated as A 220164 for both.

HIGHER COURTS

There followed a series of attempts to persuade higher courts to dismiss Carole Tregoff's case.

On October 14 Judge Walter J. Fourt of the State Appeals Court denied, without comment, Carole Tregoff's writ to prohibit her prosecution. Neeb contended his client was being maliciously singled out.

On October 19 a petition was filed with the California Supreme Court to have Carole Tregoff tried separately. Neeb contended, once more, that prosecutors had maliciously pursued his client and had violated her constitutional rights. This, too, was denied without comment.

On October 23 Neeb asked the United States Supreme Court to consider the same question. This request was refused by Justice William O. Douglas.

And on October 27 it was back to the California Court of Appeals again with a second request. This time Neeb and Bringgold contended that the county grand jury could not grant immunity to a witness to testify about crimes committed outside their jurisdiction. The conspiracy was said to have taken place in Nevada. They moved that all charges be dismissed again, and once more were refused.

Neeb's last attempt to have the case dismissed: again to the United States Supreme Court seeking a writ of certiorari, a petition claiming his client had not received constitutionally guaranteed justice. Miss Tregoff was asked certain questions in Judge Miller's courtroom, he argued, after she was deemed a suspect by Whichello; those answers led to her arrest and violated her constitutional right not to give evidence against herself. This would be pending as the trial began.

Finally, on November 5, with no more reasons to delay their appearances, the two defendants entered their pleas before Superior Court Judge John G. Barnes in Pomona. Both pled "not guilty."

Grant B. Cooper succeeded in transferring the trial to the Los Angeles Courthouse. "The courtrooms are bigger over there, Your Honor," he explained, "and they're closer to all the attorney's offices. And," he went on, "the defendants would get hot lunches there. Out here they get only sandwiches, Your Honor, cold sandwiches."

Cooper had patiently waited while Neeb and Bringgold made their series of appeals, but now was reported anxious to begin. His clients were starting to backlog. He had been retained to defend movie star Sterling Hayden at his trial for contempt of court. Hayden had taken his four children on a year-long cruise aboard the yacht *Wanderer*. Although he had custody of all four, their mother had been unable to see them, as the court had ordered.

Whichello asked D. A. Bill McKesson for an assistant. He was assigned Clifford Crail, a thirty-year veteran of the office.

After getting the trial moved to Los Angeles, Cooper next filed a petition with the District Attorney's office asking that it be conducted outside of Los Angeles County due to prejudicial pre-trial publicity. Wanting separate trials, Carole's lawyers said they wanted to stay in Los Angeles. Cooper's motion was denied.

A quick series of challenges by both the District Attorney's office and Cooper resulted in assignment of the case to Judge Walter R. Evans. The challenges were entered under a new state law that allowed each counsel to make one objection without having to provide cause or reason.

Evans presided as Superior Court Judge in the mountainous northern California area of Mono Lake. He actually made his home in Pasadena, however, where he lived with his wife and daughter.

Just days before the trial was to begin, Robert Neeb had to withdraw as Carole's primary counsel. His firm's senior partner, Jerry Giesler, was seriously ill, and Neeb needed to attend the firm's business matters. He would maintain an intense interest in the case and make many appearances in Carole Tregoff's defense. Donald Bringgold would be responsible for the day-to-day management of her defense. The young, soft-spoken, University of Minnesota graduate had recently been acquired by Giesler's firm. He was to be assisted by the always direct—and sometimes abrasive—Rexford D. Eagan, known as the "gunslinger."

Part II

The First Trial

one

Jury Selection and Pretrial Motions

A few of the hundreds of spectators that came to watch the
defendants arrive each day of the trial. *Getty.*

TUESDAY, DECEMBER 8, 1959

IT WAS A cool, blustery, rainy day in Los Angeles. A
quarter of an inch of rain would fall on the first day of the
trial, held for one day only in the old Hall of Justice building
across the street from the recently built county courthouse.

125

"Please be seated!" It was Evans's second request for order. He straightened some papers, then looked up; the small room was packed with the most it could accommodate, just fifty; all but two were seated.

"We have no place to sit down, Your Honor." Cooper said, hunching his shoulders up. "The other defendant and her counsel along with the prosecutors have taken all the chairs. Look!"

Most people had been waiting since 6:00 A.M. to get a good seat. About half of the people were reporters and photographers. Before Evans's entrance, a smiling Finch had his picture taken with Reverend Henry Kent of West Covina's Presbyterian Church, and then with his dad, who gave him a hug and wishes for "best luck."

In a nearby jury room fifty people waited to be assessed as "finders of fact."

Dr. Bernard Finch and his attorney were still looking for a place to sit.

"Would the bailiff please find some chairs for Mr. Cooper and his client so that we might get under way." Thus Evans issued his second command of the trial. He was a tall, slightly overweight jurist who had wanted to be a judge so much that he decided to commute from Pasadena to Mono Lake. Mono Lake was known mostly for its water. Los Angeles had been gulping it since the California aqueduct connected the two areas in the '20s.

Evans wore his black horn-rimmed glasses most of the time. Regarded as even-tempered and fair by most, his calm, monotone voice would contrast with the defense attorneys', most dispositioned for drama.

The chairs arrived and the two men settled behind the defense table. Cooper started arranging papers. The room was noisy and crowded; by the end of the day Evans obtained permission to use the larger Department Twelve in the new court building across the street.

Judge Evans asked if there were any matters to be heard before jury selection got under way.

"Yes, Your Honor," Cooper rose. "We move that the trial be transferred out of the Los Angeles area. I feel that my client cannot get a fair trial here. There has been very prejudicial pretrial publicity about this case, and I am prepared to present evidence that it would be impossible to select a jury that has not already formed an opinion of my client's guilt."

"We would object to such a move, Your Honor." Bringgold spoke, still seated. "My client has limited funds, and it would be a hardship for her to move her defense out of the area. We would move that my client be tried separately from her co-defendant."

Whichello was last. "This is all a ruse to get the two trials separated, Your Honor, nothing more. We object to both motions and request that they be dismissed so that we can get on with the trial."

Evans advised that he would hear evidence on Cooper's motion. He then asked, "How much time will you need to present your motion, Mr. Cooper?"

"Oh, about a day and a half. I plan to call a witness who conducted a public opinion survey for my firm." Cooper crossed his arms in front of him and continued, without blinking an eye. "I will also call Mr. Whichello and myself to the stand."

The room buzzed with excitement and some nervous giggles. Evans hammered his gavel to quiet the crowd. It had taken, as expected, little time for the flamboyance of the attorneys to be on review.

"I also," Cooper continued, not waiting for the crowd to quiet, "will call Judge Albert K. Miller and District Attorney William McKesson."

The noise crescendoed even higher as the gavel slapped at the wood of Evans's desk.

Cooper first called Dorothy Corey, who worked for Facts Consolidated, a Los Angeles public survey company.

"We found that 46% of the people surveyed thought Dr. Finch was guilty of murder, and 54% had no opinion. Of the undecided group, 60% thought he could not get a fair trial in Los Angeles," Corey reported.

Next, no less than ninety newspaper articles were entered, one by one, into evidence.

"Look at this one here, Judge." Cooper held a tabloid high. The headline read, "Judge Thinks Finch Guilty." Albert Miller had been interviewed by several reporters after the preliminary hearing. "How can my client get a fair trial in this county if the people have been reading headlines like this?"

Next: a sixteen-millimeter film of the interview Whichello gave to reporter Baxter Ward. The courtroom darkened, a projector rattled, and the two men appeared on a small portable screen the bailiff had erected at the front of the courtroom. They were joking and laughing. Whichello announced, "These two people are guilty of murder in the first degree, Baxter. There is no doubt in my mind."

Cooper turned off the projector; the lights came on.

"What person could be a juror on this case with an open mind after having seen a television show like this?" Cooper reasoned.

He was done for the day. The press was anticipated the excitement of the next day when Fred Whichello was to be a witness, again.

WEDNESDAY, DECEMBER 9, 1959

A few more of the hundreds of people waiting for a look at the two defendants would get into the larger Department Twelve of the new Superior Court building. It had one hundred ninety-nine spectator seats; extra chairs were brought in so that fifty more could be admitted.

Today, as they would every day, Dr. Finch and Carole Tregoff walked by the group of would-be spectators, seeming to ignore the insults and sneers. Some would yell "Adulterer" or "Murderer." Photographs of the scene show faces of indignation and disgust.

Inside, the parties arranged themselves as they would for the next few weeks. To the right of the swinging half-door was the prosecutor's table. Whichello was closest to the center, with Crail to his right. On the other side of the space between prosecutors and defendants was Cooper, closest to Whichello; to his left was Finch, then Eagan and Bringgold sat between Carole and Bernard. Neeb, when present, would be to Carole's left.

The jury box was to the spectators' right. Today it was empty.

Before court was convened, Bernard Finch and Carole Tregoff were photographed sitting at the defense table, talking quietly.

When Bringgold arrived he immediately sat between the defendants, whispering something to Carole. She looked away for a moment, then said something in return.

A reporter standing nearby caught Bringgold's attention. "What were Carole and the Doctor talking about, Don?"

Bringgold didn't look up. In a flat monotone he replied, "The quality of cold meat sandwiches at our county jail facility."

"All rise," the bailiff commanded. "Superior Court of Los Angeles County, Judge Walter R. Evans presiding."

Evans walked in from a small door next to the jury box. "Be seated," he said quietly. Then looking at Cooper, "I see we have enough chairs today, Mr. Cooper."

"Yes," Cooper smiled broadly.

Evans asked him to present his first witness.

"I call myself to the stand," Cooper announced.

"You still intend to call yourself, counselor?" Evans's head cocked slightly to the side.

"Yes." Cooper was walking briskly to the witness stand; his left arm pressed a folded newspaper to his side. He was in vintage form.

After being sworn as a witness, he proceeded to make a statement that there had been certain "hallway conversations" between himself and Fred Whichello.

"He told me that he had no evidence whatsoever that my client had first denied that he was in Los Angeles at the time of the slaying, Your Honor, then he turns around and gives this press interview." He held up the newspaper, moving it around in front of him, first to the judge, then to the courtroom.

"The story reads 'Deputy D. A. Whichello was quoted as saying Dr. Finch's alibi was 'blown away' by the statements of Miss Tregoff made to the Las Vegas sheriff's investigators. That's not gentlemanly conduct, Your Honor, and I submit that Mr. Whichello was trying to convict my client before he ever entered a courtroom."

Whichello's face slowly reddened. He had not expected Cooper to attack him personally. He tried to pass it off as a cheap legal maneuver. Still, it bothered him. After almost thirty years of dedicated service to his office, his integrity was being impugned in open court.

"And look at this," Cooper's voice rose. He was showing headlines of a *San Gabriel Valley Tribune* issue announcing the "murder kit." "Mr. Whichello has already labeled these contents as murder weapons belonging to my client. He doesn't even know who this case belongs to or where it came from. These are matters to be determined by a court of law."

He then held up a newspaper with a forty point headline that read "Murder for Hire Plot Revealed."

"The D. A.'s office had a press conference in which they announced that they had decided my client had hired some man in Minnesota to kill his wife. I don't know how we could find twelve men or women who haven't already decided what happened the night my client's wife died."

Cooper stepped down and walked slowly to his chair, past Fred, who did not look up. A few moments passed; quiet settled onto the room, broken occasionally by a cough. The defense attorney looked at the prosecutor and announced, "I call Mr. Fred Whichello, Your Honor."

Cooper would keep his adversary on the stand for one and a half days of testimony, hammering at his ethics and motives. He was convinced his client had been treated unfairly. His questions would fuel an intense rivalry with Whichello, who in pretrial interviews had routinely cast Bernard Finch and Carole Tregoff as adulterers and murderers, hatching their scheme from a bed of greed.

"He loves to get me on the stand, Your Honor, and it never serves any useful purpose," Whichello respectfully protested as he walked to the witness box.

The Deputy D. A. was sworn. Cooper then waited for a few moments as he pretended to be organizing his papers. The tension in the room was rising, and he was the focus of attention. Whichello looked down at his trouser's legs, occasionaly picking off a piece of lint.

"Now Mr. Whichello, did we have a conversation in the halls of the Citrus Municipal Court, prior to my client's being held for arraignment, concerning the source of this newspaper story here?" He held up a newspaper with a headline, "Finch Says In Las Vegas the Whole Time."

Whichello: "We may have talked about it."

Cooper: "And did you not tell me that you were the source of that story, and that you told the press that Carole Tregoff Pappa, and I quote, had 'blown his story?'"

131

Cooper was at the witness stand now, his right arm resting on the dark oak rail; he was glaring at Whichello, who straightened noticeably, then settled back in his chair.

"Absolutely not," the prosecutor spoke as his face reddened, "I don't know where they got that story, Mr. Cooper, and neither do you."

Cooper would drag the deputy D. A. through each of the ninety newspaper stories that named Whichello as a source of information, one at time.

Cooper: "How about this story? Did you not describe a certain attaché case as a 'murder kit' in this interview?"

Whichello: "Yes, I did say that the kit could be called a 'do-it-yourself murder kit.' I didn't think up the name, though. I believe Captain Ryan may have coined the phrase."

Cooper then asked about the Minnesota telephone call Fred had made to Manly Bowler, assistant to District Attorney William McKesson. In this conversation Bowler was advised that James Cody would testify that he had been hired to murder Barbara Jean Finch. Shortly afterward, the assistant D. A. had given the news to the press.

"Yes, I phoned my office about the results of the interview with Mr. Cody. It's my job to advise the District Attorney on the status of my cases."

Whichello was briefly cross-examined by his assistant, Clifford Crail.

Crail: "Do you give information freely to the press without regard for how it will affect any subsequent court proceedings?"

Whichello: "No. As a matter of fact, I get daily complaints from them that I don't give them enough information."

Crail: "And did you at any time give information to the press with the intention of harming the defendants or prejudicing any potential jurors at their trial?"

Whichello: "Absolutely not, I would never do such a thing."

THURSDAY, DECEMBER 16, 1959

When Grant B. Cooper entered the courtroom, he could see a conference in progress at the prosecutor's table. A group of men were speaking in hushed tones, excitedly, often interrupting each other. Seeing Cooper they quieted; as he walked by they moved to the far right, next to the jury box, and started whispering again.

Talking with Fred Whichello were Captain William Ryan, District Attorney William McKesson, and his assistant, Manly Bowler. McKesson and Bowler were being briefed by the other two on statements they had made to the press. McKesson had been appointed to finish a partial term as District Attorney. In a few months he would run for the office in the general election.

"I call William McKesson to the stand," Cooper announced. The press would celebrate his boldness: The lone defense lawyer calling the District Attorney to the stand!

"I was at a convention of district attorneys in San Francisco when Mr. Bowler called me about the news of a man in Minnesota who said he had been hired to commit a murder," McKesson said.

Cooper: "Isn't it unusual for you to be contacted about such specific items in a case?"

McKesson: "This wasn't a usual case. There was a lot of attention being focused on the Finch-Tregoff case."

Cooper: "Oh, so you took a special interest in this case?"

McKesson: "Everybody did."

Next: Manly Bowler.

Cooper: "Now Mr. Bowler, when you released the information that there was a man in Minnesota who said he had been asked to murder Mrs. Finch by Dr. Finch and Carole Tregoff Pappa, don't you think that made people think the two were guilty of murder?"

"The press and the public have a right to know." Bowler was moving nervously in the chair. Then he added, "They were breaking down the door to the D. A.'s office, trying to get information about this case. Every day I was handling complaints that we were not giving them enough information. I had reporters from all over the world in my office."

FRIDAY, DECEMBER 17, 1959

Fred Whichello was reading the morning's *Los Angeles Times*. He wasn't reading the usual front page recap of the trial; he was reading a short item on the second page.

"Old Reb Williams Near Death" was the headline for the report that the last living veteran of the Civil War, Walter Williams, was taking his final breaths.

As a child, Fred often heard people talk of what they had done during the Civil War or what they thought of Lincoln, Davis, Lee, or McClelland. He had been with the D. A.'s office since 1933.

ALLEN SILL

"These were the last of the gutsy prosecutors," Chief Sill told me. "These guys knew what they were doing. Nowadays, a young lawyer gets out of school, works for the D. A.'s office for a few years to get some trial experience, then they join the big law firms for the money. But these old-timers—well it was their career, their life, to be a prosecutor."

Cooper's attacks on Whichello and his office had been brutal and merciless. Today the sides would make their arguments about where the trial should take place and whether the defendants should be tried separately.

After listening attentively first to Cooper, then Whichello, Evans denied the motion for a change of venue.

Then Bringgold argued to have Carole tried separately. It was a vital part of her defense strategy; she still had been the only witness to testify she was at the scene of Barbara Jean Finch's death. And she would not have to testify against herself.

Bringgold's motion was denied also. Citing costs to the taxpayer as a concern, Evans decided the two would stand together. He also announced jury selection would begin after the noon recess.

The press described Carole as more relaxed than at previous hearings and dressed more conservatively; her hair was shorter, combed back into a "French roll." She had gained about ten pounds. She would wear the same checkered dress, with a high collar, for the rest of the trial. Finch would wear the same blue suit, with pants too short, and a narrow black tie without the clasp, mandatory for the day.

Although his attorney gained much of the attention of the newsmen, Dr. Finch always played to the crowd—recognizing certain people by name, flashing one of his broad, confident grins.

Allen Sill attended some of the trial sessions.

ALLEN SILL

"He would come in, walking fast and confident, waving to people he knew. I remember one day he saw me and gave me the biggest smile and said, 'Hi ya, Chief, how's the family?' Why, he didn't know my family; he didn't even know if I *had* a family. It was all a big show."

135

Jury prospects would be brought in groups of twelve. Cooper would question all twelve first. Then Eagan would survey them, followed by Bringgold. Finally, Crail and Whichello asked questions.

Judge Evans would act as host and introduce the people.

"And your name, sir, is Louis H. Moeller? Is that right?"

"Yes, that's right," a short gray-haired man said. "Only it's pronounced with a 'u' sound and not an 'o' sound—Moeller. It's a German name, Your Honor."

"Well, Mr. Moeller," Evans used the corrected pronunciation, "do you have any reason that you could not serve as a juror on this case?"

"No," Mr. Moeller said, "but I bet the defense does. I used to be the warden of the Iowa State Penitentiary."

Cooper never looked up, "Move to excuse, Your Honor."

Still of the opinion his client could not get a fair trial in Los Angeles, Cooper would ask each prospect the same series of questions: "What magazines do you read?" "Which newspapers?" and "Have you formed any opinions about this case?"

Each defense team could object to as many as thirty prospects without stating a reason, and an unlimited number were there a "cause."

Cooper was questioning Louis Werner. "Have you ever seen the popular television show *Mr. District Attorney*, Mr. Werner?"

Werner: "Yes, I've seen it."

Cooper: "Do you think the fact that the D. A. is always a hero would affect your judgment as a juror?"

Werner: "No, I don't think so."

Whichello was out of turn. "How about *Perry Mason*, do you ever watch him? He's always a hero, too."

Cooper: "Your Honor, I would request that Mr. Whichello await his turn to ask questions."

Evans: "Agreed. Mr. Whichello, please."

All were waiting for Cooper to continue. Instead, he was listening. His chin was lifted up, head twisted slightly clockwise and moving first to the right, then the left. Slowly he turned around, still moving his head.

He turned abruptly to Evans, stood straight, and announced, "Your Honor, there is a movie camera being operated in here. I can hear it."

All counsel and defendants turned and looked back at the crowd. The room was quiet. Evans listened and heard nothing.

He looked over at his bailiff, "Did you hear anything?" The bailiff lifted his shoulders slightly and rapidly shook his head from side to side.

Cooper's eyes were wide; he pointed to the back corner of the room on his left. "It's not going now, but I heard it over there."

"Well, go look around for the camera," Evans commanded.

Two bailiffs started walking up the center aisle of the room, each scanning a side, row by row. The spectators were suddenly on trial; the accused, accusing. Cooper remained standing, arms folded in triumph.

As the bailiffs approached the back of the room, one of them noticed to his left there was one man, the only person, not looking back toward him. He was small, wearing wire-rimmed spectacles and a white, short-sleeved shirt with a thin, black tie. The bailiff stopped and fixed his eyes on the man who was still looking straight ahead. The other bailiff came over. The man was obviously trying to ignore them. By now, all had noticed.

"The fountain," he said in a trembling, high-pitched voice. "It was the water fountain."

The room was still silent.

"The water fountain. See." He got up and walked to the fountain just a few steps away. "It makes that sound. I was just getting a drink." He pressed down on the silver button and the water spurted up making a mechanical, swishing sound.

The high drama over, all turned to the front of the room.

Mrs. Sadye B. Bullene was next.

Asked if she were impartial about the defendants, she said, "Well I've formed opinions and changed them, and changed them back again. First I thought they were guilty, but now I'm not sure. I just can't get enough information from the papers."

"Move to dismiss." Cooper and Eagan spoke at the same time.

TUESDAY, DECEMBER 15, 1959

"Well a friend of mine is a former patient of Dr. Finch's." Margaret Slater was answering Judge Evans's question concerning associations she may have had to the parties involved. "And I do have a trip planned for after the holidays. Will this last that long?"

The drone of jury selection was tedious.

As Rexford Eagan was questioning Elba Colette of Arcadia, he heard a loud yawn from the prosecutor's table. He glanced over and saw Clifford Crail's hand cupped over his mouth.

"Well, are we boring you?" he asked.

Crail jumped to his feet, embarrassed. "Your Honor, I object to the lack of dignity Mr. Eagan is displaying in the courtroom."

As the gears of justice turned in Department Twelve, in a nearby courtroom Marie Anne Lidholm was involved with another one of Dr. Finch's legal problems, her civil suit. She had filed for recovery of $100,000 in damages, including headaches, nervousness, and sleeplessness she claimed to have suffered since his attack.

WEDNESDAY, DECEMBER 16, 1959

Covina was celebrating the appointment of one of its hometown boys to the head coach position at the University of Southern California. John McKay was the surprise choice.

Another son of Covina was being observed, on trial for his life, by a junior high school government class from nearby Eagle Rock. As the two dozen children were shown to the seats reserved for them, the teachers quieted them down with a few minutes of shushing.

At the front of the courtroom Judge Evans was having a conversation with his clerk, Melvin La Valley. The clerk was about to call the one hundredth prospect.

"What do you mean? You mean there's nobody else?" Evans asked

"Right, Your Honor. This is the last prospect. Down here we call fifty prospects at a time, and this is the end of the second group," La Valley explained.

"All right, put out a call for fresh jurors; we'll need them by tomorrow." Evans was presiding over the trial that would set a record for numbers of prospective jurors called.

Prospect number one hundred was James A. McCartin of Tujunga.

Whichello: "Do you have any friends in the law enforcement field?"

McCartin: "Well, yes. I have close friendships with a number of county sheriffs, and a couple of highway patrolmen."

Whichello: "Is that all?" He sounded hopeful.

McCartin: "No, my father and his brother were both F. B. I. agents."

Bringgold and Cooper both spoke: "Move to dismiss."

FRIDAY, DECEMBER 18, 1959

In the chambers of Judge Walter Evans, Grant Cooper appeared to be testing the waters for a possible plea bargain. Some observers speculated his brutal attacks on Whichello had been an attempt to set the stage for an agreement to reduce the charges against his client.

Whichello: "What's that again?"

Cooper: "I told you, my client is willing to stipulate that he fired the fatal shot."

Whichello: "Well, he can change his plea at any time, Grant. Are you telling us you want to change it?"

Cooper: "Well, I can tell you he's not prepared to plead guilty to murder, Fred. He will say he fired the fatal bullet. That's what I have to offer. Now you tell me what you might have to offer."

Whichello rubbed his chin with his right hand, looked down at the floor, then back at Cooper. "I think we can let the jury decide on all the facts concerning Mrs. Finch's death. And," he looked at back to Evans, "we will ask for the death penalty for both defendants."

Cooper showed no emotion. "Well, in that case you can expect Dr. Finch to take the stand and tell his story and we can let, as you said, the jury decide."

No more is known of the plea bargaining conversation. Many thought Cooper was trying to plead his client guilty to manslaughter.

Now it was official: Bernard Finch would take the stand. It would be the anticipated high point of the trial.

There was one other point of business Cooper raised before the meeting adjourned: rumors that Barbara Jean Finch had made secret tape recordings of Finch and Carole at one of their "love nests." Cooper wanted to know if the prosecutors had them.

"Also, Judge, there have been said to be certain recordings and wiretaps made of my client while he was at his Monterey Park apartment. Mr. Whichello has released this information to the press in his continuing attempt to try my client in the media."

Whichello reddened and sat up straight. "I have heard of such tapes, but I do not possess them."

The prosecutor waited for any words from Bringgold and Eagan. But the two were silent. He looked at them for a moment, then asked, "Well, uh, how about it? Is Mrs. Pappa going to testify in her defense?"

Bringgold: "We haven't decided."

Evans advised all sides he would recess the case until after Christmas. The next court session: December 28. He was also able to get the group to come to a "gentlemen's agreement" to show discretion in discussions with the press.

"No problem," Whichello had acquiesced.

During the last few days of 1959, there would be a series of "strategy sessions" attended by all the defense counsel, Carole Tregoff, and Bernard Finch. "These meetings are all business," Rexford Eagan would tell reporters.

Carole had been a Christmas present; she would be twenty-three years old on December 25.

DECADE ENDS

And the '50s ended. It had begun with the Korean conflict and Joseph McCarthy.

But McCarthyism faded and "Ike" ended the Korean war and managed an economy boom; many moved to the suburbs and told their children to "fit in." Instruction in conformity was aided by reels of television sitcoms that showed all how to act, dress, and speak. Most behavior was expected, and life was easier and less complicated that way.

The decade closed with pockets of "beatniks" spreading across the country, criticized for their dress, literature, and morals—a hint of what was coming.

The primaries, the national conventions, and the election of 1960 would draw much attention. But the country—and the world—would not forget to watch the Finch-Tregoff trial in Los Angeles. Proceedings began in the first week of the year. Those looking for conflict, drama, and pathos would not be disappointed.

two
Opening Remarks of the Prosecution

First Jury. *Getty.*

MONDAY, JANUARY 4, 1960

OUTSIDE DEPARTMENT TWELVE, Grant Cooper and Fred Whichello held each other by the lapels of their coats; neither was moving.

"Turn a little more toward me, Mr. Cooper." A young photographer was framing them for the next day's edition. "Legal Giants Come to Grips," he thought to himself, composing a headline.

Cooper was in the left of the frame, and Whichello to the right. Each had grabbed the other's coat with his right hand. The left hand was at the other's right elbow. "Almost like a professional wrestling pose," the photographer mused.

"Now look mean," he instructed them; the flashbulb popped and fizzled.

The trial was to begin.

Jerry Giesler, in his 1960 book *The Jerry Giesler Story, as Told to Pete Martin*, would write of the advice he gave to young lawyers in his firm, including which jurors to avoid in a murder case.

"Avoid grouchy people or those with narrow, hard lives," he instructed, "or those with meticulous, routine jobs requiring attention to tedious detail."

The twelve jurors were:

- Alfred W. Alm, a treasury agent from Eagle Rock who would be chosen as foreman
- Daisy B. Prior, a West Covina resident
- Gertrude E. Mann
- Irene Fluhr
- Floyd G. Jones
- Louis Werner
- Beatrice P. Hindry
- Samuel Jacobson
- Mrs. Rebecca Reynoso, an Hispanic
- Genevieve E. Lang, also of Eagle Rock
- Dolores Jaimez, an Hispanic man and postal clerk
- Eddie L. Lindsey, a black man, also a postal clerk.

Six women and six men. The jury had three people considered "minorities" at the time: Jaimez and Reynoso, both Hispanic, and Lindsey, an Afroamerican. The rest were middle-class whites.

Cooper had no more challenges and could object to no more juror choices. Bringgold and Eagan had challenges left that they could use in Cooper's aid, but they did not.

Cooper asked for more challenges and was refused.

"I wouldn't deny the motion if I had the slightest doubt that the defendants can get a fair trial. I think the six women and six men in the jury box are alert and honest and down-to-earth jurors." Evans replied. He then denied, once again, Carole's motion to have the trials separated.

Defense table. First Trial. *Getty.*

Cooper made a motion not to allow the prosecution to use Barbara Jean's divorce attorney's statements regarding the "death threats" Finch had allegedly made against Barbara Jean Finch. He reasoned that it was hearsay evidence. Evans agreed the statements were hearsay, but denied the motion, noting that hearsay may be used in a murder case to describe a victim's state of mind.

Robert Neeb was present, full of motions. He moved Carole's statements to Clark County sheriffs and West Covina Detectives and her testimony at Dr. Finch's preliminary hearing, that led to her arrest, not be allowed. This latter would be known as "Exhibit 60" for the prosecution. Evans took this under advisement, promising to rule on it before testimony began.

Cooper then rose and again personally attacked Whichello. Fred had told the press who his witnesses were to be.

"Your Honor," he began, "Mr. Whichello is at it again. He has released a list of fifty witnesses he intends to call."

Evans had seen the list published in all the local newspapers.

"I strongly protest the release of this list," Cooper continued. "It was a breach of our gentlemanly understanding reached in chambers a few days ago. We had, Your Honor, all agreed to use discretion and good judgment in any statements to the press."

Evans had no choice; he reluctantly issued an "anti-talk" order to all counsel: "All counsel will refrain from making any and all public appearances and public statements to the press, radio, television, or otherwise as to any phase of the case, as to what is going to be proven or what the effect of the testimony might be or might have been."

Whichello squirmed in his chair. It was Cooper's last stab before the men squared off for trial. Evans then leaned back and took in a deep breath as he looked around the room. There were the usual mulling sounds heard when large groups were idle from business—mumbles, giggles, and an occasional cough. To his left was the jury, twelve men and women and the four alternates. Most of them were looking out at the larger group that had come to witness their judgment. One older, heavy-set man in the front row had his hands together resting on his large abdomen. He was blankly looking at the wall opposite him; his face showed no emotion.

Closest to the jury, Crail and Whichello were talking and pointing at a drawing that showed the layout of the Finch property to be used in Fred's opening remarks. Ryan was behind them, listening and watching them point, occasionally nodding.

In the seats of the courtroom Evans spotted Dr. Finch's father. The man had a grim expression and was looking randomly around the courtroom, as though wondering why all these people wanted to share in his family's misfortune.

The judge's wife and daughter were sitting in the front row behind the prosecutors; the two were not looking at him. His wife was studying the jury and his eight-year-old daughter was looking at all the attorneys. She had heard her dad talk about them at home; her mouth was half open.

On his right was a special section reserved for photographers and certain others. There he saw Carole's father and stepmother. Both were looking at the prosecutors. Mrs. Tregoff was to the left of her husband, holding onto his arm with both of hers, talking to him.

On the other side of the aisle from Whichello was Cooper, watching each juror intently, his arms folded in front of him, his chin up slightly. To the right of Cooper was Dr. Bernard Finch, reading a copy of the prosecutor's opening statement, just distributed; his elbows were resting on the table. There was no expression on his face and he was very still, studying.

Rexford Eagan was to the left of Finch, leaning back reading the same statement. Evans had heard he was a former football player, in the backfield somewhere he thought, and a usually feisty ex-marine and World War Two veteran. Eagan had a wry smile on his face. He would occasionally shake his head from side to side.

Donald Bringgold was looking directly at him. He had no papers or briefcases in front of him. It was as though Bringgold had been assigned only to observe. His left thumb was rubbing his chin as he continued to look at Evans; the jurist felt a twinge of unease and looked at Carole, sitting at the end of the defense table, farthest from the jury.

The judge knew that Carole might not be there if she had said nothing. *More attractive even than her photos,* Evans thought. The young woman seemed composed; her eyes were wide, her mouth open slightly. She looked directly at the jury, never seeming to keep eye contact with any; her eyes, instead, darted from one to another. Sitting straight, her left arm was flat on the table.

Finally: Robert Neeb. Evans had noticed the senior partner in Giesler's firm never spoke while court was in session, and had learned from one of the clerks of a particular instruction Neeb would give to his clients and co-counsel. "Never talk to me in court; you can write me a note or wait till adjournment, but never talk me. I want to see and hear everything."

Although Evans had presided during a part of the trial of Caryl Chessman, the rapist-kidnapper who was eventually executed at San Quentin. He knew this would probably be his most noteworthy case.

It was time to start.

"Mr. Whichello." After one slam of the gavel.

"Yes, Your Honor." He was walking to the left of the courtroom carrying an easel that was carefully positioned so all could see it. "I have a few diagrams I will be showing." Crail had followed, carrying a stack of thick, stiff, three-feet by two-feet paper boards. He placed the boards on the easel, squaring them neatly. The first was seen to have three large headings, each with a letter in front of it; and under each of these were three to four subheadings.

Whichello's opening statement would last three and a half hours. He told the jury of his faith in their ability to determine an appropriate verdict after they had heard the facts and reminded them, officially, that the two defendants were on trial for murder. Then he outlined the details of his case. With his dry, professorial monotone, he first went over the three main groups of evidence they would hear. The prosecutor was "lanky," as described by some, and so, at times, were his sentences. Sometimes, at the end of a long sentence, jurors would have furrows between their eyes.

"The first thing that we propose to prove to you, and I have given a capital *A* to that topic, is the murder itself. That will necessarily involve largely the evidence of the evening of July 18, 1959, at and in the vicinity of the Larkhill Drive home in West Covina.

"Let me outline that these topics are not necessarily tied into reality, but are principal subdivisions of the subject matter we will take up.

"In topic B," he pointed to the next heading where "MOTIVES" was scrawled, "we intend to reflect to you the motives or reasons for the commission of the murder on July 18, 1959, and we expect that topic to include three subdivisions because we expect the evidence will reflect three sorts of reasons for this murder."

Some of the jurors leaned forward, squinting to read the smaller print of the first subheading.

"We will consider the first subdivision under *MOTIVES* what we might call the *TRIANGLE*—the title given to situations where three persons are involved, two married, one on the outside of the triangle anxious to change that relationship." He was standing between the easel and Evans, pointing with his right index finger.

The next subdivision was *MONEY*.

"The second subdivision under *MOTIVES*, which we feel the evidence will reflect, can bestated by the one word: *MONEY*. It was to each defendant's actual advantage that this murder be committed."

HATRED was next.

SUNDAY TRIBUNE A3

je of Evidence Aimed at Dr. Finch, Carole

Attack on
nan Charged

'rice Spiral Seen as
Result of Steel Pact

Rise in Steel Prices Expected
Unless Productivity Increased

PROBLEMS

Macmillan
Beginning
Africa Trip

KOREAN WOMEN

Fred Whichello lays out his case. *Valley Tribune.*

"The third motive which we feel the evidence will reflect will be also simply reflected by the word *HATRED*. And this motive, of course, incorporates some aspects of motives one and two, this third being based on frustration in connection with the first two subdivisions."

He was at the third main heading now, pointing to CONSPIRACY.

"I will now proceed to another class of proof, which we will call the *CONSPIRACY*. Here we refer to evidence which principally bears on the planning, the meeting of the conspirators, the statements made at that time which would particularly tend to show the conspiracy, and will also tend to show that the murder itself was premeditated."

Whichello occasionally digressed into laborious, long, one-sentence paragraphs. "With regard to this last group, there is certain evidence which tends to show certain admissions and things which the law classifies as admissions and certain statements made by the defendants which tend to connect them with the occurrence, and which together with the other evidence in the case are such as to reflect the offense as charged."

He previewed some of the testimony to show Finch had a pattern of violent behavior against his wife.

"Miss Lidholm," he was describing an attack in May, 1959, "will testify that she heard loud noises from the bedroom occupied by Doctor and Mrs. Finch and that next morning there was blood on the pillow and that Mrs. Finch appeared the next morning with a Band-Aid on her forehead.

"Another woman will tell you she saw the wound under the Band-Aid and that Mrs. Finch told her she was afraid of Dr. Finch. And Mrs. Finch's attorney will also testify to seeing the cut on May 19, 1959, that it required stitches, and that Mrs. Finch made statements indicating fear of her husband."

A second assault would be described.

"There will also be testimony that Dr. Finch threatened to tie her up and run her over a cliff in a car, and that on one occasion he sat on her chest for a lengthy period, and that he threatened he had people in Las Vegas whom he could hire to kill her."

Whichello wanted to show that Finch was strapped financially.

After referring to Mrs. Finch's control of all the family assets, "The prosecution will also introduce evidence that on May 1, 1959, Dr. Finch gave a check to the business manager of his West Covina Medical Center for $3,000, which purportedly carried the signature of Mrs. Finch and was drawn on her own private banking account. The handwriting on the check, experts will tell you, and the signature were not written by her, but were either a tracing or an attempt at simulating her signature and handwriting."

And he announced that he would also convict the two of adultery.

"These two defendants shared a series of what might be called 'love nests'..."

Finch jerked up straight, glaring at the prosecutor. Carole grabbed the edge of the table and squeezed, her knuckles noticeably whiter.

"...as early as 1957."

"We purport to show that there were quarrels between Dr. Finch and Mrs. Finch for some time and that Dr. Finch had moved out of the South Hills residence in May of 1959. And that also in May he rented an apartment with *Mrs.* Pappa under the name Mr. and Mrs. Evans," he walked two steps toward the jury, "and he and *Mrs.* Pappa came around there a few times a week, often with the doctor wearing his white coat."

And he would go over how Finch had helped Carole rent her apartment in Las Vegas.

"We will also show that in Las Vegas, Dr. Finch engaged the apartment there for Mrs. Pappa and that when he did so, he made this statement: 'As soon as I clear up my affairs in L. A.,'" he paused, waiting for all the jury to look, "'I will join her.'"

He used the rest of the afternoon court session detailing what each witness would say, after which all counsel approached the bench and agreed the jury should see the Finch residence. Court would convene at 1:15 P.M. on Larkhill Drive, West Covina.

three
Court Session at Larkhill Drive

Valley Tribune.

TUESDAY, JANUARY 5, 1960
1:30 P.M.

I⊤ WAS "LADIES' day" at South Hills Country Club. The early afternoon was cool; temperatures would not rise above seventy-five degrees. Except for the eucalyptus, most of the trees had no leaves. The dozen groups of four that were scattered about the front nine holes of the course could see and hear the yellow school bus grind and cough up Larkhill Drive to the Finch driveway. Already there were about thirty cars that had carried the attorneys and the press. The women golfers would look at each other, nod knowingly, then continue play.

The bus stopped, straddled across the driveway. Its door squeaked open and the jury filed out. Soon fifty people were gathered at the base of the hill below the Finch residence, next to a six-foot-square white sign that had been mounted on two four-by-four-inch posts. It read NO TRESPASSING BY ORDER OF SUPERIOR COURT, STATE OF CALIFORNIA. Already parked next to the sign when the bus had pulled up were a Chevy Nomad, a late-model T-bird with its soft top on, and a Corvair coupe. Two reporters leaned against the Nomad, smoking, waiting for court to convene.

The golfers could easily hear the annoying chatter of the group on this otherwise quiet day as it walked up the long driveway. Often, an intruder would look down into the valley, pointing to a home or familiar building. Soon, all were arranged in front of the garage.

Dr. Finch surveyed the unkempt yard, unmowed for six months. Many of the carefully placed bushes and trees were dead for lack of water.

Many would note the home had an awkward, cold design. The front formal entrance was a fifty-foot walk from where guests parked. The more direct route to the house: through the small door at the back of the garage, across the lanai—the patio and pool area—and inside through heavy, sliding-glass doors.

Joyce Hoffman had been a babysitter and housekeeper at the Finch house before the couple hired Marie Anne Lidholm. She would later talk to me by phone.

INTERVIEW WITH JOYCE HOFFMAN
BY TELEPHONE, MAY 3, 1992

"It was me who told them they needed to hire one of those exchange students I had heard about. They needed somebody that could live-in. They were on the go too much for somebody like me. Then they hired the Swedish girl."

As for the house, "The house was laid out strange; I never did get used to it. You know it was designed by Dr. Finch himself. It always reminded me of a clinic or a hospital. It was cold. To get to the front door from the driveway you had to walk about fifty feet. The quickest way into the house was through the back of the garage to that sliding patio door."

"My first witness," Fred began, "Marie Anne Lidholm, first came through these patio doors after hearing screams for help." They were standing in the inner court of the home, next to the pool. As he began, a dry wind moved some fallen eucalyptus leaves in small funnels about the group and rustled others still atop.

Carole Tregoff and Dr. Bernard Finch stared blankly into the pool as Whichello spoke; it had been drained of water. It was one of the few places they could look without meeting the eyes of others.

Whichello was taking his time. He wanted the jury to imagine the screams for help and the sound of the door sliding open. He paused, studying each juror, most with eyes fixed on the two defendants. One, Geraldine Lang, was less than three feet from them; she studied Carole. Mr. Dolores Jaimez was at the back of the group watching both defendants, his face broadcasting more emotion.

Photographs of this day show Carole sad and tearful, usually with a handkerchief to her eyes. She is always to

155

one side of the group with Bringgold standing between her and the jury.

"When she got to this door here," Fred was on the move, "she noticed her mistress lying on the concrete floor." He made sure all saw where the light switch was. Then he pointed to some blood stains that had been sampled; small lines of chalk circled the dark stains. "And there were stains on the convertible that was parked here, of which I will show you pictures. The car motor was running, and the radio was playing quite loudly.

"About here, we found fragments of a rubber glove, similar to those used by a surgeon." Then he walked back into the garage, grabbed a rake, and started walking down the hill that led to the home of Raymond Finch, Sr.

Cooper wondered what the rake was for, but said nothing. This was Whichello's time.

Fred turned. He was halfway down the hill and the group had not followed. He yelled, "Now if you'll just follow me." They moved across the driveway and through a ten foot stretch of tall, dry weeds, then down a half dozen earthen steps carved out of a steeper part of the hill. The women walked slowly, studying where their heels would land.

"Here is where the body was found by Officer Rund," Fred announced after all had caught up with him. Some were standing at the top of the steps. "Now I will show you the location of the body." He put the rake down with the handle pointed back to the steps.

Cooper was standing to Fred's right; Don Bringgold was to his right, then the taller Evans and Neeb. Cooper could keep silent no longer. "Is the handle the victim's top or bottom?"

Whichello spoke in his business-like tone. "That would be her head. Her feet were pointed this way, toward the country club over there. The body was lined up like this."

He backed up to a hedge and put his right arm out to the side and his left behind him. "See. And the victim was on her back, like this." He bowed his back as far as he could. "Her left leg was kind of bent underneath her."

Cooper nodded, then looked to Neeb.

"This is very confusing to me, if I might interject, Your Honor." Neeb interrupted. "If I can't get an idea of how the body was situated, I doubt the jurors can either."

Mild consternation jumped into Whichello's face. "What do you mean? The body was like I said. The head was up this way, the legs were over there," he was drawing with his hands, "and the left leg was—"

"Lie down and show us, Fred." Cooper wiggled his right hand down at the dried grass between them.

Photos from session at Lark Hill drive. Upper right just minutes before Whichello was photographed lying down on the job.

Fred turned to Cooper, hands at his hips.

"Actually, it's not a bad idea, Your Honor. I think we'd ail like to actually see how the body was found." Neeb agreed.

"I'm not lying down on any grass!" Fred's face was red. He turned to Evans. "Now maybe someone else could lie down and I could—"

Cooper: "You have the best knowledge of this."

Neeb: "And you've seen the actual photographs, Mr. Whichello."

Fred took a deep breath, then moved his arms to the side, palms up. "Oh, all right. Anything to help educate the court, I guess. Well, this is a first for me, Your Honor."

Neeb took a step to his right, distancing himself from Evans.

Whichello handed a small stack of papers to a nearby Ryan, slowly lowered himself into the dry grass, then methodically situated his arms and legs. "Okay, counselors, her left arm was down behind her and her left leg—"

The group was startled by several loud pops and fizzles; three photographers had been hiding behind the hedge near Neeb and the other defense counsel.

Fred's right hand rose, too late to block the flashes. He glared at Neeb, then Cooper. He looked back at the hedge; the photographers were gone.

He moved his arms and legs back to their positions, talking slowly and watching the two senior defense counsel.

The group went up the steps to the asphalt driveway and looked to the west, down the hill toward Citrus Street. The prosecutor was pointing across the road, just to the right of the tenth hole's tee. "You can see there the home of Mr. Mossberg, where a car was stolen within minutes of the murder."

Whichello looked over toward the house of Bernard Finch's father, Raymond. There were some photographers waiting at the front door, cameras held up. The doctor came out of the front door, wiping away tears. He had not seen his mother in months. His head was down as he walked past the newsmen. One reporter stepped forward as though to ask a question, then back, saying nothing.

Evans adjourned court, instructing all to reconvene in Department Twelve at 9:00 A.M.

four
Testimony of Marie Anne Lidholm

WEDNESDAY, JANUARY 6, 1960

FRED WHICHELLO WAS angry. He studied the photograph on the front page of *The Examiner* as he wiped his glasses clean with a handkerchief. Irritated, his head was rapidly shaking from side to side.

Above the picture was a large, bold headline: "Deputy D. A. Lies Down on the Job."

The man for whom he was waiting walked by and shuffled sideways to his seat at the defense table.

"You're behind this, Bob. I know it. You've got the press in your hip pocket and everybody knows it. It was a cheap trick getting me to lie down like that and it wasn't gentlemanly!" Whichello pounded the desk with his fist.

Robert Adam Neeb was a founding member of the Los Angeles Press Club and was still its general counsel. He glanced at the prosecutor, then back to a stack of papers he was arranging. "Good morning, Fred. What's the matter?"

Fred's voice rose a notch, his words coming faster. "Don't act like you haven't seen this!" He held up the paper, pointing at the picture. "And don't pretend you didn't know those photographers were there when you tricked me into lying down. Pictures and headlines like this degrade the decorum of the court." He slapped the paper on the desk.

Neeb said nothing. Years later, his daughter, Rosemary, would tell me "Anything and everything was fair. An attorney would show no quarter to his opponent."

This was the first day Hollywood starlets would make an appearance at the trial—a publicist's dream. Terry Moore had her picture taken with Grant Cooper. The two are shown sitting in the spectator seats, chatting. In standard litany she was quoted: "I'm gaining experience for an upcoming movie." Other stars would later interview Finch and Tregoff, their stories and photographs appearing daily on the front pages of a tabloid-sized evening newspaper with the daily-running headline, "Impressions."

Eric Ambler, the *Life* magazine reporter, was to title his feature, "The Shock of the Fascinating Finch Affair." Some would feel insulted by his story's subtitle: "Noted Mystery Writer Describes the Courtroom Circus."

He would write: "The sight of these ladies, pad and pencil in hand and skirts hitched up becomingly, being photographed while they interview the eagerly cooperative Miss Tregoff and Dr. Finch, is troubling. Are a man and a woman really on trial here for their lives?"

A quiet, unassuming nineteen-year-old Swedish girl was sitting in the witness chair. She had taken her thick, dark-framed glasses out of their case and was putting them on, wanting to see the people who were to question her. She was wearing a dark blue, pleated schoolgirl dress and a simple white blouse. It had been cool that morning when she left the Pasadena home of her family's friends, the Stewarts, so she had draped a sweater over her shoulders. She looked calmly at the crowd gathered to hear her. There were two hundred fifty people in court; most were studying her, some taking her photograph.

Clifford Crail questioned her first, asking for a description of the alleged attack by Dr. Finch on his wife, a few weeks before her death. She spoke in her heavy Swedish accent.

"One Sunday morning, about the middle of May, Mrs. Finch called me into her master bedroom. I saw blood on the pillow and sheets of her bed. She told me 'My husband tried to kill me last night'

"Then she said, 'He tried to put my clothes on and put me in a car and run it over a cliff where it would explode.'"

Cooper was standing, "Your Honor, this is all hearsay evidence."

Evans allowed the testimony to continue, citing certain exceptions to exclusion of hearsay as evidence. "I will allow the questions, but the jury must accept the testimony only as showing Mrs. Finch's state of mind at the time of her death."

Marie Anne continued: "On that same day she packed her clothes and moved out of the house. She told me she was going to file for a divorce. She said she was going to stay with two women friends in Hollywood and would check by telephone each morning to see how everything was. Mrs. Finch stayed away about three weeks, and the day she moved back in, Dr. Finch moved out."

Dr. Finch had taken the couple's red Chrysler. Barbara Jean would be driving the Cadillac. Toward the end of June, less than three weeks before the murder, Dr. Finch had returned to the residence, hoping to exchange cars. He had planned a drive to Las Vegas and thought the Cadillac was better suited for the long desert drive.

Crail: "Was there any difficulty in the exchange of the cars?"

Lidholm: "Yes. He came about noon, wanting to exchange cars. They were arguing in the master bedroom. I couldn't help overhearing because they were talking so loud. He said, 'Give me the car keys,' and she said, 'I don't have them here; they're in the car.' Finally, Mrs. Finch came rushing down the hall into my bedroom and said, 'Marie Anne, call the police!' Dr. Finch came to my door and she looked at him and said, 'I'm not going to let you push me around and throw me on the floor.' He said, 'What do you mean by that?'"

She told of one of Dr. Finch's more curious visits home before the murder. It was July 9. Barbara Jean Finch had not been at home. He showed Marie Anne how to use a gun that was kept in the library.

Crail: "What kind of gun was it? A rifle? A revolver?"

Lidholm: "I don't know. A long one, I think a rifle."

Dr. Finch had said that he wanted her to know how to use the weapon were burglars to break into the isolated home.

She then spoke of hearing Mrs. Finch's car come home the night of the murder. Her bedroom window faced the pool and garage area, and her window had been open that night.

Crail: "How long was it after you heard the car come into the drive before you heard Mrs. Finch call out?"

Lidholm: "It was one or two minutes. It was taking longer than usual for her to come inside, and I remember wondering if something was wrong."

Crail: "What did you hear her say?"

Lidholm: "She yelled 'Help!' It was a terrifying sound; I knew something horrible was going on. I heard her when I was in the bathroom and again when I rushed into my bedroom and put on my bathrobe. I yelled out for Patti and the two of us went to the lanai door. We started for the garage, but then I thought that maybe she should stay inside. We could hear a horrible sound like something being slammed around. That's when I stopped and told Patti to go back into the house and wait for me." She stopped, looking down as though to prepare herself for the description of what came next.

Her quiet voice echoed through the large, otherwise silent, room.

Lidholm: "I ran along the pathway towards the garage and I entered the garage from the side door and I turned on the light."

Crail: "And what did you see there?"

Lidholm: "First I saw Mrs. Finch lying on the floor. I think she was unconscious; she was not moving."

Crail: "Where was the defendant, Dr. Finch?"

Her voice rose slightly.

Lidholm: "He was somewhere between me and Mrs. Finch. He rushed towards me immediately after I turned on the light. He bashed my head against the wall several times, the same wall the light switch is on; he banged my head several times, knocking me unconscious."

Crail: "And what do you remember next?"

Lidholm: "The next thing I remember I was leaning against the north wall of the garage, just sitting there. Dr. Finch went to put me into the Chrysler car and that was the first time I saw any gun in his hand."

Crail: "What do you remember next?"

Lidholm: "When I woke up he was standing in front of me. He fired a shot at me and told me to get into the back seat of the car."

Crail: "You then entered the car?"

Lidholm: 'Yes. Then he ordered Mrs. Finch into the car. He pulled her around the back of the car and pushed her in. Then he ran back around and got in the driver's side. When Dr. Finch started the car, she ran away and he ran around the front of the car and then out of the garage, after her."

Crail: "What did you do then?"

Lidholm: "I waited for a few seconds, then I ran inside to phone the police. Patti met me at the patio door and asked me what happened."

Crail: "Did you hear anything as you were running into the house?"

Lidholm: "I heard Mrs. Finch yell 'Help' again."

Cooper objected one final time, claiming this was hearsay, and again was overruled.

Crail: "You then phoned the police?"

Lidholm: "Yes. As I was phoning the police, I heard another shot. Then Patti and I went outside to see if we could find Mrs. Finch."

Crail announced he was finished with his witness. All were left with the image of two young girls on an asphalt driveway looking into the darkness for Barbara Jean Finch. Most appreciated their bravery for going back outside after shots had been fired and many concluded at this time that Marie Anne might have been another victim had Patti not been at her side.

Cooper rose to cross-examine the chief witness against his client; he would take three hours, standing near the witness most of the time, his back to the jury, his right arm on the witness box rail. He would look directly at her, sometimes talking gently and slowly, sometimes brutally confrontive. Marie Anne was nervous at this point. The pitch of her voice rose slightly and as she occasionally looked away from Cooper, she would also look away from the jury.

She told me later of her thoughts, "I just wanted to help find the truth. I was just trying to help and remember as best I could. Those lawyers, and they were very good lawyers, got me so confused sometimes."

Cooper first asked her if she remembered receiving any telephone calls from Dr. Finch the night before the murder—an indication, perhaps, that the doctor was expected.

Cooper: "Miss Lidholm, do you remember a phone call on July 18 from the Las Vegas operator asking if Mrs. Finch was there and your reply that she was not there, but would be back later?"

165

Lidholm: "I don't remember. There were a lot of phone calls."

Cooper: "Do you remember later that evening, about 8:00, the operator calling again and asking for Mrs. Finch?" Lidholm: "I cannot be sure."

Cooper: "In other words you have received many such calls from Las Vegas, many times?"

Lidholm: "Yes."

He briefly asked about the day in May when she saw the blood on Mrs. Finch's bed.

Cooper: "On the day you saw her bandaged, did she appear frightened?"

Lidholm: "Yes. She told me about everything and said, 'I want you to know everything in case something should happen to me.'"

He moved on.

Cooper: "Would you demonstrate, on me, how Dr. Finch held you when you say he grabbed you and banged your head against the wall?"

The young girl stood up and leaned forward. She put both palms over Cooper's ears.

Lidholm: "It was like this."

Cooper: "Thank you." He paced twice to the jury box, then turned. "Now, in your first statement to Captain Ryan you said that Dr. Finch had a gun in his hand when you entered the garage. Would you mind telling me, Miss Lidholm, how he could have a gun in his hand and still hold you with both hands as you have just shown me."

Crail's objection was overruled.

Lidholm: "It was not right, the first time I said it. I remember now that he did not have a gun when I first saw him."

He walked to his desk and grabbed a small stack of stapled paper, holding it up.

Cooper: "This is a copy of the statement you made to Captain Ryan, Miss Lidholm. Do you recall making statements to him that you heard shots while you were still in your bedroom, before you went outside?"

Lidholm: "I don't remember what I said. If it is down there, I must have said it."

Cooper: "At this time, then, you don't remember hearing shots before you left the house. Is that correct?"

Lidholm: "No." Her voice cracked. Her mouth was dry.

Cooper took his pipe out of his coat pocket and held it like a gun, pointing it at Marie Anne.

Cooper: "Now when you were leaning up against the wall, you say Dr. Finch fired a gun and told you to get into the car?"

Lidholm: "Yes."

Cooper started pointing the pipe up, then down, then to all sides.

Cooper: "Was he holding it like this, or this, or this?"

Lidholm: "I don't know which way it was pointed."

Cooper: "But you do say you distinctly remember seeing white smoke come out of the gun."

Lidholm: "Yes."

Cooper: "And you are certain then," he paused, "quite certain that the gun was fired while you were in the garage and not when you were in your bedroom?"

Lidholm: "Yes, quite certain."

Marie Anne had at first said both she and Mrs. Finch had entered the car from the driver's side.

Lidholm: "I corrected that because it was wrong."

Cooper went on for another hour. He had discovered minor discrepancies in her many statements about exactly when Dr. Finch had turned off the light and about whether the patio lights had been on or off. She could not remember if she walked or was dragged to the passenger side of the car. In some statements she had said she blacked out when her head was banged against the wall; in others she had not.

Cooper: "How could you remember any of these things if you were unconscious?"

Crail rose and objected.

Cooper returned to the fact that she had not mentioned to Ryan in her first statement that Finch had fired a shot in the garage.

Cooper: "Didn't you consider that important?"

Lidholm: "I don't know. I just know I do my best, and tell as much as I know, and I can't do any more, Mr. Cooper."

Her voice was strained. She started shaking her head from side to side as she talked. Whichello leaned forward, his head tilted up, resting on his knuckles.

Cooper slowly walked back to his desk. There he picked up an inch-thick stack of bound paper. Then he strolled back to the witness stand, thumbing through the report.

Cooper: "Now, Miss Lidholm, I know you have been as careful with your testimony as possible. I'd like to read to you your testimony at the preliminary hearing of Dr. Finch.

"You were asked 'All the while the doctor was moving around the car, you didn't see anything at all in his hand, did you?' and you answered 'No.' Now did you so testify, Miss Lidholm, as I have read?"

Lidholm: "Yes."

Cooper: "And in your statements to Captain Ryan and Sergeant Hopkinson and in the deposition taken in my office on November 27, you did not mention you saw a gun in his hand as he ran around the car?"

Lidholm: "That is correct."

Cooper stepped a few feet away. He looked at the jury.

Cooper: "Miss Lidholm, are you still willing to testify that you saw a gun in the hand of Dr. Finch that night and that he fired that gun?"

Whichello watched intently, his hands cupped in front of his mouth. Marie Anne's chin rose slightly, just as it had when the group of newsmen questioned her in West Covina.

Lidholm: "Yes, I saw him with the gun and he fired it at me."

Cooper looked down and walked back to the defense table. He shuffled through some papers, only wanting to appear as though he were searching for something. He was gathering himself.

Cooper: "Miss Lidholm, there appear to be quite a few discrepancies in your various statements. Which one are we to believe?"

Her eyes were red. She had been on the stand the entire day. Taking a deep breath, she spoke slowly.

Lidholm: "I know there are some differences with my statements to the police on that night, but since then my English has improved and I have had time to think things over."

He moved slowly toward her; his head was cocked back, mouth slightly open. Sounding angry, his voice was measurably louder with each question.

Cooper: "Well, did he have a hat on? Did you think that over?"

Lidholm: "I am uncertain."

Cooper: "Did he have a coat on? Did you think about that?"

Lidholm: "I don't know."

Cooper: "You have testified previously that he may have had a coat on. Did you have time to think about that?"

Lidholm: "I was so confused. I thought hard and I remember now, I..."

Cooper: "So he may or may not have—"

He never finished his sentence. Marie Anne had both her hands over her ears; head shaking quickly from side to side, she was sobbing loudly. Court was recessed for the day. Evans appeared uncomfortable after Cooper's questions. He had allowed them, most thought, because this was a capital case.

After court that day Crail and Whichello both talked of the much-anticipated testimony of Dr. Finch. Most observers thought a "self defense" strategy, taking advantage of the discrepancies in Lidholm's testimony, was most likely.

"One other thing for sure, Fred," Clifford Crail said as the two walked through the courthouse parking lot.

"What's that?" Fred asked.

"It's going to be one hell of a story."

five

Testimony of Patti Daugherty
and other witnesses

Valley Tribune.

THURSDAY, JANUARY 7, 1960

PHOTOGRAPHERS MET PATTI Daugherty in the parking lot; she was escorted by her father, Lyle. Both smiled briefly at the men. Patti wore short white gloves and carried a small purse. She was twelve years old and, in heels, as tall as her father.

Her father would usually have his hand at her elbow, ready to steer her, guarding her from the attention.

DAN LEONARD

"She was very pretty," Dan remembered. "I always had a crush on her. She was a cheerleader in high school. Occasionally I would muster the courage to talk to her; she always would say 'Hi' and be very polite. She was a kind person."

ALLEN SILL

"I remember being there that day. I didn't hear any of the testimony—I had to get back to the station—but someone had asked me to take some judge from Pakistan down there. I remember his name, Sarafutallah."

I was looking at the newspaper photo as the former chief spoke. There they were: Sill and Sarafutallah talking with Fred Whichello. The Pakistani was short, slim and well-groomed; both he and Chief Sill were looking at the beaming Whichello.

"You know," Sill said, "Everybody wanted to be a part of this thing, in one way or another. This judge from Pakistan wanted to be able to tell people in his country that he had been here. He asked me to introduce him to Judge Evans and Finch. So I did. Then before I could get out of the courtroom to get back to West Covina, the producer of the Tom Duggan show called me up."

Duggan aired a weekly Saturday night show that featured unusual or provocative guests. Joe Pine would emulate him in later years.

"They wanted me to bring this judge over for the show the next night. So I did. They introduced me on the show, too, as one of the men that brought Finch back from Las Vegas. It was an exciting time."

Marie Anne was brought back for a few questions. Rexford Eagan asked her to confirm she had not seen Carole Tregoff the night Barbara Jean died. Clifford Crail asked about the injuries she suffered and the subsequent headaches and incoordination she still had.

Patti Daugherty walked to the witness box. She had been calm, smiling politely, and brave up to this point. But as soon as her name was called she began crying. Her father escorted her to the stand. Seated, her head was down; she was taking slow, deep breaths. Lyle stayed a few moments, talking quietly until she calmed.

"Thank you, Mr. Daugherty," Evans said as the protective father was returning to his seat.

This was her first sworn testimony. She would stay calm, her voice quivering slightly, her face frozen into a polite smile.

Clifford Crail examined for the prosecution. He walked slowly to the witness box. He wanted to put his witness at ease, as much as possible; she was the best corroboration to the testimony of his main witness, Marie Anne.

Crail: "I want you to know, Miss Daugherty, that you are among friends here. Many of the jury have children of their own, and I do."

She smiled stiffly, looking at him directly in the eyes.

Crail: "Why, even Mr. Cooper has a few of his own."

Cooper: "I have five, counselor."

There was a ripple of laughter.

173

Crail: "Now tell us what your relationship to the deceased woman was?"

Daugherty: "You mean my Mom?"

Crail: "Uh, yes, Barbara Jean Finch."

Daugherty: "She was my mother." She appeared confused for a moment.

Crail: "Do you recall the events at your home on the night of July 18 last?"

Daugherty: "Yes, I was at my house with my brother Raymond and Marie."

Crail: "Do you recall how you were spending your time on that evening?"

Daugherty: "We were watching the Miss Universe Pageant on television from Long Beach. It was just over and I went to bed. I was just going to bed..." She stopped; her lower lip quivered.

Crail: "What happened then?"

Daugherty: "Marie Anne came out and she was standing by my bedroom and calling to me. She said, 'Patti, come quickly!' or something like that. We ran to the lanai door and started to run to the garage. When we got to the garage she turned and told me to go back into the house."

Crail: "Can you tell us what you heard when you were running to the garage?"

Daugherty: "Yes, I heard my mother. I could hear her clearly. She was screaming, 'Help, help, Marie Anne!'"

Crail: "What else did you hear?"

Daugherty: "I heard footsteps, or what sounded like footsteps, then someone hitting against the wall of the garage. Then Marie turned to me and said, 'Go back into the house!'"

Crail: "When you went back into the house, did you hear any other sounds?"

Daugherty: "I heard one gunshot."

Crail: "Where was Marie at this point?"

Daugherty: "She was not on the patio or in the house and I assumed she must have been in the garage."

Crail: "When did you see her next?"

Daugherty: "I saw her running toward the house." Then we went inside and called the police. That's when we heard the second gunshot. Then we went outside." She paused, looking down. Her face was more contorted, tears appearing on her cheeks.

Carole's attorneys were asked if they had any questions. Bringgold waited until she composed herself.

Bringgold: "Miss Daugherty, did you at any time see Miss Tregoff that night?"

Daugherty: "No."

Cooper had no questions. He was anxious to get the girl off the stand. His client had slowly slumped onto the table during the girl's testimony. Now he was resting his head in both palms; he did not move.

Crail, aware of Dr. Finch's remarks to police in Las Vegas, anticipated testimony that some of the murder kit items were obtained from the garage on July 18 and were to be used on the family boat.

Crail: "Just one thing more, Miss Daugherty. Did you ever see any pieces of rope in your garage?"

Daugherty: "No."

Cooper asked two questions at this point. He walked to the small table in front of the judge's bench and opened the brown attaché case, taking out two small pieces of clothesline-sized rope.

Cooper: "Now, Miss Daugherty, did you ever see two pieces of rope like this in your garage?"

Daugherty: "No."

Cooper: "Do you think you could remember everything that was in the garage on that night?"

He was walking back to his chair now, just starting to sit down.

Daugherty: "No, of course not. I couldn't remember everything that was there." She giggled. A small ripple of sympathetic laughter crossed the room.

Cooper took a deep breath, "No more questions, Your Honor."

Eagan asked again if Patti had seen Carole that night.

"No." And Patti Daugherty was finished.

Evans thanked her and told her she was excused. She stood up, and then had to sit down. The brave twelve-year-old could start crying now, and she cried as her father walked up and led her out of the courtroom.

Someone brought Bernard a birthday cake after the court session. He was forty-two years old.

FRIDAY, JANUARY 8

Frank Meehan, on patrol for West Covina Police July 18 when the call came from the Finch residence, was testifying. He was describing some of the pictures he had taken at the crime scene.

Meehan: "And about here is where the attaché case was that Dr. Finch, that is the older Dr. Finch, found."

Whichello: "What did you do when you were shown the case?"

Meehan: "I immediately took it into the lanai area and began inspecting the contents."

Whichello brought the case to Meehan and asked him to describe the contents.

Meehan: "First I noticed this smaller shaving-kit bag, it had a box of .38 caliber ammunition inside it, a total of twelve cartridges in all. Also I noted a flashlight, two three-foot lengths of three-eighth-inch rope, this squarish-looking bottle containing a clear fluid which we later identified as Seconal, this smaller bottle that was labeled 'Seconal

50 mg' which had some tablets in it, and another smaller bottle containing some reddish capsules."

Meehan was shuffling through the case, putting the items on the railing of the witness stand as he spoke.

Meehan: "Here's the bottle that had the small hypodermic syringe with '20 cc' written on it, a needle, a similar but larger syringe with '50 cc' written on it. This syringe was wrapped in this brown paper."

Whichello had seen the items many times; he stood back now, to Meehan's left, watching the jury study each item of the "murder kit."

Meehan: "...an unopened package labeled 'latex rubber surgeon's gloves.' Here's the knife, it's an eight-inch carving knife; a large, folded sheet of latex; and a cellophane-wrapped object labeled 'latex rubber bandage.'"

Whichello noticed that some of the jury were no longer looking at the contents, but instead were looking at Dr. Finch and Carole Tregoff.

Meehan: "This is an envelope of loose powder which I understand is used by a surgeon. He puts it on his hands to make putting on the gloves easier. This one is open. It was found with an empty similar glove package. This is a roll of wide elastic bandage, a sanitary napkin, and an empty envelope labeled 'latex surgeon's gloves.'"

Meehan had all the items laid out now. He looked at Fred, who was still studying the jury.

The next witness was fingerprint expert Del Freeman of the Sheriff's Department.

Freeman: "I dusted the case and its contents for fingerprints. I have found two which match those of Dr. Finch. The first is a thumbprint on this bottle of Seconal, and the second..."

Cooper interrupted. Most thought he was going to object to the line of questions.

Cooper: "We can save everybody a lot of time here, Your Honor. We will stipulate that the case and its contents belong to Dr. Finch."

Fred turned, looking surprised, saying nothing. This was unexpected. Rex Eagan, for Carole Tregoff, was not at a loss for words, however. He was quickly on his feet, wanting his client to have no association with the kit whatsoever.

Eagan: "We would be happy to join in that stipulation, Your Honor."

For a moment no one spoke. Eagan sat back down. Evans waited for Whichello.

Evans: "Mr. Whichello?"

Whichello: "Uh, so stipulated."

Dr. Gerald K. Ridge was the county coroner. A short, thin man, he wore his customary bow tie. His hair was in a crew cut and he had small, dark-rimmed glasses.

He was standing in front of a crude, hand-drawn human form. It had a round head, arms slightly out from the sides, and legs drawn too small. In the chest area were some wavy horizontal lines that were supposed to be ribs. Standing between the jury and the drawing, Ridge pointed to a small dot on the drawing's chest.

Ridge: "In back, there was a round gunshot wound, here in the left back region next to the shoulder blade. Following this wound track inward, I noted the wound extended forward and toward the right and slightly downward. In its course it caused damage to the left pulmonary artery, which was the immediate cause of death."

Whichello: "Doctor, could you move back slightly? Some of the jury cannot see."

The coroner shuffled backwards, clearing his throat.

Whichello: "Now Doctor, were you able to determine the caliber of the gunshot wound?"

Ridge: "Not exactly, it could have been..."

Cooper was on his feet for yet another surprise.

Cooper: "We will stipulate that the wound is .38 caliber, Your Honor."

Evans looked over to Whichello; the prosecutor said nothing as he studied Cooper. Clifford Crail nodded affirmatively from the prosecutor's table. "We would so stipulate," he said.

Evans: "So stipulated." He waited for Fred to continue. "Mr. Whichello."

Whichello: "Uh, please continue, Doctor."

Ridge: "Of course. I also found on the deceased a horizontal laceration involving the right upper eyelid and eyebrow area. After I removed the brain I noticed an irregular fracture in the very thin blade of bone over the right eyeball, and another fracture in this thin blade of bone here."

He was pointing to a bone near the right temple of his drawing.

Ridge: "I also observed other skull fractures. Here, there were two in the left back part of the skull. In addition, I found the following wounds."

He carefully listed his findings, pointing to each area with a pencil.

Ridge: "The outer left upper arm was bruised as though someone had been grabbing it, the outer lower forearm was reddened just above the wrist, and halfway up to the elbow an abrasion was present. The outer portion of the right arm and right elbow had abrasions and contusions. The lower portion of the upper right arm and part of the lower arm closest to the body had several minor abrasions."

The jury was intent. All were studying the drawing as Ridge told of the wounds Barbara Jean Finch sustained the night she died. Finch was watching also, his chin settled onto both palms.

Ridge: "There were also abrasions and contusions on the middle finger and base of the right thumb, on the right leg in front of the right knee. The right ankle and foot had several contusions."

Whichello asked for some conclusions from his expert witness. "Could either of the head fractures been caused by a blow with the butt of a pistol, or say by her head being smashed into a hard object, like a car roof?"

Ridge: "Yes."

Whichello: "Or maybe she fell, Dr. Ridge. Could she have fallen on the lawn and suffered any of these injuries?"

Ridge: "The characteristics of the terrain, particularly of the driveway and the lawn is such that it is very unlikely that these wounds were sustained in any way such as falling down the steps or on the lawn. We also should remember that the garage was the only place where there was evidence of blood.

Ridge sat down. Most thought Whichello was finished and the witness would be cross-examined by Grant Cooper, but instead, the prosecutor walked to the exhibit table, picked up the "murder kit" case, and returned to the witness stand. Cooper's eyebrows were slightly raised.

Whichello: "You saw Officer Meehan go through the objects in this kit, Doctor." He put the case on the witness box rail and began taking out its contents, holding each up high before placing it beside the case. "Are these items, here, that I am showing you, typical of what a doctor might carry?"

Ridge: "Well, some are. I suppose a butcher knife is unusual."

Evans reached for his gavel but the snickering quieted on its own.

Whichello: "Now, Dr. Ridge, you see these syringes here. I have a 20 cc syringe and a 50 cc syringe. Could either of these have been used to inject a fatal air embolus into Mrs. Finch?"

Cooper: "Objection, Your Honor, on the grounds that this calls for speculation on the part of the witness. It is not justified in this case. One could speculate a thousand ways to kill someone with these instruments found in the bag."

Whichello: "Your Honor, with most of these exhibits the jury can reason for themselves and no expert evidence is necessary. But in the case of this particular item, expert advice is necessary. The circumstances show that the doctor equipped himself with various ways to kill and..."

Evans: "The objection is sustained, Mr. Whichello."

Whichello: "Very well. Dr. Ridge, is air embolism taught in medical school?"

Cooper: "He's still doing it, Your Honor."

Evans: "I'll allow that question, Mr. Cooper."

Ridge: "Yes."

The prosecutor next picked up the bottle labeled "Seconal." He held it up in front of Ridge and shook it; it was about half full of liquid.

Whichello: "About how much Seconal is in this bottle now?"

Ridge: "About 15 cc. The usually dose is about 1 to 2 cc."

Whichello: "And what would happen if all this liquid were injected into a person?"

Ridge: "Rapid unconsciousness, perhaps coma and death."

Whichello was again looking at the jury.

Whichello: "And would you, say at autopsy, be able to detect the presence of this substance?"

Ridge: "Seconal is not routinely checked for. Just alcohol."

Whichello: "Everything else then, Doctor, is customary for a physician to carry around with him?"

Ridge was rummaging through the case.

Ridge: "Clothesline would also seem unusual. It's possible a shaving-kit might be carried, although I never have. And I have never carried .38 caliber ammunition around in my case."

There was more scattered laughter. Cooper, irritated, turned and glared at the crowd. Evans's gavel landed once.

MONDAY, JANUARY 11, 1960

Los Angeles was drenched with the largest rainfall of the season. One and a half inches of rain would arrive from the Pacific. A drying jury watched two men scuffling at the front of the courtroom.

Grant Cooper and Dr. Gerald K. Ridge wrestled for control of a .38 caliber pistol.

It was the beginning of Dr. Ridge's cross-examination. The two were standing in front of the witness box. Cooper was nearer the jury, holding the gun in his right hand. Ridge, wearing the same bow tie, was to Cooper's right. He had his right hand on the gun and his left on Cooper's wrist.

Cooper: "It's okay, doctor. Try a little harder!"

Ridge tried pushing the attorney's hand as far down as it would go, all the time wiggling the gun. It never came out of Cooper's hand.

Cooper: "Fine, thank you, Doctor. I think that's enough. Now tell me, do you think that the bruises on Mrs. Finch's hands and wrist, that you pointed out to us last Friday, could have been caused by a stuggle for a weapon, such as we just had?"

Ridge: "Yes." He was breathing harder as he stepped back into the witness box. "All the injuries I observed would be consistent with such a struggle."

Whichello and Crail glanced at each other. They wondered if Bernard was going to tell a story of an accidental death during a struggle.

Cooper would next entertain the courtroom by mocking the labeling of the attaché case as a "murder kit." He brought the case and the other items to the witness stand.

Cooper: "Now, the prosecution has called this bag and its contents a 'murder kit.' Let's look at some of these items. These tablets, for instance. Wouldn't it be pretty hard to get somebody to swallow them against their will?"

Ridge: "By mouth, yes. However, they could be inserted into the body cavities."

Cooper: "Hmmm, I see. Well, how about these syringes. Would they be ordinarily found in a doctor's bag?"

Ridge: "Of course."

Cooper: "You didn't find any needle marks on the deceased, did you, Doctor?" Ridge: "No, none."

Cooper then went through the other items.

Cooper: "There are some bullets here, too. Obviously if one were going to shoot someone, one wouldn't need these other items."

Ridge: "I suppose not."

Ridge admitted that even the knife and rope might be used by a physician, in some instances.

Cooper: "These other items, as a pathologist and physician and surgeon, the more reasonable uses for these are for innocent purposes?"

Ridge: "That is correct."

Cooper: "So why did the prosecution call this a 'murder kit?' Do you have any idea, Doctor."

Ridge: "I..."

Cooper: "You could stab someone with this, I suppose." He held up the knife. "Or you could stick the handle down someone's throat, thereby suffocating them." He held the knife handle over his wide-open mouth as his head tilted back. Laughter began in the back of the courtroom. "You could tie them up with this rope and inject them with some Seconal."

Whichello was flushed.

Cooper: "I just wonder why they called it a 'murder kit.' Look at this. What could this be used for, Doctor?"

Ridge: "It's an elastic bandage, usually used to hold a wound dressing in place, or for support of a sprained ankle or wrist."

Cooper: "Oh, yes. Let's see." He was holding the wrap in his left hand, his right hand was at his chin, two ridges appeared between his eyebrows. "Sure. One could wrap this bandage around the neck and strangle someone." His hands were around his own neck now, his eyes wide and round. The laughter in the courtroom was too much for Evans. The gavel came down twice.

Cooper asked Ridge about the .06 percent level of alcohol found in Barbara Jean Finch as part of her post-mortem exam. He established that such a level could affect her judgment.

As Cooper asked his last question, Whichello looked up, appearing puzzled.

Cooper: "Now Doctor, could Mrs. Finch have been shot somewhere else and run to the bottom of the steps where she was found?"

Ridge: "Absolutely not. Due to the nature of her wounds, she died within a few seconds of being shot."

Cooper: "So she could not, say, have been shot in the garage and then run down the hill?"

Ridge: "Impossible."

Whichello next called James E. Chick, owner of Chick's Sporting Goods in Covina. Mr. Chick told of selling Bernard Finch a .38 caliber pistol in 1950.

Captain William Ryan followed.

Ryan: "I found no rings on the body, not even a wedding ring, and we did not find a handbag, either." He coughed and hacked as he would for the rest of the day's testimony. He had come down with the epidemic flu that had invaded the area. His smoker's hack was even worse with the infection.

Whichello: "Did you talk with Marie Anne Lidholm on the night of the murder?"

Ryan: "As I recall, I talked to her only once. I may have spoken to her briefly again. I spoke with her about 2:00 A.M. We were all outside in the lanai area of the residence."

Whichello: "What was her appearance? What emotional state was she in?"

Ryan: "She was upset, not crying or anything like that, just upset."

Whichello: "And what did she say to you that night, Captain Ryan?"

Ryan: "I asked her to report briefly on what had happened that night." He had his hand-written notes in front of him now. She said that she and Patti Daugherty, Mrs. Finch's daughter by a former marriage, were just going to bed when they heard screams and what she thought were shots. She ran to the garage and observed Dr. Finch, who forced her head back against the wall of the garage."

Whichello walked to the exhibit table and picked up a key ring with about six keys on it.

Whichello: "Do you recognize these, Captain Ryan?"

Ryan: "Yes, I received these from Clark County Sheriff's Investigators when I went to there to question the suspect, Dr. Finch. They had found them in his possession when he was arrested."

Whichello slowly walked back to the exhibit table and picked up the attaché case, talking as he returned to Ryan.

Whichello: "Now, did you find any that fit this case?"

Ryan said nothing. He set the case down on the rail in front of him and opened it with a small key on the chain.

Whichello smiled slightly as he took the exhibits back to the table.

Whichello: "Now did you, yourself, make any search around the perimeter of the house?"

Ryan: "No."

Whichello: "Did you see anybody else doing that?"

Ryan: "No. We were from time to time in the area around the garage and the pool, but as far as searching around the house, I did not do anything like that, nor did I see any other officer doing so."

Whichello: "What were the light conditions that night? How well could you see?"

Ryan: "It was a very light night as I recall. I don't remember if the moon was out that night or not."

Whichello: "Would you have seen anybody hiding in these bushes on the north side of the house?"

Ryan: "Oh, absolutely. We would have seen anybody in there."

During Cooper's cross-examination of Ryan it was shown the latter had possibly misunderstood the maid during her first statement to him, that she may have said she heard "shouts" and not "shots" when she first heard sounds from the garage.

TUESDAY, JANUARY 12, 1960

Holding her own court today: Dorothy Kilgallen, who was talking with Bernard Finch. The writer and talk show guest was interviewing him for her upcoming book *Murder One*.

She would write "The doctor was completely relaxed, sometimes even boyishly enthusiastic, as we talked," and, "This man accused of murder radiated the most convincing kind of charm."

Finch asked, "Why have you come three thousand miles to cover this story, Dorothy?"

"Well," she began, "the newspaper world makes a distinction between a 'good' and a 'cheap' murder trial."

"Oh." He rubbed his chin. "I see. It's partly because I'm an educated man, and people wonder. Very interesting."

Also in court that day as the "celebrity reporter" for the "Impressions" series: actress June Lockhart.

Whichello was about to begin the *heading B-Love AF-FAIR* portion of his case. He would first call Barbara Jean's divorce attorney, Joseph T. Forno, to the stand to tell of events that warned of the violence to come on July 18, 1959.

Cooper's strenuous objections to the testimony as hearsay evidence would again be overruled by Evans, who allowed it for the jury to see Mrs. Finch's state of mind at the time of her death.

In answering Whichello's questions, Forno said, "Mrs. Finch told me that Dr. Finch had said he was going to take her in the car to the desert, kill her, and leave her there. She mentioned the gun on a number of occasions. Also, she stated that Dr. Finch always carried a gun, and she asked me if there was any way I could get the gun away from him."

Then a chilling prediction of events to come: "She told me that if anything ever happened, she would run down the hill to her father-in-law's house, where it would be safe."

She had sued for the divorce in May, after alleging her husband had beaten her in the master bedroom of their home. And, not uncommon for the time, she had asked for virtually all the family assets in the settlement. Until the case could be heard, she had been given control of all the family's property and money, including revenues from the West Covina Clinic and Hospital.

"Dr. Finch had stated a desire to reconcile at this time," Forno continued. "But Mrs. Finch thought it was a trick to get back into the house so that he could kill her. She agreed to the reconciliation attempt only after Dr. Finch agreed to a strict restraining order that kept him from coming to the property to harass her or even telephoning the residence.

"Mrs. Finch called me on June 26, saying that her husband had ignored the restraining order and had come to the house demanding that she trade cars with him. She told me that he had hit her during an argument over the matter, and that he had driven away in the Cadillac, leaving her the Chrysler."

Barbara Jean had called the police to report the attack and the fact that a restraining order had been violated. "But," concluded Forno, "she told me Dr. Finch got on the phone with Officer Handrahan and talked him out of filing any charges."

In his cross-examination Cooper chose not to challenge the attorney's memory of those events, but instead focused on an unexpected development.

Cooper: "Do you, Mr. Forno, have a man who works for your office—his name is Adair?" He was shuffling through some papers as he walked to the witness stand. "Yes, here it is: Herbert S. Adair, Jr.?"

Forno: "Yes, Mr. Adair works for my office on occasion." Forno moved slightly in his chair, crossing his legs and then his arms. He was not used to being a witness and appeared uncomfortable.

Cooper: "What did he do for you with regard to Mrs. Finch?"

Forno: "He acted as a sort of bodyguard because she was afraid of her husband."

Cooper: "Now was he with her on the night of July 18, last, acting as her bodyguard?"

Forno: "Yes."

Cooper: "In fact, he was a member of the same tennis club as Mrs. Finch, and frequently would go with her there. Is that correct?"

Forno: "Yes."

Cooper: "He frequently would be with her at late hours. Is that correct, Mr. Forno?"

Forno: "Yes."

Cooper: "Acting as her bodyguard?"

Forno: "Yes."

To support the "love triangle" portion of his case, Whichello had the managers of two apartment complexes in Monterey Park testify the two defendants shared the units, at different times, for two years before the murder.

After the noon recess the jury was again treated to an unusual sight: Fred Whichello with a dress draped across his back, standing about six feet from the witness stand, facing away from it. He was crouched slightly down, as though running. Several of the jurors were coughing and hacking. The flu virus had moved into a few more people. The man in the witness box was standing, pointing a gun at the prosecutor.

Whichello: "Like this, Mr. Cromp?"

Clifford Cromp was a ballistics expert from the sheriff's crime lab.

Cromp: "Yes, the bullet entered the body at about this angle. The gun would have been slightly above the level of the shoulders, from about four to six feet away. The bullet had a definite downward trajectory."

Cooper kept Cromp on the stand for an hour, carefully dissecting his conclusions and questioning the validity of his facts. And he eventually succeeded in bringing the expert to concede on a point vital to his client's defense.

Cooper: "So then, it *is* possible that the gun could have been discharged from as little as two feet away, say during a struggle. Is that what you are saying now?"

Cromp: "Well, it's possible, but not likely."

Cooper: "Is it possible or not?"

Cromp: "Yes."

As Cooper was using the physical evidence to show the gun may have accidentally discharged during a struggle, witnesses to the contrary were arriving in Los Angeles.

It was 2:30 P.M. and James Cody, having arrived from Minnesota, was walking into the terminal of Los Angeles International Airport. He was accompanied by two Minneapolis municipal policemen. And driving from Las Vegas, through a rare desert rain storm, was Donald Williams, Carole Tregoff's lifelong friend, who was scheduled to testify for her prosecutors.

WEDNESDAY, JANUARY 13, 1960

Spectators were disappointed and angry.

"I've been waiting in line since six this morning," said one.

"They could have told us this earlier," whined another.

They were looking toward the front of the courtroom. The jury box was empty and Judge Evans was talking to all counsel.

Bringgold was coughing and hacking; he spoke in a nasal tone.

"That's fine with me; I've got the same thing," he said.

Several of the jurors were sick with "virus-Q," as the flu had been dubbed. And Bringgold was quite ill, also. One juror, Floyd G. Jones, had been sick for two weeks and when he got worse, his physician ordered him to bed for at least two days.

"We better just adjourn till Tuesday," Evans advised the group. "I'd rather wait until the original jury is healthy instead of going to the alternates. Anyway, I hear some of the alternates are sick, also."

On Sunday, Carole Tregoff Pappa would be simply Carole Tregoff. Her divorce decree from James Pappa would be final.

six

Testimony of Donald Williams, James Cody, and Others

TUESDAY, JANUARY 19, 1960

"Carole told me that she would be 'quite happy if Mrs. Finch was out of the way, permanently.'" Donald Williams was uncomfortable in the witness box. He blushed easily and seemed to know his crimson face was visible to all. He cleared his throat frequently and shifted in his chair continuously. He was a good-looking man, with short, curly hair and a cleft chin.

"You know, it's not very often," he told the court, "that you are asked to sling the first arrows at a lifelong friend. I'm not comfortable doing this, Mr. Whichello."

The witness continued. "She moved to Las Vegas in May and stayed with my family a few weeks before Mrs. Finch was killed. She said she just wanted to 'get away from the mess in L. A.' She told me that Mrs. Finch had been engaged in certain objectionable activities with regard to her divorce from Dr. Finch."

Williams was a student at the University of Southern Nevada, later to be called University of Nevada at Las Vegas.

He had been advised some might consider him an accessory to murder and was testifying with immunity from prosecution.

"So one day Carole asked me if I knew anyone who could gather evidence for their side of the divorce suit against Mrs. Finch.'" He cleared his throat. Not once in his testimony did he look at Carole.

"I asked a friend of mine, Dick Keachie. I had gotten to know Dick when we were both bellhops, one of my summer jobs. I asked him who he might know and I learned that a friend of his named Cody might be interested. And that was all I had to do with it."

Whichello showed him a picture of Barbara Jean Finch. She was posed in a tennis outfit, racket at the ready, radiant.

"I was asked by Carole to deliver this picture of Mrs. Finch to Cody, which I did."

Then Williams finished by telling how Dr. Finch had approached him about three weeks later.

"Dr. Finch was quite upset. He told me that Cody had cheated him out of some money, about $1,200, and he needed to talk with him right away. I told him I would look around for him."

The first witness after the noon recess was on the stand.

"Well really, I'm a sort of writer-producer-director-actor in the motion picture business. I used to just act, but now I'm trying for diversity." Mark Stevens, friend of the Finch family and fellow member of the Los Angeles Tennis Club, was testifying for the prosecution.

"Mrs. Finch was afraid for her life. She had told me on many occasions she had been threatened many times. I remember once he approached her at the tennis club and she ran from him, into the women's dressing room. She told me that once Dr. Finch had beaten her, then sat on her chest for four hours before allowing her to call for help." Stevens continued.

The actor spoke of many things that day, but Whichello wanted his testimony in a particular area.

192

Whichello: "Did you have any conversations with her about her plans to protect herself?"

Stevens: "I told her she should get herself a gun and she said 'no.' She told me she had never even seen a gun, didn't know how to use one, and would be scared to death to even have one. I walked her to her car that night and got her to take a jack handle from me. I put it in the back seat of her car."

Finished, Stevens went through the doors at the back of the courtroom. A tall black man in a marshal's uniform got up and followed him out.

"Excuse me, Mr. Stevens," the black man said. Stevens did not slow. "Mr. Stevens." He was louder.

Stevens turned. Then, thinking the man wanted an autograph, he took a pen from his coat pocket. "Sure, who should I make it out to?"

"Well, it's a bill, sir. Actually it's a writ from Small Claims Court saying that you still owe $536 to the Villa Capri restaurant."

Photographers were all around them, bulbs flashing. Stevens was at a loss. Then, regaining his composure, he smiled and shook the man's hand, taking the writ.

"Oh sure. Great place to eat, the Villa Capri. You know, I was sure I paid this." Smile fixed, he was gone.

Down the hall, Rexford Eagan was talking to some reporters about the witness he knew Whichello would be calling tomorrow.

"We will show what kind of deals were made with these low-life hoodlums to get them to testify."

WEDNESDAY, JANUARY 20, 1960

The witness for Wednesday had been anticipated by spectators for some time. Four hundred people were lined up outside Department Twelve's doors. Marshals, seeing the larger-than-usual crowd, asked for help from the other courtrooms. Still, the doors burst open and an uncontrolled crowd quickly filled the 250-plus seats that were available.

James Cody, sometimes known as Jack or John Cody, had been sentenced to an additional year of confinement after walking off the prison farm in Minnesota. In exchange for his testimony, he was granted immunity for any crimes connected with the death of Barbara Jean Finch.

Cooper studied Cody as he walked to the witness box. To him this was a visitor from the dark side of human existence that had slithered in to strike at his client. The short, slightly-built convict was sworn. His face, paler than at the grand jury hearings, was framed by the same dark, short-curly hair. His eyes were pale blue, his face seldom showing any expression.

This witness concerned Cooper more than any of the others; he had nothing to lose, having discredited himself before anybody else could. He was a self-professed liar, pimp, con artist, and alcoholic. He made his living cheating other people. He had no remorse and no guilt about testifying to what he could do, or to what others would have him do.

Cody began, "I was first introduced to Carole by Donald Williams and Richard Keachie. It was on July 1, 1959. The three of them came to my apartment in Las Vegas. I asked Carole if she wanted to go get something to eat while we talked and she said, 'Okay.' So we went to Foxie's, downtown. We went, just the two of us. Williams and Keachie had other business to attend to."

Whichello: "What was said at that July first meeting?"

Cody: "She asked me if Don had approached me on this matter and went on to ask how much money I would need and how she wanted me to do it."

Whichello: "And what did she want you to do?"

Cody looked confused. He glanced from Whichello, then to the crowd. He thought everybody must have known by now.

Cody accuses. *Getty.*

Cody: "She wanted me to kill Mrs. Finch."

Evans had to gavel the crowd down; gasps and nervous chatter had erupted.

Cody: "I told her Don had explained everything and that I thought I should get $2,000 for doing the job. She said she thought $1,000 was more reasonable, and we dickered around, you know, back and forth for a little while. Anyway, with the expense money I told her I would need—to buy a weapon and a car—we finally agreed on $1,400. She was going to give me $300 up front and the rest when the job was done."

Carole's right elbow was resting on the table, her hand on her cheek, hiding part of her face from the jury. Finch was looking directly at Cody, his arms and hands directly in front of him.

Whichello was standing in front of the jury box, in front of the juror on the end, so that Cody was looking toward them as he spoke.

Cody: "She drew out some maps on napkins. One was a map of the Finch house and the other was a map of how to get to an apartment in Hollywood that Mrs. Finch had. Carole told me, 'If Mrs. Finch is not at the West Covina residence, she would be at the Hollywood apartment.' It was named the Hollywood Hills Motel or Hotel, or something. Anyway, I had the address and a map of how to get there."

Whichello: "What else was said at this meeting?"

Cody: "She told me it should look like a robbery, and that I should take the woman's rings and jewelry. I told her I would do it in my own way. Then we decided to do it on the following weekend, the Fourth of July weekend. Carole said that Dr. Finch goes to a tennis tournament in San Diego every Fourth of July, and that he would have a good alibi."

Carole was looking down at the desk top, her hand still at her face.

Whichello: "Now did you, Mr. Cody, at any time intend to kill anybody?"

Cody: "There was never a doubt in my own mind; I knew I was not going to do it at all." He answered quickly.

Whichello: "Then why did you agree to do it?"

Cody looked confused again. After a pause he answered, shoulders slightly raised.

Cody: "To get some money. I needed the money. She wouldn't give me any that night, but she said she would give me some by the next morning. I told her that I was going to fly to Phoenix after I got some money, and then take a bus to L. A. and do it over the weekend. Then she took me out to McCarran airport and bought me a one-way ticket to Phoenix."

Whichello: "When did you see Carole Tregoff next?"

Cody: "The next morning. She met me at the restaurant again, as we had agreed. I was surprised to see her. I told her I didn't think she was going to go through with it."

Whichello: "And what did she say?"

Cody: "She said 'I've made up my mind, Jack. If you don't do it, Dr. Finch will, and if he doesn't, I will.'"

Evans again had to quiet the crowd. It took longer this time. The buzzing would be louder, lasting longer as Cody's testimony continued.

Cody: "Then she gave me $330 that she had in an envelope." He looked over at Evans. "I told her, 'Carole when I get on the plane you cannot recall me, I am on my way.' She said, 'Good luck, everything is fine.'"

Whichello: "When did you leave Las Vegas?"

Cody: "The next day, on July 3. I drove my car to the airport and cashed in the airplane ticket. Then I drove to Los Angeles. I returned to Las Vegas on the night of July 5."

Whichello: "And when did you see Miss Tregoff next?"

Cody: "That same night. About 7:30 P.M. that night she came to my apartment and we went to Foxie's again. She asked me if I had done the job and I said 'Yes' and that I had done it with a shotgun at the Hollywood apartment. She asked me what car Mrs. Finch had been driving, and I told her it was the Chrysler. She said, 'That's right,' and handed me an envelope with the rest of my money in it. It was about $900."

Whichello: "Was there any further discussion at that time?"

Cody: "Well, she was smiling. She was very happy. It was the first time I had seen this girl happy. I asked her what about and she said she was happy because 'it was taken care of.'"

Several gasps were heard, followed by whispering sounds.

Whichello walked to his table. He looked through a few of his notes and then was back to his post at the jury box railing.

Whichello: "Now, when did you next see her?"

Cody: "I was at Foxie's the next night, with Dick Keachie. She drove up outside. Looked real nervous. I went outside and she asked me, 'Are you sure that you killed her?' I said 'Yes' and she asked me, 'Are you sure Mrs. Finch didn't make you a better deal?' I said, 'No, I didn't even talk to her. I just shot her and put her into the trunk of the car.' Then I told her I had taken some pictures and mailed them to myself and that they would be arriving in the mail soon. I had seen that in a movie once—somebody mailed pictures to themself."

Whichello: "When did you first meet Dr. Finch?"

Cody: "It was at my apartment the next day. Carole came to my door and asked me again if I was sure that I had shot Mrs. Finch and I again told her 'Yes.' I told her that if she wanted, we could ride into L. A. and I would show her the body in the car trunk. Then she asked me if I would talk to Dr. Finch, so I said, 'Sure.' So she went and got him and brought him to my door. He asked me how I had done it, and I showed him how I had shot her in the chest with a shotgun. I told him she was at the Hollywood Motel or Hotel or whatever. Then I asked him, 'Why do you ask?' He said, 'I just got through talking to my wife and she is very much alive.' I told him that was impossible as I had just shot her."

Whichello: "Then what did he say?"

Cody: "He said, 'Oh, my God, a tragic mistake has been made.' He told me that Mrs. Finch's girl friend must have been the one who got shot. Then he told me to go back and do the job right. I told him the car with the body in it was behind a schoolhouse. He asked me what had happened to the jewelry the woman was wearing. I said I had given it to the friend who helped me. Then he asked me if I was sure that I was willing to try to do it again and I said, 'Sure.'"

Whichello: "Did he tell you anything to say when you did the job?"

Cody: "Yes, he said to tell her before I shot her that 'This was for Bernie' or 'was from Bernie,' or something like that. Then I tried to talk him out of it." He shifted in the chair and cleared his throat. "I told him that killing his wife for money was not worth it, that he should be very proud to take Carole to a new town and to start a new business. 'If Carole loves you, that's what is most important,' I told him."

Whichello: "And what did he say?"

Cody: "He said Mrs. Finch was no good, that she had him in a bottleneck, and then he asked me if I would need any more money. I said, 'Sure.'" A pocket of snickers was heard toward the back of the room. "I would need another gun and another hundred dollars,' I told him. He offered to let me use a shotgun that he kept in the trunk of his car, but I told him I would rather get another one."

Whichello: "When did you see Miss Tregoff and Dr. Finch next?"

Cody: "That night we went out drinking together with another couple, some friends of theirs. I got plastered and passed out. When I came to, I was on a plane bound for Los Angeles and someone had placed ninety dollars in my pocket. I stayed in Los Angeles that night and flew back the next day."

Whichello: "When did you see Carole and Dr. Finch after you returned the second time from Los Angeles?"

Cody: "I saw Don Williams after I got back. He asked me if I had been working and I said, 'Yes.' Then he told me he wanted his cut of the action for helping out and that Carole and Dr. Finch wanted to see me again. I went to Carole's apartment. She was very upset, and she told me that the doctor was very angry because I had not done the job."

Cody leaned forward in the chair, his arms half extended in front of him, palms up. He sounded fatherly. "I told her I had not been able to do the job. I told her, 'Carole, I've been around this sort of thing all my life. You do not know what you are getting into. Murder is a pretty big beef.' When I was finished she said, 'Jack, my mind is made up.' Then she told me again, 'If you don't do it, the doctor will, and if he won't, I will do it.'"

Evans quieted the crowd after more gasps and whispers. "She was in on it from the start."

Cody: "Then the doctor came out of the other room. He was angry all right. He asked me what I was doing in Las Vegas. I told him that I had to establish an alibi for myself. I told him not to worry. I said, 'I've got somebody reliable to do the job for us. He's Spanish.' Then Finch seemed to relax, so I left."

Whichello: "Did he say anything else?"

Cody: "Just as I was leaving, he told me not to worry. I didn't know what he meant. So I asked him, 'What do you mean?' and he said, 'Don't worry about me; I'll establish an alibi for myself.'"

The courtroom filled with chuckles; Cody wore an 'Eddie Haskell' smirk. Finch's head was down, his face red.

Whichello: "And a few days later, on July 12, did you see them again?"

Cody: "Yes. It was a Saturday I believe. The doctor came to my room at the Desert Motel. He was really upset. He asked me whether I was sure I was going through with it. He told me, 'You can back out now if you want to. It's got to be done, and I'll do it if I have to.'"

Bernard was glaring at Cody now. Carole was glancing at each jury member.

Whichello: "Now did he give you money again?"

Cody: "Yes, I told him I would still be able to do it and that I would need a hundred dollars again. He ran out and cashed a check and came back within a few minutes. He gave me a hundred in cash and told me to get going on it right away."

Whichello: "Did you see Dr. Finch or Carole Tregoff after this?"

Cody: "No, I never saw them till today."

Whichello: "Did you ever at any time intend to kill anybody?"

Cody: "I just did it for the money." More snickers from the back of the room. "After I figured they wouldn't give me any more cash, I left town on the sixteenth."

Whichello paused; he was walking back to his table, left hand on his hip, right hand on his chin. He knew the witness's credibility would be targeted during cross-examination.

Whichello: "Did you at any time contact a law enforcement officer about these events?"

Cody: "No."

Whichello: "Now, when you were first contacted by Officer Ryan and myself, you refused to discuss these matters, is that correct?"

Cody: "Yes." He cleared his throat and moved forward in his chair. "Do you want the truth about that, now? I mean about what happened?"

Whichello: "I want the truth about everything, Mr. Cody." He looked quickly at the jury.

Cody: "I was just waiting for Dr. Finch to send somebody up to help me out. You know, to keep me from getting any additional time. When nobody came, I called my own attorney, Mr. Fish. He told me to talk about everything."

Whichello: "So at no time were you offered, say, a 'package deal,' whereby if you testified, you would get special treatment of any kind?"

Cody: "None whatsoever." His voice was raised as he looked at the jury.

"I have no further questions, Your Honor." Whichello was through. Had he a choice, many thought, he would not have used such a person for his case. He would much rather have had witnesses like Marie Anne. Cody's testimony had been necessary to convict the two on conspiracy charges.

Cooper was the first to cross-examine Cody. He strutted to the witness box slowly, like a street fighter closing on his next opponent. His head was tilted back so that he looked at Cody through the bottom of the lenses in his glasses. His mouth was slightly open, and his eyes did not blink as he stared at the man before him.

Cooper: "Now Mr. Cody, you were a fugitive from justice. Is that true?"

Cody: "Yes. I had escaped from a Minnesota workhouse in January of 1958. I came to Hollywood with my girl friend, Joy Hickman."

Cooper: "And how did you support yourself?"

Cody: "By my wits." He was cocky now, sitting back in his chair, relaxed.

Cooper: "I don't know what that means. What sort of wits do you have?"

Cody: "Well, I worked at a photographic studio for a little while, and Joy kept bringing money; she would wire for money from back home. Sometimes I would make money playing pool."

Cooper: "And where did you go from Hollywood?"

Cody: "Las Vegas. I moved there around December of 1958. I worked as a shill for one of the casinos."

Cooper: "And you testified you left Las Vegas on July 16 of 1959."

Cody: "Yeah. I had heard that this guy Finch was looking for me, and common sense told me to get out of town."

Cooper: "You wanted to 'blow town' because you had cheated him out of some money?"

Cody: "Yes."

Cooper: "Now, when the detectives questioned you, in Minneapolis, about your connection with Dr. Finch and Miss Tregoff, you didn't want to talk to them at first, did you?"

Cody: "No."

Cooper: "You were afraid of being charged with a crime, weren't you?"

Cody: "Yes, conspiracy. My lawyer told me I was involved in a conspiracy."

Cooper: "So then, at risk to yourself and out of the kindness of your heart, you decided to talk with the authorities?"

Cody: "No, it was on the advice of my lawyer."

Cooper: "Now you say that when Don Williams approached you, he was the first one who mentioned anything to you about a murder?"

Cody: "Yes, I think it was Don, but I can't recall anything about it. I think it was Don who said something about a murder."

Cooper: "And you were not interested in committing a murder, is that correct?"

Cody: "No."

Cooper: "Did you at that time decide you would go along with he idea of committing a murder just so you could get some money?"

Cody: "I did not know about the murder until I talked with Carole."

Cooper: "What did Don Williams say to you when he showed you this picture?" He was holding the prosecution exhibit of a picture of Barbara Jean Finch.

Cody: "He said, 'Study this picture. Study it well.'"

Cooper: "And the next person you talked to about this so-called conspiracy to commit murder was whom?"

Cody: "Carole. She said she had a job for me and she asked if Don had explained it to me. I said he had, and then she asked me how much I wanted. I said I wanted $2,000. She said $2,000 was too much, and that she had told Don $1,000."

Cooper: "So at this point you were not aware of, exactly aware of, what it was that she wanted you to do?"

Cody: "Yes."

Cooper: "So you were dickering about a job and you didn't even know what it was?"

Cody: "I may have known the specifics, I can't remember."

Cooper: "Well, what do you remember?"

Cody: "She said 'No' to the $2,000, that she was thinking more along the lines of $1,000. She told me what she wanted me to do. She told me she wanted me to kill Mrs. Barbara Jean Finch."

Evans's gavel fell three times to quiet the crowd's buzzing. Carole's forehead was resting on her left palm.

Cooper: "So you are sure that the word 'murder' was used?"

Cody: "I guess I can't remember for sure."

Cooper: "You realize that this is a very important point, Mr. Cody."

Cody: "I'd just rather shut up about it for now."

Cooper: "You'd rather shut up about it? Very well." He walked triumphantly back to his table. "Then you went along with this 'idea' that you weren't quite sure what it was, in order to make some money. Because you live by your wits?"

Cody: "That's right. We settled on $1,000 for the job, $100 for a car, and another $100 for a gun and expense money."

Cooper took a moment behind his papers at the defense table, a habit usually indicating a change in his line of questions.

Cooper: "Did Dick Keachie ever tell you that this job would require someone that was slick and a 'ladies' man?'"

Cody: "Yes, Keachie said the job required someone who was slick and that he wasn't slick enough. And that he had to be a ladies' man."

Cooper: "So would you say that you are a 'ladies' man,' that you have," he paused again, "a 'way' with the girls?"

Cody: "I hope so."

Cooper: "Didn't you tell Carole that you could 'have your way' with any girl within twenty-four hours?"

Cody: "No, no, I didn't say that."

Cooper: "You didn't? Well, didn't Don Williams ask you how you got such a good-looking girl friend in Las Vegas?"

Cody: "He may have; it's a common question."

Cooper: "What did you do when you went to Hollywood, purportedly to kill Mrs. Finch?"

Cody: "I went out drinking with another girl friend, I got plastered, and the next thing I knew I woke up, and it was the fifth of July."

Cooper took another couple of moments, strolling in front of the jury box, garnering attention as he prepared for another point.

Cooper: "During your conversation with Carole at the restaurant where you say you told her you would do the job of killing Barbara Jean Finch, what was her reaction?"

Cody: "She was happy, she seemed to relax, she seemed thrilled."

Cooper: "'Thrilled'? Now, Mr. Cody, what did she do to make you think that she was thrilled that you were going to go off to Los Angeles and kill somebody?"

Cody: "Well, she was tense and then she relaxed."

Cooper: "Do you have any regard for the truth, Mr. Cody?"

Cody: "Yes, I have."

Cooper: "But you have no regard for it when it suits you not to. Is that correct?"

Cody: "Depends on who I am dealing with."

Cooper walked back quickly to the witness stand. He raised his voice; his face was red now.

Cooper: "You say these things, remembering that you should tell the truth and that there is a jury and persons charged with murder in this room?"

Cody: "Yes."

Cooper: "You are not exaggerating a tiny little bit?"

Cody: "No, I am trying to tell the truth."

Cooper: "You told the District Attorney's office that she was 'thrilled?'"

Cody: "Uh, well I guess so. If it's down there, I guess I said it."

Cooper: "I don't want you to guess, Mr. Cody. Did you or did you not tell representatives from the District Attorney's office that she was 'thrilled?'"

Cody: "If you say so, then maybe I did. You know how somebody can be frowning and then the next minute they aren't frowning?"

Cooper: "Did she say anything?"

Cody: "I don't recall. I think she did mention something."

Cooper: "Are you sure you are not trying to help the D. A.'s office for your own purposes?" Cooper was leaning forward; he was inches away from Cody, staring directly into the man's eyes. Cody was looking down.

Cody: "I am just telling the truth, that's all. Just like the guy, my attorney, told me to." He was still looking down.

Cooper eased up. He would be calm for his next few questions. He needed the jury to follow his reasoning closely.

Cooper: "And then, you gave her some fatherly advice; you tried to talk her out of it."

Cody: "Yes, I think I just told her 'Carole, are you sure you want this done?'–or something like that."

Cooper: "But why would you try to talk her out of it if you were conning her for some money. Was that part of your act?"

Cody: "Uh, the money was not that important to have this woman killed."

Cooper looked at the jury.

Cooper: "So then you must have gone to the police to have kept this from happening."

Cody: "No." He stopped, then looked at the jury. "No," he was explaining now. "I was a wanted man, you know; I would have been arrested."

Cooper: "Now let's review what else you told Carole. You told her that you would kill Mrs. Finch, and that was a lie, wasn't it?"

Cody: "Yes."

Cooper: "And you told her that you had killed Mrs. Finch. That was a lie also, wasn't it?"

Cody: "Yes."

Cooper: "And you told her that you had put the body in the trunk of a car and hidden it behind a schoolhouse. That was a lie also, Mr. Cody?"

Cody: "Yes."

Cooper walked back to his position in front of the jury box.

Cooper: "What did you ever tell Dr. Finch about yourself? For instance, did you ever tell him you about your prowess as a lover?"

Cody: "I suppose I did."

Cody seemed quite nervous now. His voice had climbed to a high pitch, almost squeaking. He was fumbling for words, rambling without the prompt of questions. "The doctor told me about his clinic. He said that if I ever were on the lam or in trouble and wanted a place to hang out, he could put me in his clinic. I said, 'That would be silly, now wouldn't it! After killing your wife, I would stay at your clinic. You could come in and give me a shot and eliminate me, too." He rose slightly from his chair, still crouched, pointing at Finch with his left index finger. "There's no way I would ever go to that man's clinic."

Cooper: "Oh, no? Well, when did you remember this part, the part about Dr. Finch inviting you to his clinic?"

Cody: "While I was in Minneapolis in jail." He was sitting down now, rubbing his forehead with his left fingers.

Cooper: "Was there anything else that you thought about and remembered in the jail there?"

Whichello objected and was overruled.

Cody: "There were a number of things. I tried to tell Mr. Whichello about them when I came out here."

Fred Whichello was rubbing his forehead with his fingers now.

Cooper: "These are all things that you did not remember when you testified at the grand jury, including the fact that Dr. Finch had told you to say, This is from Bernie,'"—Cooper was mocking Cody, talking with a New York gangster accent—"just before you were to shoot Mrs. Finch. Is that correct, Mr. Cody? You remembered them after you went back to jail?"

Cody: "Yes, I suppose so."

Cooper: "Anything else you remembered, back there in Minnesota?"

Cody took a moment to think, his hands were together as looked up to the ceiling.

Cody: "Yes." He looked directly at Finch. "He said he liked my girl friend, Joy, and that he would like to meet her some time."

Cooper: "And then, as I recall, you said that Dr. Finch took you out in public with some of his friends, and that you 'got plastered.' Is that right?"

Cody: "Yes."

Cooper: "How many of his friends did he introduce you to?"

Cody: "About four."

Cooper: "And he took you out in public, and introduced you by your correct name, *Cody*?"

Cody: "Yes."

Cooper took another pause. He was ready for his next point.

Cooper: "Now, Mr. Cody, you told Carole that you were a 'ladies' man,' now didn't you?"

Cody: "No, that's not true. I never did brag about being a ladies' man, to her or anybody."

Cooper: "And isn't it true that you were told by both Dr. Finch and Carole that Mrs. Finch had evidence against them in the divorce proceedings and that they were anxious to make it a sort of stand-off by getting some evidence against her?"

Cody: "I don't recall. I mean, no."

Cooper: "You were given her home address, the address of her hairdresser, the location of the tennis club, all to follow her, weren't you? And you said you would get the evidence against her even if you had to sleep with her yourself, didn't you?"

Cody: "No, that's a lie." He was shouting. "I was supposed to kill her."

Cooper cross-examined him for eight hours. Rexford Eagan was next.

Eagan: "Do you use any other names?"

Cody: "Yes, I have used John Lorrie. And Jack is a nickname for John."

Eagan: "Why did you use the name John Lorrie?"

Cody: "I was on the lam for writing bad checks."

Eagan: "And you have used other names?"

Cody: "Yes, I have used my first two names, John Patrick. I used those after I escaped from the prison farm."

Eagan: "Was that an *honor* farm, Mr. Cody?"

Cody: "No." He chuckled briefly. "There were a lot of bars there, not much honor."

Eagan: "Did you desert from the army in 1953 and thereafter receive a dishonorable dis—"

Whichello: "I object, Your Honor. My witness is not on trial for his military record. We know he's a hard-drinking fighting-Irishman who has had certain brushes with authority in the past."

Evans advised Eagan that the objection was sustained.

Eagan: "When you first met Miss Tregoff, were you under the influence of alcohol?"

Cody: "Yes, I am positive I was not sober."

Eagan: "And at that or any time did you discuss with Miss Tregoff your alleged prowess with women?"

Cody: "I may have, I don't recall."

Eagan: "You have testified that you were hired to murder a woman."

Cody: "Yes."

Eagan: "Would you commit a robbery or a holdup for money?"

Cody: "I might be tempted."

Eagan: "Tell us, Mr. Cody, would you lie for money?"

Cody: "Yes."

Eagan: "Your Honor, for the first time in this witness's testimony, I agree with him. I have no further questions."

Whichello objected to the remark and had it stricken.

FRIDAY, JANUARY 22, 1960

"I would testify without hesitation that the person who wrote the name 'Barbara J. Finch' on the check was not the same person who signed this signature card." Donn E. Mire was a nationally recognized handwriting expert; he was being questioned by Fred Whichello.

Mire was standing in front of the witness box. Between him and the jury were two two- by-three-foot enlargements: one of a signature card from Citizens National Bank and the other of a check for $3,000.

D. Bryce Rose, the comptroller for the West Covina Hospital, had just testified Dr. Finch gave him a check, with Barbara Jean's signature, for $3,000 in May. Rose was instructed to cash it at the Covina branch of the California Bank and to return with two $1,000 bills and two $500 bills.

"The signature was either copied or traced," Mire continued, "but the check was not signed by the same person who signed this signature card."

Cooper cross-examined Mire, getting him to admit that his specialty was not an exact one, and that possibly a person under stress could sign something in an uncharacteristic way.

Cooper: "So it is possible that she did sign the check, Mr. Mire?"

Mire: "Oh sure, remotely. It's more likely that Dr. Finch signed it though, in my opinion."

Cooper was caught off guard, not expecting the answer.

Cooper: "The witness is answering questions I haven't even asked, Your Honor. I move his last answer be stricken."

Evans: "Mr. Mire, I don't see how could you make such a statement unless you were to examine Dr. Finch's handwriting also."

Mire: "But I did."

Evans: "Who asked you to do that?"

Cooper sighed and sat down.

Mire: "Mr. Cooper. He gave me some checks signed by Dr. Finch yesterday and asked me to look them over."

Evans: "The answer stands."

Betty Jean Behr, who knew the Finches as a fellow member of the Los Angeles Tennis Club, told of Barbara Jean's last night alive.

Fred Whichello started by showing her a picture of Mrs. Finch.

Behr: "Oh yes, that's Barbara Jean, all right. I knew her approximately a year. We would meet occasionally and play tennis. I last met with her about 2:00 P.M. the afternoon of her death. We stayed at the club and had a couple of drinks, and then we went to dinner at about 8:00 P.M. at Kelly's Steak house, which was about fifteen minutes' driving time from the club."

Whichello: "Did you and Mrs. Finch go in your car?"

Behr: "No, there were four of us. She went with Mr. Adair in her car, and I went with my husband, John, in our car. We had dinner. They finished before we did and left about 9:30."

Whichello wanted to establish what valuables Mrs. Finch had when she was seen last.

Whichello: "Was she carrying a purse with her?"

Behr: "I positively saw her with a purse at dinner. I had no cigarettes and she took hers out of her purse and gave them to me. I remember because I spilled half of them on the table. The purse was white; I remember because it matched the white dress that she was wearing. It was average size, what you would call a 'clutch bag.'"

Whichello: "Did she have a watch or any jewelry?"

Behr: "She had earrings and a watch, but I'm not sure about any other jewelry."

Cooper cross-examined.

Cooper: "Had you ever seen Mrs. Finch smoke?"

Behr: "Well, not actually, no. Could be the cigarettes were Mr. Adair's."

Cooper: "But you are still sure she had a white purse, some earrings, and possibly a watch?"

Behr: "Yes, I'm sure."

Cooper: "Can you describe Mr. Adair for us, Mrs. Behr."

Behr: "Oh yes. He was tall, had dark hair, and was very good-looking, about thirty or forty years old."

Whichello was ready with the parade of those made car-less after the murder. Carl Mossberg was first. His home was across Citrus Street, next to the tenth tee.

Mossberg: "I have this bell hooked up, you know, so I can tell when somebody comes down the driveway, because my driveway is so long. It's like the ones at the service stations. You know, somebody drives over the hose and 'ding,' you know about it at the house. Well, it went 'ding' about midnight. I didn't think anything of it, because I figured somebody was coming home. Next morning I got the phone call about my car being stolen, and I figured out they had been driving out with my car."

Cooper: "Did you see who drove your car out of the driveway that night, Mr. Mossberg?"

Mossberg: "Well, no."

William D. Booth was the Los Angeles Police Department patrol officer who found Mossberg's car.

Booth: "It was about 5:30 in the morning. The sun was just coming up and I was on my way to work; I was working day shift that day. I couldn't get to work. There was a car parked across my driveway, up close to the garage, you know, like somebody was trying to hide it there or something. I checked the registration, which was on the driver's sun visor. Then I called Mr. Mossberg and told him where his car was. Then I notified West Covina Police Department."

Cooper: "Officer Booth, did *you* see who parked the car in your driveway?"

Booth: "Oh, no."

Leon Serruys lived three blocks from Booth's house in La Puente.

Serruys: "Yeah, I got up Sunday morning and noticed my car was gone. Just gone. I never noticed a thing during the night. I notified the sheriffs and I got a call from Las Vegas police later that day that they had found my car in front of a repair shop."

Cooper: "Did *you* see who stole your car, Mr. Serruys?"

Serruys: "Uh, no. I must have been asleep when it was stolen. I mean, I was asleep."

Esker Oxley lived across the street from Serruys and said she heard the car start up and leave early Sunday morning, shortly after midnight. Mrs. Ann Reynolds, who also lived across the street from Serruys, thought she had seen "a man" that night.

Reynolds: "It was about midnight, maybe a little after, I'm not sure. I was watching the late show on TV. I heard a man running down the street, and I was alone in my house. I was scared. So I got up to make sure the door was locked. I looked over to Mr. Serruy's house and saw a man getting into his Cadillac; the car's inside light was on."

Whichello: "Now before this you saw the man running. Is that correct?"

Reynolds: "Yes, he was running next to the curb toward Alwood Street. He didn't have a hat on. He was wearing a light-colored sport shirt and slacks, no coat or suit or anything. I made sure my door was locked and went back to watch the late show."

Cooper: "Now, Mrs. Reynolds, do you know who stole Mr. Serruys's car?"

Reynolds: "Well, no, I thought it was Mr. Serruys at the time. I mean it was his car, so I thought it was him driving off in it."

Judge Evans had asked all counsel to meet in his chambers.

seven

Exhibit 60; Second Testimony of
Marie Anne Lidholm

"Miss Tregoff was under arrest from the time she walked into the Las Vegas Sheriff's Office. The precedents are clear, Your Honor." Bringgold was setting the stage to have Carole's sworn statements to Las Vegas and West Covina police not be admitted as evidence. He had learned that two reporters had interviewed Ray Gubser of the Clark County Sheriff's Office the day after the murder.

"I have called two Las Vegas reporters to be witnesses for us on Monday, Your Honor. They will testify that Miss Tregoff was in custody when she was being questioned. She was not advised of any rights, nor of the fact that what she said could be used against her," he continued.

Evans looked at Whichello. "What do you know about this, Fred?"

"They've been singing this song all along, Your Honor. The fact is that Carole was not under arrest and she gave her statements freely. The fact that she may be guilty should not make her statements inadmissible, or the basis for a mistrial. What kind of sense would that make!"

Bringgold stiffened. "It's that disregard for my client's civil rights which has been a disgrace during this entire case." As he talked to Evans, he jabbed an index finger toward Whichello.

Evans waited for the tension to ease. "Mr. Whichello, if the girl was under arrest, if there need be any clarifications of prior testimony made, you need to recall some of your witnesses."

"Of course." Whichello's voice lowered slightly. "I'll ask Captain Ryan to contact Las Vegas and see if there is any truth to this allegation. I'll call the officers as witnesses if necessary. Anything to clear up this matter."

Bringgold was not through. "We also contend, Your Honor, that Miss Tregoff was detained, and therefore under arrest, during her testimony at Dr. Finch's preliminary hearing. Her statements at that hearing, offered as prosecution Exhibit 60, should not be allowed for the same reasons."

Evans had telephoned Judge Miller at the beginning of the trial. "Judge Miller says the girl was in his office as a courtesy to her. You know the press was hounding all the witnesses, especially her."

"We know it is unusual, Your Honor, but we would like to ask again that Judge Miller be called as a witness. We will contend she was being detained in his office, and have information to substantiate the same." Bringgold knew that Miller, as a sitting judge, did not have to testify.

"You're aware he has immunity from subpoenas, Mr. Bringgold. He doesn't have to testify," Evans lectured.

"He can voluntarily testify, Judge Evans. Especially if," he waited until Evans's eyes met his, "he were encouraged to help us try the facts of this case. As court officers, of course, we are all finders of fact, sir."

Evans took a deep breath. "I'll see what I can do."

MONDAY, JANUARY 25, 1960

It was cool and damp in Los Angeles. It would not rain, only drizzle tenths of an inch for the day. And the temperature would stay in the low sixties.

Fred Whichello was sitting at his desk, rubbing his forehead, and looking at some papers in front of him. He had just informed the court Captain William Ryan was to be recalled.

Whichello: "Now, Detective Ryan, you remember that you have previously testified that to your knowledge, defendant Tregoff had never been in custody in any respect at any stage of the early proceedings of this case. Is that correct?"

Ryan: "Yes."

Whichello: "Now, did you have a conversation after court had adjourned last Friday which qualified that statement."

Ryan: "Yes." He cleared his throat and shifted in the witness chair. "I called the Las Vegas Sheriff's Office last Friday afternoon and spoke with Lieutenant Gubser. In that conversation he mentioned to me the fact that Mrs. Pappa had been technically placed under arrest by himself on the occasion of her being in his office on July 19, 1959."

There was a stir in the courtroom. Evans lowered his gavel three times.

Ryan: "Lieutenant Gubser stated that he and Detective Powell were going out for coffee and they had asked Carole if she wanted to go. She had said that she would stay as she wanted to see Dr. Finch as soon as possible. They told her she would not be able to see him until Chief Sill arrived from West Covina. They then told her that she was technically under arrest and that she could either stay on her own at the station or they could book her. At that point she decided to go with them to get some coffee."

Whichello: "During the preliminary hearing for Miss Tregoff at Citrus Municipal Court, you will recall that Lieutenant Hiram Powell, with the Las Vegas sheriffs, had said that at no time was Miss Tregoff under arrest. Do you recall that?"

Ryan: "I asked about that, and uh," he cleared his throat again, "they said that when Gubser was asking her if she wanted to go out for some coffee with them, that at that point," he cleared his throat a second time, "Detective Powell was still in the other room and he did not hear the remarks about her being in custody."

Just before court was adjourned, Evans called all counsel to the bench. He informed them that he would have to be in San Francisco for a few days to clarify issues that had come up in connection with some of his evidentiary rulings in the Caryl Chessman case.

Bringgold was quietly jubilant about Ryan's admissions.

"We got a break today and we are going to pursue it for all it's worth." He was talking to the usual crowd of reporters that gathered in the hallway outside the courtroom at the end each session. "It's obvious now that the police kept the fact that my client was in custody a secret, deliberately, so that her testimony could be used against her. She was asked to make a statement to Las Vegas authorities and not advised of any rights."

"Is Judge Miller going to appear, Don?" One reporter asked.

"It would be helpful, but—"

"Yes, he is." Everyone looked at a reporter from the *Los Angeles Times*. He had already filed his story for the morning edition. The other reporters were quiet for a moment, then all circled the man from the *Times*. "You see," he straightened from a relaxed slouch, "I phoned him at his house and he told me he wanted to be here today. He has the flu, and his doctor ordered him to stay in bed for a week. He's seventy-five years old, you know. But he will try to appear tomorrow, he told me."

Bringgold was taken off guard. He had learned to expect anything with this case, but he hadn't expected a reporter to tell him who the witnesses were to be.

"We welcome Judge Miller's decision to appear and look forward to his help in determining the facts." Bringgold was walking away from the group; most of the reporters didn't notice he had left. They were questioning the *Times* reporter about his conversation with Judge Miller.

TUESDAY, JANUARY 26, 1960

"When is that boy going to decide what he's going to do?" Fred was reading the morning edition of the *Los Angeles Times*, waiting for court to start. It was his custom to arrive early; he would usually be reading a paper as the others came in and settled. He was reading a story about Governor Ed Brown's son, Gerald. "He's decided not to go into the priesthood," the story quoted his mother. "Instead he will attend medical school and study psychiatry."

Marie Anne Lidholm was back on the stand. She had asked her mother to return a letter she had written in May. It told of the argument and altercation occurring in the master bedroom. The press had been given a copy before the day's session.

MARIE ANNE LIDHOLM

"They kept calling me back to testify." Marie Anne would tell me later. "All I wanted to do was help with finding the truth. There I was, a nineteen-year-old girl who had never lived away from home before, being asked all these questions by the lawyers.

"Every time I testified I felt like I was living it all over again."

She was reading: "During the night Dr. Finch tried to kill Mrs. Finch. Mrs. Finch absolutely now wants to have a divorce. She told me everything in the morning. He had

219

hit her and she had fallen against the corner of a bed table and got a deep cut on her temple. He had tried to make her dress and then had tried to get her out into the car. He then threatened to drive her over a ridge and that if she didn't change her mind about the property and the divorce he had a man in Las Vegas that he would pay thousands of dollars to kill her."

Cooper's cross-examination of the girl was gentler and less confrontive this time. He asked again how Dr. Finch had instructed in the use some of the household's rifles in case a 'burglar' were to be discovered.

Lidholm: "You just had to push a safety lever and then it was ready to go. He told me to use it if we ever had any prowlers."

And Cooper asked again about any phone calls Mrs. Finch may have received from her husband on the day of her death.

Lidholm: "Yes. She told me she got a phone call from Dr. Finch. I remember now. She didn't discuss with me the nature of the call. She had received the call some time Saturday morning."

Whichello and Crail were speaking quietly as she left the stand. "What is so important about the rifle, Cliff?" Fred was asking. Crail shook his head from side to side. "Or the phone call?" They concluded both items would be important elements of the doctor's story.

Evans slammed his gavel once and the room quieted. "Mr. Whichello, I understand you have some witnesses to call, as a means to clarify some previous assumptions."

"I call Ray Gubser, Your Honor." Whichello stayed in his chair.

Gubser first went through the details of how he had gone to Carole Tregoff's apartment with two uniformed officers and Powell and found Finch asleep. They had searched the apartment, put him under arrest, and returned to the station in hopes of getting a preliminary statement.

Then he told of his first contact with Carole Tregoff. Bringgold and Carole were leaning forward during this part of his testimony, never taking their eyes off the veteran investigator.

Gubser: "When we got back to the station I had a message that a Carole Tregoff had asked to speak with the officers who had arrested Dr. Finch. After a while we went back to her apartment. We couldn't rouse her after knocking on the door for five or ten minutes, so we asked the manager to let us in. I told the manager that Miss Tregoff was expecting us and we couldn't rouse her. So she came down and opened the door and let us in. Miss Tregoff was in bed, sound asleep, so after we woke her up we went into the other room while she got dressed."

Whichello: "And what did she say when she came out?"

Gubser: "She offered us a soft drink and we all sat down—Hiram, her and me–and talked for about ten minutes before she commenced to asking questions about Dr. Finch. She told us she had been with him, and then I asked her if she would mind coming down to the police station and giving a formal statement. She said, 'Sure,' so we all drove back to Headquarters."

Whichello: "Now, before you go on, Lieutenant Gubser, at any time was she placed under arrest, in handcuffs, or did you make any deals with her about immunity if she agreed to testify? Anything at all like that?"

Gubser: "She just said she wanted to make a statement."

Whichello: "So what she said was voluntary. You did not coerce her in any way?"

Gubser: "No, she just wanted to make a statement. So we went back to the station and had her make out her statement. The stenographer was new and apparently there were several mistakes that Miss Tregoff wanted to correct, so the two of them went into the other room and typed it up together; then she came back and read it a final time and signed it."

Whichello: "Was she under arrest at this time?"

Gubser: "No, not at all. She was just making a statement. Then we all went back into the Detective Bureau and I remembered that none of us had had any lunch. So I asked her if she wanted to go out and get something to eat with us. She said 'No,' that she would rather wait and see Dr. Finch as soon as she could. Powell stepped outside and I was following him. It was at this point that I stopped at the door and told her that she would have to stay until Chief Sill and Detective Ryan arrived from Los Angeles."

Whichello: "What exactly did you say to her."

Gubser: "I said, 'You know, you're going to have to wait until the officers arrive from West Covina.' They just wanted to talk to her, that's all. I told her something like, 'I guess until then you could consider yourself under technical arrest as a material witness. You can either stay here voluntarily or I could book you. It's up to you.' Then she decided she was hungry, and the three of us went uptown to get a sandwich. We came back to the station and waited for Ryan and Sill. They got there about 8:00 P.M."

Whichello: "Was she in a cell? Was she booked? Was she physically restrained?"

Gubser: "No, no, it was just an office, about sixteen feet on a side. It wasn't a cell. We were all in there."

Whichello: "Then what happened?"

Gubser: "After the West Covina detectives were through with Finch, we let Miss Tregoff visit with him while we were present. Then we drove her back to her apartment and let her off."

Whichello: "And that was it?"

Gubser: "That's the last I saw of her until today."

Donald Bringgold had his chance, finally, to cross-examine the man who, he contended, had arrested his client, asked her to incriminate herself. Curiously, Gubser had not appeared at Carole Tregoff's preliminary hearing.

Bringgold: "You were the gentleman in charge of this investigation in Las Vegas, is that correct?"

Gubser: "Yes, I was in charge."

Bringgold: "Why was it you were not present at Miss Tregoff's preliminary hearing?"

Gubser: "I," the two were inches apart now, "uh, had pressing business. I was requested to appear at the Citrus hearing in July, but I had pressing business."

Bringgold waited; the policeman looked to the side.

Bringgold: "What business was that, Lieutenant?"

Gubser: "Could have been a court case. I don't recall. I was busy, so I sent Hiram Powell down to represent us."

Bringgold: "You, then, were the gentleman who told the two reporters that Miss Tregoff was in custody?"

Gubser: "I may have; I suppose it might have been me."

Bringgold: "And since you were busy at the time of the preliminary hearing, you sent Officer Powell to represent you. He, we are told, was not aware that Miss Tregoff was in custody. You two never had a conversation whereby you discussed the fact that she was in custody? Officer Powell never knew, as far as you know, she was in custody?"

Gubser: "No, no, never."

Bringgold stared directly at Gubser for a moment, then walked to the jury box as he spoke.

Bringgold: "Now you say you got a telephone call from Miss Tregoff saying that she wanted to talk to you about the arrest of Dr. Finch?"

Gubser: "Yes. I was busy booking the doctor at the time, so Hiram took the call. After he told me, we drove over to her apartment again."

Bringgold: "You didn't just phone her back?"

Gubser: "No." He cleared his throat again.

Bringgold: "Isn't it a bit unusual, when a person calls you and asks for information about an incident, isn't it unusual to go to their apartment, knock on their door, get a key from the manager, and enter the apartment and wake them from a sound sleep."

Gubser: "Well, I guess it was pretty unusual, yes."

Bringgold: "Tell us what you did when Miss Tregoff asked to go to the washroom."

Gubser: "Yes, I remember the incident. I instructed Sergeant Butcher to show her where the washroom was."

Bringgold: "And did you have any other instructions for Sergeant Butcher?"

Gubser: "Yes. I instructed him to wait outside the door until she came out, and to return her to us."

Bringgold called the two Las Vegas reporters who had been at Las Vegas sheriffs headquarters on Sunday when Carole and Bernard were giving their statements. They would be questioned by Eagan.

The first to testify was Gene Tuttle, news editor for the *Las Vegas Review Journal*.

Tuttle: "I sometimes get a call from the *Los Angeles Examiner* up there. They'll ask me to cover a story for them or something. They called me about 7:30 Sunday morning and told me about the shooting and they had heard Finch and Tregoff might be headed toward Las Vegas. So I went out to see what I could find out."

Eagan: "And did you end up at the sheriff's office?"

Tuttle: "About noon I was at the station; my first contact was with Sergeant Hiram Powell. I asked him if I could have an interview with either Finch or Tregoff."

Eagan: "And what did he say?"

Tuttle: "He said I would have to wait and that maybe later I could talk with them. I asked him if Carole was under arrest, too, and he said that she was being held in 'technical custody.'"

Eagan: "Anything about 'material witness'? Was that said?"

Tuttle: "Just plain technical custody."

Eagan finished by having Tuttle state he was also a minister for the Jehovah's Witnesses church.

Fred had his hands clasped in front of him, resting against his mouth. His eyes focused on the table top.

"I'm a staff writer for the *Las Vegas Sun*. I have been following the Finch-Tregoff story since July."

Alan Jarlson was next.

Bringgold: "Now as a reporter, Mr. Jarlson, you were aware, on or about September 9 or 10 of last year, that during the preliminary hearing for Dr. Finch and the hearing for Miss Tregoff, that had already taken place, that the prosecution had continually stated that Miss Tregoff was not under arrest at any time, were you not?"

Crail: "Objection, Your Honor, this witness wasn't even there. I never saw him."

Evans: "The objection is sustained."

Bringgold: "Very well. On September 9, did you have occasion to be at the Las Vegas sheriff's station?"

Jarlson: "I was interviewing Ray Gubser about the case. We had heard Tregoff would try to get her case dismissed on the basis that she had been under arrest when she gave her statement in Las Vegas and that she was not aware of her rights."

Bringgold: "And what did you ask Officer Gubser?"

Jarlson: "I asked him directly if she had been in technical custody or was otherwise under arrest. He answered 'Yes,' she had been, as a material witness."

Bringgold: "How can you be so sure of what he said?" He was looking at the jury, standing with his hands on the rail in front of them.

Jarlson: "Well, I wrote the story." He brought out a paper from his coat pocket, opened it to the front page. "On page two is the continuation, where I quoted Gubser." Bringgold walked over to the witness stand as Jarlson turned to the second page and held it in front of him so the jury could see. Bringgold leaned close to the page, then pointed to a certain spot.

Bringgold: "Would you read this portion here?"

Jarlson: "Yes." He turned the paper around and started to read, "'Gubser said that after she had signed a statement, that was about 5 P.M., of July 19, Sunday, she was technically under arrest as a material witness to murder. He told her she had the alternative of remaining here or being booked in jail, so she decided to wait upstairs in our office with us.'" Whichello appeared uncomfortable as he spoke to Clifford Crail. Many thought Bringgold was winning in his effort to get a mistrial. The prosecutor made an unusual move to protect his case.

"I call myself to the stand, Your Honor," he said loudly after Jarlson had been excused. "I will be questioned by Mr. Crail."

Evans slowly shook his head from side to side as Whichello walked to the stand; never had so many attorneys been on the stand for one case, and a judge was due next week. He slammed his gavel to quiet the excitement.

Whichello: "I never knew she was in custody when I examined her during the preliminary hearing in West Covina. I had only come on the case July 23, that was the Wednesday following the murder."

Crail: "You decided to question her as a witness in Dr. Finch's preliminary hearing?"

Whichello: "Yes. She had consented to be a witness for me. It was during her questioning by me on the witness stand that I became suspicious that she was a suspect. During the time after she broke down emotionally and was taken to Judge Miller's chambers, I decided that she would be arrested and charged with the crime of murder. It was her own testimony that made me change my mind about her participation in the whole affair."

Crail: "So you decided to place her under arrest after she broke down and went into Judge Miller's chambers. Your decision came after that testimony?"

Whichello: "Right, after it."

Bringgold: "From her prior statements to Las Vegas authorities and to you, you had every bit of evidence you could get before you examined her on the witness stand."

Whichello: "That's a fair statement."

Bringgold: "You say she consented to be a witness. You had subpoenaed her, also. Is that true?"

Whichello: "I had subpoenaed her, yes."

Bringgold: "Now, when a person is served a subpoena, that means the person is obliged to testify under certain oaths and is subject to certain penalties."

Whichello: "Of course."

Bringgold: "She did not have an attorney?"

Whichello: "No."

Bringgold: "So then, since she was your witness, appearing after receiving your subpoena, you, in effect, were her attorney, is that correct?"

Whichello: "I would think that is certainly a matter of interpretation."

Bringgold: "And even when you became suspicious of her guilt, you continued to ask her questions. Did you ever advise her of her constitutional rights?"

Whichello: "Wait a minute." He was almost shouting. "Of course I asked her questions. She was a witness. At first I had put aside my suspicions of her guilt. Only later in her evidence did I become suspicious again."

Bringgold: "Did you ask Judge Miller to advise her of her constitutional rights?"

Whichello: "No."

Hoppi Hopkinson was next. Bringgold was asking about his conversation with Carole before she gave her statement to investigators in West Covina.

Hopkinson: "It was shortly after the newspapermen and photographers left the room. Just before she was going to give her statement to me and Captain Ryan, I identified myself to her and sat down and told her I had read the statement she had given to the Las Vegas officers. I advised her that we had additional evidence and that I wanted to take a more detailed statement from her. I told her, 'Carole, if you and Dr. Finch did sit in your apartment and planned to come over and kill Mrs. Finch, I would advise you not to make a statement.' She said she had told the truth and was willing to make a statement."

Eagan had doubts about Hopkinson's story.

Eagan: "You called her Carole, did you?"

Hopkinson: "That's right."

Eagan: "You had never met this girl before and you just sat down and called her 'Carole.' Is that what you want us to believe?"

Hopkinson: "Yes." He squirmed in his chair.

Eagan: "You knew she had been in custody in Las Vegas, didn't you?"

Hopkinson: "No, I had no idea she was in custody in Las Vegas."

"Court is adjourned until next Monday," Evans announced to the room. "I have been asked to appear in San Francisco to discuss another case. Mr. Whichello, who will you be calling as your witness?"

"Judge Albert K. Miller, Your Honor, has agreed to appear."

Miller would be one of the last prosecution witnesses. The press was ready for a spectacular appearance by the outspoken judge from Citrus Municipal Court. Over the weekend there would be several strategy conferences between Carole Tregoff, Bernard Finch, and their attorneys.

After one of the meetings Cooper announced to the press he would identify the 'mystery man' who had stolen the two cars in the minutes following the death of Barbara Jean Finch.

"I will solve this mystery," he announced to an eager crowd of less than ten reporters. "My client stole the cars. You'll hear all about it. As I have stated before, we have nothing to hide and he will appear in his own defense."

MONDAY, FEBRUARY 1, 1960

The first of a series of winter storms hit Los Angeles early morning. More than an inch of rain fell and it was raining heavily when Fred Whichello stepped out of his car and started walking to the courthouse building. "No reporters waiting outside today," he thought to himself. His head was drenched before his umbrella opened. The small ponds of water dotting the way to the courthouse were unavoidable; his feet would not dry for the entire day.

Gloria Wood, describing herself as a "TV star-recording artist-writer-entertainer," was the guest writer for the "Impressions" series of newspaper stories. "Finch Characters Unreal," she noted, writing: "Dr. Finch's amazing calm and seeming disregard of his surroundings are those of a man with nerves of steel. When I spoke to him, the discussion was the same as if I had met him at a reception or at the tennis club. He is a man with a magnetic personality and very attractive to women." Also noted: the release of her latest album, "Wood by the Fire."

This would be the critical day for Tregoff's attempt to have a mistrial granted. Robert A. Neeb would make a strong, emotional argument she had been in custody from the time she entered the Las Vegas sheriff's station to her arrest on the witness stand at the preliminary hearing for Finch; the testimony of Gubser and the two reporters, most thought, had firmly established that she was under arrest in Las Vegas.

As evidentiary matters were at hand, the jury had the day off. First, Judge Albert Miller, fully recovered from the flu, would talk of his treatment of Miss Tregoff as a witness in his courtroom, followed by Gladys Tregoff's memory of the same; the versions would differ.

"I'd like to give the layout of my courtroom there at Citrus Court. You see, it was like this. It was jam-packed with people; even the jury box had some extra chairs in it I brought from home." Miller would wander often in his answers and was reminded many times to answer simply and not elaborate.

"Objection again, Your Honor!" Cooper remained seated. "He's not answering the question. Mr. Crail is allowing his witness to talk about anything and everything he wants."

Evans: "Sustained. Judge Miller, once again, please try to just answer the questions."

Crail: "Once again, Judge Miller, please tell us what happened on the occasion that Miss Tregoff broke down emotionally and was led into your chambers at Citrus Court."

Miller: "Oh yes, I remember that quite clearly. She was being examined by the district attorney, and it came to a point in the questioning when he asked about whether or not she had ever had sexual relations with Dr. Finch. I, myself, was questioning her quite closely also because I-"

Cooper: "He's wandering from the question again. Your Honor!"

Evans: "Please, Judge Miller."

Crail: "Just tell us what you observed, Judge Miller."

Miller: "Oh, all right. She hesitated, and in an instant or two broke out into tears and began sobbing, and we were confronted with a witness on the stand sobbing. I called on the bailiff at this point to have a recess and to accommodate the young lady in the court's chambers. There were no other places for her, no place in the whole courthouse. We had people in the halls, even outside." He stopped himself.

Crail: "Then what happened?"

Miller: "He took her into my chambers. I think her mother, Mrs. Tregoff, went with her, I'm not sure. Then I lit up my pipe while some reporters lit up some cigarettes, and we chatted a little bit."

Crail: "Did you at any time instruct anyone to place her under arrest or hold her in custody?"

Miller: "Nothing of the sort. Never at any time!"

Crail: "What did you say to her after going into chambers?"

Miller: "Well, you didn't ask me why I went into the chambers in the first place." Cooper: "Your Honor!"

Evans: "Please let the attorneys decide which questions they want to ask, Judge."

Crail: "I just want to know what conversations took place after you went into your chambers."

Miller: "Very well. First of all, I told her we had some reporters from all over the world out there. I told her, 'I have had multiple requests to let these people take your picture in my courtroom and I want you to know I have forbidden it, unless you decide you desire to be photographed.' I told her, 'The court is not going to require you to submit to pictures.' Then I talked to her about the question she had just been asked before she broke down. I told her, 'It is none of my business how you answer, and I haven't the slightest idea how you would answer it, and whether you answer or not is strictly up to you. You don't have to answer if you don't want to.'" He shifted his bulk slightly in the chair, then continued.

"I told her, 'Of course, it's true that I did overrule an objection to the question by Mr. Cooper, when he said the question was out of order, but that doesn't mean you have to answer it. Just answer it if you want to.' And that's what I told her-not word for word, of course, but that's the substance of it."

Crail: "Did she make any reply to you at that point?"

Miller: "No. I pointed out the private restroom next to my chambers and suggested that she might want to freshen up a bit. She went in, and I think her mother went with her. In due time she came out; her complexion had brightened up a little bit. She came out, and she said she was 'going to answer that question.'"

Crail: "Did Miss Tregoff, at any time during her testimony, object to answering any questions?"

Miller: "No, no, never. We went back in and resumed court and she answered the question. I had the reporter repeat the question and she answered, 'Yes.'"

Eagan would cross-examine.

Eagan: "At the time the preliminary hearing took place, this young lady," he was standing in front of Cooper, pointing to Carole Tregoff with his left hand, "was in your courtroom under subpoena?"

Miller: "I don't know; the record would show. I don't remember if she was subpoenaed or not. She was there."

Eagan: "She was called as a witness by Mr. Whichello. Is that correct?"

Miller: "Yes."

Eagan: "When she was called, was she advised of her constitutional rights?"

Miller: "Everybody there, everybody in the courtroom," he was leaning forward, his voice raised for the first time, "all the witnesses and observers had been advised of their constitutional rights."

Eagan looked perplexed. He glanced at Bringgold who appeared confused.

Eagan: "And at the time Miss Tregoff was called to the witness stand, you didn't give her any other explicit instruction?"

Miller: "No."

Eagan: "You are telling us, Judge, that you had no idea that she might end up being a defendant?"

Miller: "None whatsoever. I had no idea she would be a defendant, none."

Eagan: "None?"

Miller: "I answered you. I had no idea she would be a defendant. I already told you that." His voice was louder.

Eagan: "Well then maybe, Judge, you could tell us the purpose of a Sergeant George Odle in your courtroom."

Miller: "Odle?" He shifted his weight again.

Eagan had been told, during his extensive interviews with people present at the preliminary hearing, that Miller had motioned for Odle to follow him to his chamber's door.

Eagan: "George Odle, from the West Covina Police Department. His duties aren't ordinarily connected with your court, are they, Judge?"

Miller: "No, he was there for crowd control."

Eagan: "Oh, crowd control. I see. After Miss Tregoff was led into your chambers, you had a conversation with Sergeant Odle, did you not?"

Miller: "Not that I recall. He understood what his instructions were. I had instructed him prior to the hearing as to what would be expected of him, to handle the crowd, to go ahead and use the jury box for spectators, and he helped set up some extra chairs I had brought from home to help-"

Eagan: "Isn't it true that Sergeant Odle remained outside the door of your chambers while Miss Tregoff was in there?"

Miller: "I think so. He wasn't inside the chambers, so I guess he could have been outside the door."

Eagan: "And when you went into your chambers, Judge, you found Miss Tregoff was crying?"

Miller: "I would say she was sniffling a little bit, not sobbing. She had a box of tissue there and was just sniffling a little."

Eagan: "And you informed her, 'Carole,'" Eagan's voice was higher pitched, almost singing, "'you are a guest of this court and you can come and go as you please.'"

Miller: "Yes." He glared at the attorney.

Eagan: "Is it true you told her at that time you didn't care if she answered the question or not, that you said the word 'contempt,' that you wouldn't hold her in contempt of court if she refused to answer?"

Miller: "Well, it wasn't exactly like that, I worked it differently. I didn't want to crowd her or anything."

Eagan: "Well, we'd like to know what you said, Judge. Did you say, 'If you answer this question this will be an end to it.' Did you say that?"

Miller: "In a sense I guess that's what I said."

Eagan: "At the time you declared a recess was there a court reporter present in the courtroom? When you spoke with Sergeant Odle was there a court reporter in your courtroom?"

Miller: "I told you." His voice was raised; he was squeezing the arm of the witness chair. "I didn't speak with Odle; he had his instructions from earlier."

Grant Cooper's examination of the judge would be one of the high points of the trial. His curiosity had been prodded when Miller announced that "everyone in the courtroom had been advised of their constitutional rights."

Cooper: "Judge Miller, I'm a little confused. Could you tell me how everyone in the courtroom was advised of their constitutional rights, including Miss Tregoff?"

Miller: "At the preliminary hearing, at the beginning of every hearing, I read the accused his constitutional rights.

Everyone in court hears the rights. It applies to everybody, not just the accused. These are rights everybody has."

Cooper: "You remember that I was present when my client was arraigned on July 21, a Tuesday, when my client was arraigned. You advised everybody of their constitutional rights at that time? And my client's preliminary hearing date was set for July 27?"

Miller: "Yes."

Cooper: "But Miss Tregoff was not present at that time. Are you aware of that?"

Miller: "I'll take your word for it. I haven't any idea. I didn't even know who she was at the time."

Cooper: "And at the preliminary hearing on July 27 you again reminded my client of his constitutional rights; you read that little speech about the constitution? As I recall, Miss Tregoff was present that day."

Miller: "I would say that I did."

Cooper showed no mercy. He picked up an inch-thick document, fanning through it with his thumb.

Cooper: "Well, then, why is it I can find no record of such a speech in the court records, Judge?"

Miller: "A record is a record." He was sitting back and yelling now, his face red. "You asked me if I had any independent recollection of informing him of his rights. I do have. I answered you in the affirmative."

Cooper: "Your Honor," Evans was still looking at Miller. "Your Honor, I would like at this point to remind the court that the record of that hearing is in the record and that my client was not told of his constitutional rights at that time."

Miller left, most thought, slightly bloodied. But he still stopped to talk to reporters on his way out, trying some of his old jokes; there was little laughter.

Gladys Tregoff was one of the last witnesses of the day.

Bringgold: "Were you with you daughter the entire time during that preliminary hearing for Dr. Finch.?"

G. Tregoff: "I was with her the entire time. I sat with her in the section reserved for witnesses, and I went with her into the judge's chambers after she broke down crying."

Bringgold: "What did Judge Miller say?"

After lengthy objections from Whichello, claiming Mrs. Tregoff's testimony would be hearsay, Evans allowed her to tell her recollection of the twenty minutes spent in the private chambers of Judge Miller.

G. Tregoff: "He told her, 'We are all human. Just answer this question yes or no and we will have the whole thing over with.'"

Bringgold: "Did he ever tell her she could refuse to answer if she wanted to?"

G. Tregoff: "No, I did not hear him say that, and I was with her every second."

Robert Neeb was sitting at the defense table studying some notes. He was about to make the motion to dismiss Carole's case in an impassioned address that lasted one hundred minutes. He rose slowly, walking to the front of the defense table. The focus of his argument would be Tregoff's statements to police, and Exhibit 60, her testimony in Judge Miller's courtroom. His arguments: 1. The police statements were given while she was in custody, without being advised of any rights, and 2. The court testimony was obtained after she was considered a suspect; a violation of her right against self-incrimination.

"Your Honor, it's very difficult for me to believe that we would all be talking about this issue of whether she had been under arrest or not for six months, through all of our appeals to the state and U. S. Supreme Courts, and that Sergeant Ryan would think to call Las Vegas to clarify the situation just last Friday to find out we were right all along and that she had been arrested and told that if she didn't cooperate she would be booked. It doesn't matter if she was a material witness or not; she was in custody. It has never been my practice to be vindictive in the twenty-five years I have been involved with the courts, but I simply do not believe Captain Ryan's testimony.

"From the time she was taken into the sheriff's station until the time she appeared on the witness stand, she was, in a legal sense promised immunity because she was not told the statements could be used against her.

"Mr. Whichello, by leading, suggestive, and argumentative questioning, led Carole Tregoff into a position where he could order her arrest. I believe he intended all along to have her arrested and that at no stage did he warn her of her legal rights. It is incredible that this could happen in Los Angeles County in this country, but it did.

"Judge Miller said he didn't want to 'crowd' Miss Tregoff during her testimony. He wasn't crowding her. He was pushing her all the time, pushing her to incriminate herself. This was not a way to run a court."

In closing, Neeb flailed all those he thought conspired against his client.

"There has been a consort of action between the District Attorney's office, the police, and Judge Miller, and the victim was Miss Tregoff as she walked into that witness box. I move the case against Carole Tregoff be dismissed and should this be denied, defense moves that these exhibits not be allowed as evidence."

Evans had gone to his chambers for a few minutes to ponder the question. As he returned, Neeb, sitting to Carole Tregoff's right, squeezed her hand, then whispered into her ear.

"I have every respect for District Attorney Whichello and for Judge Miller," Evans began. "I do not believe that the two conspired to treat the girl unfairly. Motion for a mistrial is denied.

"As for Mr. Neeb's objection to the admission of the testimony at the preliminary hearing, the so-called 'Exhibit 60,' I have decided to sustain it."

Excited reporters ran for telephones, many surrounded the defense table. Jubilant and beaming, Carole Tregoff pulled Neeb toward her, kissing him on the left cheek. This was the only photograph of the attorney smiling in court.

Hopes for order abandoned, Evans stopped slamming his gavel and shouted his other decision, not heard by many. "The statements made to police in Las Vegas and West Covina will, however, be allowed. Court is adjourned."

Fred Whichello was standing, putting the day's notes and reports back into his briefcase. After the reporters had talked with Carole and her attorneys, they swarmed about the deputy D.A.

"How much does this damage your case, Fred? Now that you can't use Exhibit 60?" one asked.

"It doesn't damage my case at all. Our case didn't rest solely on the discrepancies in her various statements." He didn't look up. "We still have those statements to the police and she's still got a lot of explaining to do."

He and Clifford Crail would meet later that night to discuss how the defense of Bernard Finch, M.D., might be presented. It would start in the morning. Both men were certain it would be interesting, to say the least.

With Exhibit 60 ruled inadmissable, Robert Neeb withdrew his petition from the United States Supreme Court.

eight

Opening Remarks in
Defense of R. Bernard Finch

WEDNESDAY, FEBRUARY 3, 1960

THE CROWD WAS the largest so far; six hundred people were milling about by 8:00 A.M., hoping to see the defendants, or possibly to buy a place in line for twenty dollars. The night janitors reported lines forming at 2:30 A.M.

Yesterday's storm front had passed through; the sun would peek through the overcast intermittently.

Jayne Meadows was the "celebrity reporter" for the day. She would interview Finch and find him "fascinating." Photos of the two show them smiling broadly, bent over at the waist, leaning toward each other, their faces only inches apart.

Waiting calmly, talking only occasionally, were Whichello and Crail. They had been speculating for months about the specifics of the defense. Cooper would make them wait until the end of his opening address. Although some of Finch's early statements indicated he might try to convince the jury he had acted in self-defense, some observers thought the plan called for a story of an accident. Cooper would take most of the day.

He rose and moved slowly to the jury, walking along in front of them as he spoke. He was careful to make eye contact with each, stopping his stride, if necessary, until a juror looked back.

"At no time did my client intend to murder his wife nor did he conspire to murder her," he began in a calm, matter-of-fact tone of voice.

"Dr. Finch will tell you that shortly after the birth of their son, Raymond, in 1953, Barbara began to exhibit towards him signs of sexual coolness. He will tell you that before the birth of their son they had the usual, normal sexual relationship that exists in any happy, harmonious home. But after the birth of Raymond, Junior, they drifted apart. While there was not a total abstinence, it was gradual in the years 1954 to 1955.

"This led to numerous quarrels and bickering and in November of 1956 they agreed to obtain a divorce. But this was postponed for many reasons, not the least of which was their concern for the welfare of their son, Raymond. Also, it would be hard for Dr. Finch to build his planned hospital if there were a divorce, with all its scandal and the division of the family's resources. He will tell you how he had just borrowed a quarter of a million dollars for the purpose of building their new hospital in West Covina.

"Dr. Finch will tell you that he and his wife reached an 'armistice' after November of 1956, and that each could pursue relationships outside the marriage. This was understood and agreed to by each party. Although there were arguments during this time about one issue or another, at no time did my client strike or harm Mrs. Finch in any way.

"We will show you that in contradiction to much of the prosecution's case, Barbara Jean Finch did know how to use a gun. In 1950 Dr. Finch bought a gun for the purpose, in the first instance, of doing some sports shooting, target practice. He gave this gun to Barbara because their home was located in a very sparsely populated area. We have witnesses who will tell that Barbara told them that Dr. Finch had given her the gun.

Finch and Cooper wrestle in court. *Getty.*

"Independent witnesses will also be called to show that Dr. and Mrs. Finch would take the gun out behind their house in the South Hills area of West Covina and shoot tin cans for target practice.

"Dr. Finch would take the gun with him when he had occasion to go to out at night to a house whose occupants he did not know because there had been several cases of narcotics addicts slugging doctors to obtain narcotics. He would occasionally keep the gun under the front seat of the red Chrysler convertible that he usually drove. He brought this car to the family home on an occasion when he went to see Mrs. Finch to exchange cars. This gun was left in the car at the request of Mrs. Finch.

"We will present evidence that Mrs. Finch made up the stories of her husband's attacks on her for purposes of making her divorce case more convincing. On one occasion, when Dr. Finch asked her why she was saying such things, she told him, "All's fair in love and war." At which point my client said, "If war is what you want, war is what you'll get." On July 1, Dr. Finch had a conversation with Carole Tregoff, who had been in contact with John Patrick Cody. Cody had been retained to obtain evidence against Mrs. Finch for the upcoming divorce.

"My client told Carole that a good time to do it, that is, obtain information about his wife, would be on the weekend of July 4, when my client would be attending a tennis tournament in La Jolla with his son, Raymond. Carole then relayed this message to Cody, who promised that he would get the information, even if, and I quote, 'I have to sleep with her myself.'

"My client met with Cody on one occasion and gave him the layout of the home, advising him of a likely place to park so that he could observe the house and tail Mrs. Finch should she leave. On this occasion Cody bragged that he could seduce Mrs. Finch if he had to, saying 'I never met a woman I could not make within twenty-four hours.' When Dr. Finch found out that Cody had cheated him and never intended to obtain the evidence, he threatened to go to the police if he didn't get his money back."

Cooper walked over to the exhibits table. He picked up the brown attaché case, talking as he returned to the jury.

"This is what the prosecution would have us believe is a 'murder kit.' My client will have a full and reasonable explanation for every item in here. There is a legitimate purpose for everything in here.

"And then my client will tell us about the events of the night his wife died."

Whichello leaned forward.

Cooper walked back to the defense table. He stood in front of Finch, who was looking directly at the jury.

"My client will explain that Mrs. Finch pulled the gun out of the car, and will tell how he made a grab for it and grabbed her wrists and how he struggled for the gun and wrested it from her. How afterwards she still kicked and fought and, for the purpose of protecting himself, he hit her over the head with the butt of the gun, causing her to lose consciousness."

Whichello leaned back into his chair, right arm draped over the back of it; a wry smile moved onto his face.

"As he was helping his wife into the car to take her to get aid, she took off, picked up the gun, and ran out of the garage. He did not know where Carole was and feared that Mrs. Finch might shoot her. He will tell how he found his wife near the steps leading down to his parents' home and how, when he saw her, he grabbed for the gun again, wresting it from her once more.

"He threw the gun away and it went off accidentally. He did not even know his wife was shot until she collapsed shortly afterward."

Fred's smile was a little wider now.

Cooper continued. He was approaching the high point of his presentation.

"As she lay there dying, Dr. Finch knelt down beside her and he will tell about a very brief conversation he had with her and that she died as he held her in his arms."

Fred glanced briefly at the ceiling.

Cooper paused; he slowly walked back to stand in front of his client.

"In sheer panic he ran down the hill, not knowing what to do. He had just seen his wife die. He does not remember if he had the gun or the purse or any jewelry with him or if he threw it away as he ran. He does not remember taking the cars, although he realizes he must have, somehow, in his panic, taken them and driven back to Las Vegas, where he was awakened the next morning by Las Vegas sheriff's deputies."

After a prediction that they would find his client not guilty, Cooper was through.

Evans adjourned the court for the day. Tomorrow's first witness would be Dr. Bernard Finch. "It will be quite a performance," Whichello speculated to Crail as the two stuffed their briefcases.

nine

Testimony of R. Bernard Finch

THURSDAY, FEBRUARY 4, 1960

"SAVE MY PLACE in line!" the woman sitting on the floor instructed the waiting others.

Mary Schufelt was sixty-four years old. She was obviously short of breath; perspiration dripped from her face. Firemen connected tubing from her nose to the small metal bottle one of them was carried. She had collapsed while standing in line. Doctors at nearby Central Receiving Hospital would later report she suffered a mild heart attack.

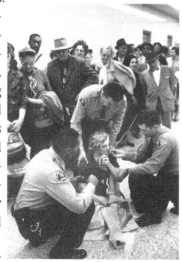

"As soon as they check me out, I'll be back." The fireman were carrying her on the litter now.

"Save my place!" *Getty.*

As they neared the stairwell to the lower floor the woman screamed her last words to the throng, "You better not give away my place!"

Extra marshals had again been borrowed from other courtrooms to control the crowd. It was the high point of the trial for many. Some were attracted by the promise of a tale of infidelity and a marriage gone bad. Others were hoping that somehow Finch would explain everything away satisfactorily, and that they could be comforted by the fact that a respected physician, a healer, would never have set out to murder his wife.

Inside, photographers asked Dr. Finch to pose with his dad. Both smiled confidently.

"So help you, God," the clerk said. R. Bernard Finch's left hand was on a Bible, his right hand held up.

"I do," he said, sitting down.

This was his first testimony. He looked out at the crowd of people, then over to the jury. All eyes were on him. Whichello and Crail seemed quite serious; both had note-pads in front of them, pens at the ready. Carole seemed to be smiling at him. Her two attorneys seemed to look at him apprehensively. He and Cooper had been through the story countless times and he had rehearsed it during his idle time in county jail. Now it was time to deliver, time to convince the jury to give him his life back.

Cooper was taking his time, waiting for the moment to build, giving his client a few moments to get comfortable in the witness box.

Cooper: "Dr. Finch," he spoke quietly, seriously. "Did you on the night of July 18 murder your wife?"

Finch: "Absolutely not, Mr. Cooper." He was sitting up straight, his voice self-assured, without the slightest hint of stress. His eyes would always be looking at Cooper or the jury for his entire testimony. Occasionally, he would talk directly to a juror, nodding his head and gesturing. Often a juror would nod back.

Cooper: "Or at any other time?"

Finch hesitated for a moment.

Finch: "No."

Cooper: "Dr. Finch, did you at any time conspire with Jack Cody or Carole Tregoff or with any other person to kill and murder your wife?"

Finch: "No, sir. I certainly did not."

Cooper: "When were you and Barbara Jean married?"

Finch: "December 22, 1951."

Cooper: "And you went to medical school where?"

Finch: "At the College of the Medical Evangelist, in Loma Linda. I graduated in the class of 1943."

Cooper: "And you began your practice with the Magan Medical Clinic of Covina?"

Finch: "Yes, sir."

Cooper: "When did you meet Barbara Jean?"

Finch: "I met Barbara Jean Daugherty in 1946. She was a patient of mine at the Magan Medical Clinic. I took care of her for some minor ailments. I managed her pregnancy with Patti in 1947. This was followed by some thyroid problems she had that I managed. She developed a goiter after the pregnancy."

Cooper: "Now in December of 1950, did you purchase a gun?"

Finch: "Yes, from a friend of mine, James Chick. He owns a sporting goods store in Covina; he was up here on the stand. It was a revolver with a four-inch barrel, just like the one Mr. Whichello submitted as evidence. I also purchased some ammunition, three boxes, I believe."

Cooper: "And why did you purchase the gun? Did you purchase it to murder your wife?"

Finch: "No, sir, I didn't." His voice lowered and became raspy; his eyes began to tear. After a moment he cleared his throat and looked back up. "There was sort of a scare went around about then. Some doctors had been called out and then hit on the back of the head, and their medical bags were stolen for the narcotics we carry. I wanted to have the gun available so if I got called out at night to make a house call on a person I didn't know or in an area I didn't know or was suspicious of, well, I would just take the gun along. I had a permit to carry the weapon, also."

Cooper: "Did you ever show the gun to Barbara Jean?"

Finch: "Oh, yes. After we moved to our house on Larkhill. The house was completed in July, and we moved right in. At that time there were only about three or four houses out in that whole area. The golf course was just planned; there was nothing. In those days I made a lot of night calls, and Barbara was afraid at night. So I'd leave the gun with her, but I wouldn't let her have the gun, you know, I wouldn't have let her have it to use until she learned how. You see, I taught her how to use it first."

Cooper: "How did you teach her how to use the gun?"

Finch: "Well, we just took out the gun and used to go out back of the house, between the house and the hill on the opposite side of where Dad's place is, and we put bottles and stuff and tin cans and just fired it, you know, like target practice."

Cooper: "Now, what kind of a shot was she?"

Finch: "She couldn't hit the side of the hill if she held the gun in one hand, so I taught her how to hold it with two hands, like this." His left arm was almost straight, his left thumb and index finger extended, his right hand was grasping his left wrist. "You see, like this she could hit bottles at, maybe, twenty-one feet away."

Cooper: "Then you lived at the Larkhill residence after 1952. Let's get back to that, Doctor. How did you and Barbara get along, generally speaking, during those early years?"

Finch: "We got along all right. We tried to develop some common interests and make our marriage work. She started playing a little bit of tennis. She didn't do much because she got pregnant the next year. Our sexual relations were normal. Our ability to like each other seemed to be satisfactory, at least. We liked each other as individuals. We didn't quarrel or bicker, no big 'silent treatment.'"

Cooper: "Now when was the child born?"

Finch: "Raymie, he was born in April of 1953."

Cooper: "And after the birth of your son, was there any change between you and your wife? I mean with respect to your sexual relations?"

Finch: "Yes. The way it happened was after Barbara had Raymie, after the usual six-week waiting period, we started having the usual sexual relationship which you expect to start. Except things weren't always right. As a matter of fact, they weren't usually right, and I always thought that it was just a fear, you know, a normal fear, of a girl that doesn't want to have another baby again right away. We used the usual contraceptive methods of the day.

"During the year of 1953 and into 1954 I became more upset about it. Our sexual experiences had resulted usually in Barbara crying and me being frustrated. She was completely unable by 1954 to reach a climax at all. She had become completely frigid. She went through the usual lines of excuses of being too tired and the whole gamut. Well, finally in 1954 I suggested to Barbara that we ought to seek some help regarding the problem. I checked her physically myself. Physically there was nothing wrong with her, nothing at all. Nothing that would cause sexual frigidity." He looked around, all eyes were still fixed on him. "Shall I continue on. Just continue on?"

Cooper nodded affirmatively.

Finch: "Well, she did not want to seek psychotherapy for this. So after much ranting and raving on my part she did finally say that she would go. I sent her to a doctor psychologist that I knew by the name of Dr. Miller, Vernon Miller, and she went down there, I thought, once a week. About a month later I saw Dr. Miller and asked him how things were going. I was surprised to find out that she had not been going at all.

"When I confronted her about this, she told me that she wanted to shut me up and that was the only reason she had said she would go. Then she told me that she had bought some books on the subject and that she was going to start doing some reading, and she did. I used to see her reading the books.

"She accumulated quite a collection of books, and she read them, but it didn't help."

Cooper: "When did you stop having sex altogether?"

Finch: "It gradually decreased in 1954 and 1955. Then we stopped some time completely in 1956. I would say in November of 1956."

Cooper: "Now some time in 1955, did Carole Tregoff Pappa come to work for your clinic?"

Finch: "Yes, I met her about three weeks after she came to work for our clinic. She was a very pretty girl. She worked as a receptionist at first, then she became my medical secretary after Mrs. Reida Ronds left the clinic. In August of 1956."

Cooper: "And when did you first suggest that you meet outside of the clinic?"

Finch: "It was in February of 1957; I invited her to have lunch with me. Then shortly thereafter I noticed we seemed to get along, so I invited her out to dinner."

Cooper: "You knew she was still married at that time?"

Finch: "Yes, I knew. I was enamored with her from the start; she was such a beautiful girl."

Cooper: "And shortly thereafter you rented an apartment together. Is that correct?"

Finch: "Yes, we got our first apartment together in April of 1957, April 15, in Monterey Park. We wanted an apartment so that we could have someplace to be alone, and Carole needed a place to keep her clothes for when we went out."

Cooper: "So then, you two had sexual relations?"

Finch: "Certainly."

Cooper: "Did Barbara Jean know about the relationship?"

Finch: "No, I chose not to tell her. Once, she saw Carole and I coming out of a grocery store together and later asked me if we were seeing each other. I told her 'No.'"

Cooper: "Why did you deny it?"

Finch: "Carole had no agreement like I had with Barbara Jean, and I didn't want Barbara going to Jimmy Pappa and telling him about it. Also, I didn't want to hurt Barbara's pride. I didn't want to flaunt the relationship in front of her. If she had become angry and proceeded with the divorce, my plans to build the West Covina Hospital would have been ruined.

Cooper: "Tell us about this 'agreement' that you had with Barbara Jean. When did you have a conversation with her about that?"

Finch: "Some time in November of 1956. It was at our home, in the evening I'm pretty sure. I told Barbara that as far as I was concerned, our marriage had become a failure, and that I was not getting anything out of it, and all I was doing was working and coming home to bickering, and if not bickering, the silent treatment, which I think is much worse, and that I thought we should consider a divorce. We discussed it, and it turned out she wasn't for a divorce. She knew it would be financially disastrous for us both and have an effect on our credit standing. So we decided mutually to do everything we could to keep our marriage looking normal to our friends, and to try to make things a little more pleasant for each other. It was an armistice between us; it was when we tried to patch things up and, you know, to make things a little more pleasant for each other.

251

"The last point of the conversation was that I was not to approach Barbara sexually any further, because it seems like that was the source of our trouble. In exchange for this, I was to have freedom of action, and could come and go as I chose, and Barbara could come and go as she chose. She wanted to take a modeling class in L. A., and she wanted a new car. These things were all done in an effort to keep her happy. I got her a new Cadillac in December of 1956."

Cooper: "And in 1957, after Carole became your medical secretary, you invited her out."

Finch: "Yes, the first date I ever had with Carole was a luncheon date in February of 1957. At first it was just an invitation for a pleasant lunch. I knew her pretty well, and I certainly liked her looks. Like I said, I was enamored with her right away."

Carole smiled, looking down at the floor.

Cooper: "Now, during this time that you and Carole were having this affair, did you discuss the possibility of marriage?"

Finch: "Certainly. We were both very aware not only of the complete failure of our own marriages, but of each other's marriage. We knew that eventually we would both be getting a divorce. I explained to Carole that my marriage had to be continued for some time. The reason for this was that I was involved in the financing of the planned West Covina Hospital, and a divorce would hurt me and my partners. Why, I eventually had to borrow a quarter of a million dollars."

Cooper: "Now, did you at any time have a discussion with Carole about the propriety of her leaving her husband?"

Finch: "Yes. She did leave her husband, in September of 1958, about a year after our affair started. We didn't think it was a good idea to have our two divorces simultaneously. We had been trying to cover up the fact we had been going out together. But after Carole told Jimmy she was going to leave him, he called Barbara and told her of our affair. Barbara was quite alarmed. She wondered if I was going to divorce her. I told her 'No,' and that just because Carole and Jimmy were getting divorced didn't mean we were going to. I told her I wanted to go ahead with our marriage the way that it was."

Cooper: "How did she react to that?"

Finch: "At the time she seemed to be reassured, but about two months later, I think in about November of 1958, I learned she was consulting a lawyer about a divorce. I told her to give me another year, and that by that time her share of the community property would be even bigger and my hospital would be in the black. She said that made sense, and that she didn't want to hurt any innocent people, meaning my business partners and the employees of the hospital. I felt better about the situation, and things seemed to go along as usual until about April of 1959, I learned that I was being followed by detectives. I noticed it when once I was being tailed on my way to the Los Angeles Tennis Club."

Cooper: "What else suggested you were being tailed by detectives?"

Finch: "One day Carole and I were at the beach and someone took our picture. Later, I asked Barbara if she knew anything about it. At first she just said, 'Could be.' But I kept questioning her about it, and she eventually told me 'Yes,' that she was having me followed. It was then I suspected she was going to proceed with a divorce and in May-May 13, I believe-she told me she was going to file for a divorce. I persuaded her to talk it over and she agreed to postpone it. We both agreed at this point to go to a marriage counselor."

Cooper: "Why would you agree to go to a marriage counselor if you had already decided to get a divorce?"

Finch: "Well, uh," he looked confused, "I guess I was trying to fool Barbara. I was trying to stall her! I needed time."

253

Cooper: "Now, on May 15, your wife suffered some wounds to her head at your home. Would you tell the court what happened that night?"

Finch: "Certainly. My wife had been suffering from the flu and was taking some medication. I woke up during the night after hearing a noise and noticed that Barbara wasn't in the bed. I looked over and there she was on the floor. She asked me 'What happened?' and I said, 'I don't know, but you have a cut on your head.' I helped her get dressed and took her down to the hospital and stitched up a cut over her eye. I was very careful, so as not to leave a scar."

Cooper: "So you didn't hit her with a gun, like the prosecution says, or shove her?"

Finch: "No. There is this night stand next to the bed with real square edges and square corners."

Cooper: "And there was no loud talking?"

Finch: "Nothing like that, at all. Barbara was sick that night."

Cooper: "Now, let's talk about this check that the prosecution says you forged. Did you fake your wife's signature on this check for $3,000?"

Finch: "No, not at all. In fact, she signed two checks that day. She was going to give me the money so that I could deposit it in my own account and then pay some of the household bills. She was very upset that day. She signed the first check and her tears fell on it, ruining the signature, so I had her sign the second one."

Cooper: "Now on May 18 were you two going somewhere?"

Finch: "Yes, that was the day we were supposed to go to our marriage counselor. We went and then drove back together. Barbara and I were to meet later that night and discuss some business matters. I phoned the house later and learned that she was gone. I did not see or hear from her for three days. It was then that I learned that she had filed for divorce on that day, the day we had gone to the marriage counselor."

Cooper: "When did you next see Mrs. Finch?"

Finch: "About three weeks later. We worked out an agreement whereby she would postpone the divorce and move back into the house; in turn, I would move out. This was about June 10."

Cooper: "You knew that there was going to be a divorce-it was just indefinite as to when it would start?"

Finch: "Yes."

Cooper: "Did you have any conversations with Carole during this time about hiring detectives to follow your wife?"

Finch: "Yes, during the time of June 10 to the 22 I had a series of conversations with Carole, who was living in Las Vegas at that time, about hiring some detectives to follow Barbara Jean, as she had done with me. I told Carole that I had been unsuccessful to get someone in the L. A. area, and I didn't know who to turn to next. I was busy with my practice and all, so I thought that maybe she might have the time to try to get somebody in Las Vegas. She said she would be glad to. We figured there are a lot of people who go up to Las Vegas and Reno to get divorces. They have to get their residencies established. I figured there must be detectives around to follow them and see what they are up to."

Cooper: "On the fifteenth of June, did you have occasion to change cars with Barbara Jean?"

Finch: "Yes. I was having problems with the cooling system on the Chrysler convertible, which I had been driving, so I asked her if she would mind trading cars with me. I called her about 11:00 in the morning from my office. She said, 'Sure, come on up and we can talk about it.' I never went inside the house. I just stood at the door and tried to talk to her about switching cars. I said, 'Look, Barbara, all I want to do is exchange the cars. Just give me your keys; my keys are in mine.' And all of a sudden she just screamed and said, 'My keys are in the car,' and turned and ran down the hall yelling, 'Marie Anne, Marie Anne! Call the police, call the police!'

"I stuck my head inside and looked down the hall and the two of them were standing there. Marie Anne was looking at her like something was wrong. I said, 'What is the matter with you? What do you mean? All I want to do is switch cars.' She didn't say anything to me. She just said to Marie Anne again, 'Call the police.' Well about that time Raymie came running down the hall to say 'Hi' to me. I picked him up and gave him a kiss, and the two of us went outside."

Cooper: "And you did trade cars?"

Finch: "Yes. Raymie and I took my bags out of the back of the Chrysler and put them in the Cadillac. The keys were in the switch of the Cadillac, just as she had told me. I kissed Raymie good-bye, and then I left."

Cooper: "Now tell us about the gun, the .38 caliber pistol that you usually kept with you, or in the Chrysler."

Finch: "I left it in the Chrysler that day, on purpose. I had previously borrowed the pistol from Barbara for an outing I had with the boat. I had gone out boating and wanted to shoot some sharks. She had told me that she wanted the .38 caliber pistol for protection at the house. I told her I would bring it back, so I left it in the Chrysler, in a small shaving bag, with some bullets."

Cooper: "Did you at some time that day have a conversation with any policeman?"

Finch: "Yes, when I got back to my apartment. I had thought that maybe Barbara was upset because she thought I wanted to make a permanent trade with the cars. She didn't give me a chance to explain that I just wanted to make a temporary trade, for a trip to Las Vegas I had planned. I phoned the house, and a policeman was there. This is Sergeant Handrahan of the West Covina Police, Dr.

Finch. Your wife called us up here and said that you had been up here beating her up.'

"I said, 'Well that's certainly a shock to me, Sergeant. All I did was go up there to trade cars with her. What does she say I did to her?' He said, 'Well, she says you came up here like you're not supposed to, against a court order, and beat her up.' So I asked him to go look at her and see if he sees anything wrong with her. You know, a bruise, a scratch, any sign of trauma at all. He came back in about thirty seconds and he said, 'Doctor, I don't see a thing wrong with the girl. Maybe her make-up is a little smeared. I don't know.' So I asked him to make sure he put that in his report, that he saw no signs of trauma, because I knew she was trying to use this to make me look bad in divorce court. He said, 'I sure will.'

"Then he told me, 'You know, Doctor, if she swears out a warrant against you for violating this court order, I'm going to have to come over there and arrest you.' So I said, 'Well, I'm sure that you cannot help that, that would be part of your job, but let me tell you this. Come and arrest me on Monday because I'm leaving for Las Vegas right now. That's why I traded cars in the first place, was for my trip. If you want me, I will be here Monday.' He said 'Okay.'

"Then I asked him to tell Barbara what she hadn't given me time to explain. I said, 'Would you tell her I am not trying to trade the cars permanently, I just needed to trade for the weekend because my cooling system in the Cadillac wasn't working.' He said he would relay the message."

Cooper: "And you were not arrested the following Monday?"

Finch: "No, sir, I was not."

Cooper: "You then drove to Las Vegas in the Cadillac?"

Finch: "Yes. I got into town and checked in at the Tropicana Hotel. I was there for the whole weekend."

Cooper: "And did you have any conversations during this time with Carole about the hiring of anyone?"

Finch: "Yes. Well, I had previously had this conversation with her about the possibility of her hiring someone, and after I got there on this trip, I asked her if she had had any luck in finding anyone. I told her what had happened that morning on the car exchange scene and how I thought Barbara was pulling another deal on me, but that things would probably be all right because the police had come and seen no injuries."

Cooper: "And what did she say?"

Finch: "She said that her friend Don Williams had located somebody and that she was going to see him some time in the near future. She was planning to go over the matter with him more thoroughly and then would let me know."

Cooper: "And at this point you gave her a picture of Barbara Jean?"

Finch: "Yes, I brought a picture of Barbara and gave it to Carole. If she were to locate somebody for doing this job, I wanted to have this person be able to identify Barbara. Nobody could follow anybody or get any evidence on her if they didn't know who she was."

Cooper: "Now, later in the day did you have a conversation with Carole and Don Williams?"

Finch: "Yes, in my room at the Tropicana. I don't remember the exact words of the conversation. I can't say any exact sentences, but the point of the conversation was that I told him I was having marital problems. I told him how she had acted at the car exchange deal. And I told him, 'We've got to get somebody to get some evidence on this girl. She's continually pulling these kind of things on me and I've got to find out what she's doing.' He said he would do his best to find someone for us."

Cooper: "Now when did you learn that someone had been located?"

Finch: "On July 1, I believe, I got a phone call from Carole. She said, 'Honey, I've got good news for you. Don introduced me to a man named Jack Cody. He's a very competent ladies' man. He's working now following a woman around Las Vegas who is here establishing her six-week residency and he's dating her. He works for her husband.'

"So I said I thought the sooner we could get him on the job the better, and that she should try to get him down to Los Angeles within the next few days. I told her the next weekend would be better because I would be in La Jolla for a tennis tournament. Barbara knew that I went every year and she would probably be playing around during this time."

Cooper: "Did you discuss the terms of the arrangement?"

Finch: "Yes. She said he wanted thirty days to do the job and that he would do it for $1,350. I told her to pay just part of it if he needed it for expenses and then pay the other half at the end of the thirty days. She told me she would do it that way. Then she said that this man had guaranteed his work, that he had said he would get this information for us and he would have information for us to use in court, even if he had to sleep with Barbara Jean himself."

Cooper: "When did you meet Jack Cody for the first time?"

Finch: "I drove to Las Vegas on July 6, after the weekend. I checked into the Sands hotel and met with Carole while I was having a beer. She said that he hadn't gotten much information and that maybe I had better talk with him myself. The next day we drove over to his apartment and I went up to the door and asked him how things went. He said he had not been able to get much information. I asked him if he still wanted the job and he said, 'Sure.' He was sure he could handle it for me and that he would leave for L. A. that night and stay as long as it would take to get the information."

Cooper: "How many more times did you see Cody?"

Finch: "Twice. The very next day we learned that he was in town and sent him a message to come to Carole's apartment. I asked him if he was going to do the job and he said, 'Yes.' We had no word from him for a few days so the following Friday, I believe July 12, I went to his room and talked to him again. Same story. He was having trouble getting the information but 'not to worry,' everything would be okay."

Cooper: "And you never saw Jack Cody after July 12?"

Finch: "No, sir, never again. I went back to Los Angeles and was there until the following Friday."

Cooper: "Then you returned to Las Vegas?"

Finch: "Yes. I flew back and met Carole at the airport. We went to the Sands to get something to eat, and it was there that we decided to take a different approach with Barbara."

Evans turned to look at the witness, his left eyebrow raised.

Cooper: "And what approach was that?"

Finch: "We decided that Barbara could come to Las Vegas and establish her residency here and we could get a quicker divorce here. I decided it was not worth the battle. I called Barbara the next morning and told her to get her lawyers to proceed so that the property settlement would be ready when her residency requirements were met. I told her it just wasn't worth the battle."

Cooper: "And, when you flew to Las Vegas that night you had this case with you?" He was holding the brown attaché murder kit.

Finch: "Yes. Carole had asked me to bring her some Seconal tablets. She was having trouble sleeping, so I put them in the bag and took it with me to the airport."

Cooper: "Let's talk a little about this bag, Doctor. Did you put together this bag for the purpose of killing someone?"

Finch: "No, absolutely not!" He was pounding his fist on the rail in front of him. "Each of these items has a legitimate purpose."

Cooper: "Very well, let's look at what's inside and talk about it. Do you need to stand up to see?"

Finch stood and looked into the case Cooper had opened. Cooper was standing to the side so that his witness would be looking directly at the jury with the case in front of him as he spoke.

Cooper: "Is everything in here that was in here on the night of July 17 when you flew to Las Vegas with it?"

Finch said nothing as he rummaged methodically through the case. He stopped.

Finch: "The Seconal tablets, and a bottle of alcohol for sterilizing. They're not here."

All looked at Fred Whichello, who was comfortably leaning back in his chair. Noticing the attention, he spoke. "Well it must be up there somewhere. Look around some." Cooper was going back to the exhibit table, Whichello joined him, and the two went through the remaining items, finding a bottle with some red capsules in it and another bottle half full of a clear liquid.

Cooper: "Now was the flashlight in the case when you left?"

Finch: "No."

Cooper: "Or the kitchen knife, or 'carving knife,' as it's been called?"

Finch: "No."

Cooper: "What about the shaving bag with the bullets in it? Where was that?"

Finch: "It was under the front seat of the Chrysler, where I left it after the car exchange."

Cooper: "Okay, tell us about this bag and these items, Doctor. What are they used for?"

Finch: "The bag was given to me around Christmas of 1958 by a business firm as a gift, possibly a drug company, I'm not sure. I was putting together an emergency kit, to be used by others. It wasn't ready to be used yet, so I kept it with me as I was getting it ready. It was the kind of kit that, say, a junior doctor would take with him if he was called to a house on an emergency. He would take the bag and use it until the ambulance arrived."

Finch got out of the witness box. Cooper moved to the other side of the case and turned to face the jury. Bernard was standing to the jury's right. As he spoke he would reach in and pull out certain items.

Finch: "I was going to add a suture kit for lacerations, so we could just grab this bag and run. Then there could have been a poison case, you know some child might eat some of his mother's menopause pills or something. We could flush out the stomach using a tube and this syringe here, to remove the poison. This elastic bandage, used for wrapping a broken arm or to apply pressure to a laceration to stop the bleeding. This syringe we would use to give some Seconal or novocaine, depending on the need."

Cooper: "Anything else?"

Finch: "And this latex drape, if you are bleeding you don't want to bleed all over the place." He hadn't stopped talking. "This is a poison kit, in case somebody swallows some poison. Here's some sterile gloves in my size, size seven and a half." He was still looking at the items when Cooper asked his next question.

Cooper: "Why did you take this entire bag with you to Las Vegas?"

Finch: "Oh, well, like I said, Carole had asked me to bring her some Seconal tablets to help her sleep. I had put the tablets in the case. Anyway, as I was getting on the plane at

L.A.X., I remembered that I had forgotten her tablets. I ran back to the car. I had locked the case and didn't have time to unlock it, take out the tablets," he was rocking slightly, from side to side, "close up the case and lock it again, so I just grabbed the whole bag and ran back. I was the last person on the plane."

Cooper: "You also had your regular black doctor's bag with you when you parked your car at the airport, did you not? It's here also, I believe." He walked to the exhibit table and returned, looking through the smaller bag. "Now what is this?" He held up a small vial.

Finch: "A bottle of morphine."

Cooper: "Would the morphine in this bottle be enough to kill somebody if it were injected?"

Finch: "Yes."

Cooper: "Which drug would be more fatal to a person if it were injected, morphine or Seconal?"

Finch: "Morphine."

Cooper: "This bag was found in your car at the airport by police. You didn't take this bag with you, did you?"

Finch: "No."

Cooper closed the small bag and put it on the witness box rail. Then he closed up the attaché case and turned to the jury. "Let's put these bags away." He walked over and put them on the exhibit table. Finch returned to the witness box.

And now, it was the moment all had been waiting for. Whichello and Crail were leaning forward. Fred rested his chin on his fists and studied the witness.

Cooper: "You and Carole drove to West Covina, that Saturday night." He was standing farther away from his client than usual, in front of Evans, his left elbow resting on the judge's desk. "Tell us what happened."

Finch: "We arrived at about 11:30 that night. Carole had worked that day at the Sands, so we left right after she got off. We parked the car and waited on the lawn of the house for Barbara Jean. She came home just a few minutes later. I thought for sure she would see us when she drove up, but I guess she didn't. She kept on going and pulled into the garage. We started walking up to the garage and got there just as she was getting out of the car."

Cooper: "Show us where she was standing, Dr. Finch." He had dragged the now familiar diagram of the house and yard over to the witness box and placed it on the left side of his witness, so that all could see where he was pointing.

Finch: "She was here, just getting out of the car, on the driver's side. I said, 'Barbara, we'd like to talk to you,' and she said, 'Well, you're not going to.' Then she turned and reached back into the car. I looked back at Carole like 'What do we do next?' And I looked back to Barbara and she had a gun, and it was pointed straight at Carole. I just charged at her and—"

Cooper: "Hold on, Doctor, not so fast. I'd like you to show us how you grabbed for the gun. Would you come down here, please."

Soon the two were wrestling for the gun, much as Cooper had wrestled with Gerald K. Ridge. Finch was to the right of Cooper, his hands grabbing at the attorney's wrists.

Finch: "I grabbed and kind of lunged like this, see."

Cooper was knocked back, almost falling. The courtroom buzzed. He regained his balance, putting his right palm over his chest, as though catching his breath.

Cooper: "Take it easy, doctor. I'm an old man. Now, show us again."

Finch: "I pointed the gun up into the air, like this. When I hit into her she hit her head on the car door, and the rest of her just jammed into the car." He still had Cooper's arms pushed up. "At this point I looked into the car and saw this shaving-kit sort of halfway under the front seat. I reached down and felt the bag and sort of shook it." He was holding

Cooper's arms up with just his left hand now. "I could tell it had something inside of it. I thought there was another gun in it, so I turned and tossed it to Carole and said, 'Take this and get out of here.'"

Cooper: "And then what happened?" His voice was slightly strained as he wrestled with the stronger Finch.

Finch: "Well, I pinned the gun to the top of the car, like this." He moved Cooper's hands down, so that the gun was pointed sideways, at the jury. One juror moved to the side.

"I had her pinned to the side of the car. I said, 'Barbara, please, put the gun down.' She didn't say anything. She tried to bite me on the arm and then she started trying to stomp on my feet with her heels. I said, 'Barbara, put the gun down. Somebody's going to get hurt with the gun.' Then she tried to knee me in the groin. I bumped her in the face with my arm trying to keep the gun pinned to the car roof. Then she tripped me. I started to fall. I didn't want to let go of her. I held on and as I fell she sort of spun around and her head hit against the garage wall, on the side."

Cooper: "Did she still have the gun at this point?"

Finch: "Yes, sir, she did. And I still had ahold of her hands. She started yelling 'Help!' She yelled a half dozen times. Then I heard somebody coming."

Cooper: "What did you do then?"

Finch. "I kicked her in the feet, which made her lose her foothold. Then I stepped around to the right side of her, like this, and yanked the gun away from her. Then I hit her with the gun, hard like this."

He had Cooper pushed back against the witness box. His left hand was on Cooper's shoulder and he was holding the gun with his right hand. The gun was backward, so that the handle end pointed away. Finch moved the gun up once, then down, stopping just inches from Cooper's face.

Cooper: "Dr. Finch, why did you hit your wife?"

Finch: "I thought Marie Anne was coming with the rifle that I had taught her to use in case of burglars. I wanted to render Barbara unconscious so there wouldn't be any more wrestling around for the gun. I didn't want either one of us to get hurt, that's all. After I hit her, I dropped the gun and ran to the doorway here." He walked to the diagram and pointed to the small door of the garage that connected to the lanai area.

"I got to the door just as Marie Anne was coming in. I grabbed her shoulders and pushed her back against the wall. I only intended to pin her against the wall so that she couldn't use the rifle. She hit the wall awfully hard and she was dazed. I eased her down to the floor and said, 'Marie Anne, I'm sorry, but you don't know what has been going on out here.'"

Cooper: "Then what?"

Finch: "I heard Barbara Jean starting to move, so I walked over and picked up the gun. Then I came back to Marie Anne. I said, 'Marie Anne, don't worry. I'm not going to hurt you.' Then I helped her get up and we started to walk to the car.

"Then I felt, all of a sudden, these hands grab my hand and try to get the gun away from me. Barbara had seen me walk by, and my back was to her. I jerked my hand up, and that was the first shot. The gun went off as it was pointed out the garage door. Marie Anne said, 'Oh, no!' and real quick scampered into the back seat and laid down in the back like this." He leaned over onto his left side as far as he could. "She started to cry and she just stayed there.

"Then I turned to Barbara. She didn't say anything. I jerked the gun away from her, and she just went right back down on the garage floor again, but she kept her eyes open. I turned around and I looked at her and immediately I saw this blood on the side of her neck coming from her right ear. I knew when I saw that she had a skull fracture. I put the gun down on the top of the car and went around behind Barbara and grabbed her around the waist and helped her to her feet. Then I sat her on the edge of the front seat on the driver's side of the car."

Cooper: "What was your purpose in putting her in the car, Doctor?"

Finch: "Why, she was going to the hospital. She had a skull fracture." His eyebrows rose up making furrows in his forehead. His hands were in front of him, palms up.

"Then," he pointed his right index finger at Cooper, "I told her, 'Barbara, give me those keys or I'm going to slug you.' She had scooted over to the passenger side and was digging around in her purse to try to find the keys. She was digging around for them with her right hand and I still had her left hand pinned down with my right hand. She couldn't find them, so I was still holding her left wrist, and I reached over and put the gun down and grabbed the purse away from her and started looking through it myself with my left hand."

Cooper: "Did you find them?"

Finch: "No. All of a sudden I noticed the music on the radio. Then it occurred to me that in order for the radio to be playing, the keys had to be in the switch, so I looked in the switch and there were the keys, right there. I wanted to start the car, so I let go of her with my right hand and reached for the keys. All of a sudden Barbara was out of the car. She had grabbed the gun, which I had moved to my left leg, and she went out, just like that.

"I immediately went out of the car and ran to the front of it. I kept the car in between me and Barbara because I knew she had the gun. I banged the lights out of the car so it would be dark. I saw her at the back of the car for a few seconds; then she was gone. At first I was relieved because I felt safe; then I remembered that Carole was still outside, so I ran outside to see if she was safe." His voice showed more tension now. It was more hoarse and higher pitched. He looked, for the first time, down—at Cooper's shoes.

"I found Barbara Jean at the top of the steps that lead to my father's house, just at the edge of the blacktop of my home's driveway."

He paused and took a deep breath. His right palm was at his forehead slowly rubbing it back and forth.

Cooper: "Take it easy, Doctor. I know this is hard for you." He was at the witness box now.

Finch: "Yes, it is difficult, Mr. Cooper." His voice was huskier now, his fingers were shaking with a fine tremor. He took another deep breath and sat up straight, looking directly at Cooper.

Cooper: "What happened then, Doctor?" He spoke slowly. After his question he moved back from Finch, to a spot at the jury box rail.

Finch: "I saw the gun in her hands and jumped to the side. I landed about four feet from her. She started to run towards me at that point. I reached out and grabbed hold of her left wrist to keep her from turning any more towards me. I pounded her across the hand to knock the gun from her; it fell onto the blacktop. Then we both reached for the gun. I got to it first because she had fallen back a little bit when I jerked the gun away from her." He waited.

Cooper: "Then what happened?"

Finch: "I just reached down and got the gun. She was right, well, she was close to me and her hand was maybe two feet away from the gun when I got to it. I was a couple of feet ahead of her. Well, I just grabbed the gun and got up and straightened up to throw the thing away. Like this. I—" He had his left hand just below his chin, palm facing out. His left elbow was raised up, just above the level of the shoulder.

Cooper: "Did you have any of your fingers within the finger guard or on the trigger?"

Finch: "Well, obviously I must have. I don't know. I have no idea for sure."

Cooper: "Now, you threw it in the manner you are showing us?"

Finch: "Yes." His left arm had not moved.

Cooper: "And it went off?"

Finch: "It went off." He was nodding his head up and down.

Cooper: "Now, Doctor, after it went off, do you recall what happened to the gun? Did you throw it? Did you drop it? Did you keep it in your hand?"

Finch: "Mr. Cooper, I don't know what happened to that gun after it went off." He was shaking his head from side to side now. "I don't know whether I finished throwing it, whether I put it in my pocket, whether I stuck it in my belt. I don't know what I did with it at that time. Maybe I just dropped it right there. I just don't know."

Cooper: "Following the flash from the gun, what did you do?"

Finch: "I went over to the edge of the hill and out of the corner of my eye I saw Barbara starting to run down the path to my Dad's house. I ran over to the edge of the hill and looked down. I was looking for Carole. I saw Barbara running down the steps. It was then that Barbara fell. She just crumpled up right down the steps."

Cooper: "What did you do?"

Finch: "I took a look over at her. Then she sort of got up and sort of flopped over, and then she went down back over against the edge almost and she didn't move. I went over to her immediately.

"She was lying flat on her back with her arms either out like this, or maybe up, pointing up." He had his arms straight out at the sides. "I don't know for sure which. And with her right leg—no, I think it was her left leg straight out. I think it was her left leg straight out and her right leg curled up, in a position that made her so that her hip was turned out. I don't remember which leg it was for sure. I think it was the right leg, so the hip was turned out and the leg curled up, I—"

Cooper: "At that time did you know that she had been shot?"

Finch: "No. My first thought was that she had just stumbled on the stairs in the dark. Then, as I went down the steps and took a look at her—before I got to her—I saw her leg curled up and I thought she had broken her leg. I went running around to the side of her and I knelt down by her, right near her waistline, and started to feel over toward her leg." He paused. Another deep breath. "Shall I tell you what I said?"

Cooper: "Yes, of course, Doctor."

Finch: "I said, 'What happened, Barbara? Where are you hurt?' And she said, 'Shot in the chest.' I was amazed; I just couldn't do anything for a second. And then, and then, I said to Barbara, 'Barbara, just stay real quiet. Don't move a thing, don't move your arms or legs. Don't move a thing. Just lay real quiet. I've got to get an ambulance for you and get you to a hospital.' I got up and took two steps towards Dad's breakfast room door and I heard Barbara say 'Wait.'" He sighed deeply.

Cooper: "What then?"

Finch: "I came back and knelt down beside her."

The jury's attention was riveted on Finch at this point. Most were leaning forward on their elbows.

Finch: "She sort of, sort of moved her arm, sort of lifted her hand up like this. I thought she wanted me to hold her hand so I reached down and did. Then, I said, 'What is it, Barb?' She sort of opened her mouth a couple of times to say something, but she didn't. Then she spoke and her voice was very, very soft. I could hardly hear it, Mr. Cooper, it was very soft." He was breathing faster and more heavily as he spoke, his voice sounding as though he was shouting a whisper.

"She said, 'I'm sorry, I should have listened.' I said, 'Barb, don't talk about it now.' I said, 'I've got to get you to the hospital,' and she said, 'Don't leave me.' I started to cry."

He was barely able to talk now. His chest was heaving with each breath.

"After a little bit she said, 'Take care of the kids'; and then she went limp. I checked for her pulse right away. I reached and felt her neck for a carotid artery pulse right away. There was none. She was dead. I pulled her chin up and checked for respirations. There were none. She was dead. I said, 'Barb, Barb, Barb,' each time a little louder, but she couldn't answer me, I—"

He was sobbing now, moaning, his contorted face buried in his hands. Carole was quietly crying also, handkerchief to her eyes. And about four of the women jurors were openly crying, wiping tears from one eye, then the other.

Finch continued to sob, breathing in heaves. Evans called a recess and the doctor was led from the room by his attorney, through the side exit. A dozen or so spectators were noted to be crying as well.

SATURDAY, FEBRUARY 6, 1960

Dr. R. Bernard Finch was giving a press interview at one of the visitors' desks at the Los Angeles County Jail.

"Sure shakes you up after you relive it," he explained to a group of about ten.

"Were those her exact words, Doctor, her last words?" One asked.

"Yes. She said to me 'I'm sorry, take care of the kids.'" He spoke up so that the two or so reporters at the back of the group could hear. "When you have to describe something terrible like that, it's like reliving it again. You know I was on the stand for three days. It's a lot of tension on the stand. I just broke down. I was okay in about an hour."

MONDAY, FEBRUARY 8, 1960

Finch would be finished with his direct examination by Cooper today, and the prosecution would have its long-awaited chance to cross-examine.

"I walked back up to the garage and sat, sobbing, on the running board of the convertible, on the passenger side of the car," he described. "I checked around for Barbara's belongings. I picked up her purse. Then I thought, 'Maybe she's alive.' I guess I just wanted to believe that she was. I ran back down and examined her again.

"I guess I suddenly panicked. The next thing I knew I was running as fast as I could across the golf course at South Hills Country Club. I don't remember having anything with me. I just remember falling down once. I might have had the purse and the gun with me at that time. I just don't remember. I was in a daze. I don't remember stealing those cars, but I guess I must have. I got back to Las Vegas somehow; the next thing I remember I was asleep at Carole's apartment when the policemen came in and woke me up."

A brief recess was called after Cooper announced he was through questioning his client. The two prosecutors were talking; they had long ago decided Fred Whichello would be the first to question Bernard Finch.

Finch had returned to the defense table for a last-minute conference with his attorney before his cross-examination began. The two stood, Cooper with his right arm around Dr. Finch; he pulled him near, whispering.

Whichello was talking with Crail as the two looked over the list of questions they had prepared. They had discovered what they thought were glaring contradictions in Finch's testimony as compared to the physical evidence. They would focus on these and on their view of his story as an irrational fairy tale, one moment amazingly detailed, another mysteriously obscure.

Many would describe Whichello's cross-examination as tentative and overly-cautious. Most news stories would talk of his inability to keep Finch focused and of the witness's wandering at will through testimony that only helped his own cause.

Fred would eventually ask the doctor to confess to adultery. In a conference in Evans's chambers the day before, Whichello announced he had subpoenad two of Finch's former mistresses; they were to appear in open court and describe the affairs. Cooper suggested the women not be subpoenaed, that it would serve no purpose and, surprising Whichello, said his client would be happy to give details of the affairs under cross-examination and save them the embarrassment.

The mistresses, to be known as "Mrs. X" and "Mrs. Y," were both former employees of the West Covina Hospital and Medical Clinic.

CONVERSATION WITH
WEST COVINA PHYSICIAN

The doctor who employed Mrs. Y after she left the hospital approached me one day.

"They sent investigators out to my office to talk with her," the older doctor told me. "You know, before the trial they asked her about Finch. It was a bad experience for her. They asked if he preferred strange positions or had any perversions, that sort of thing.

"Later we learned she was to be 'on call' as a witness, and that if Finch would agree to admit to the affairs, she didn't have to go."

"Well, I suppose that saved her some embarrassment," I observed.

"Mrs. Y was a nice person. You know she was separated from her husband when she dated Finch; had been for some time. They should have called her 'Miss Y.'" He was taking something out of his wallet. "People got mixed up with that guy because he was a charmer, you know, a good-looking guy who knew what to say." He was now holding a three-inch by five-inch clear plastic envelope in his hand.

It was, I suspected, an icon.

"In fact, they gave me a subpoena, also. I keep it in here. I was just 'on call' like she was." He carefully took the document from the plastic sleeve, unfolding it slowly; it would one time tear at the middle, I thought, but not this time. My friend had indeed been subpoenaed to tell whatever he knew of Mrs. Y. And he had kept the document in his wallet for more than three decades.

So two more mysterious entities were added to the story at this point, Mrs. X and Mrs. Y.

First, Fred would get some more detail from Finch about the early years of his marriage to Barbara Jean.

Whichello: "When you were first married, were you in love with your wife?"

Finch: "Yes, I think we all like to tell ourselves that we are in love when we get married."

Whichello: "Does that mean you have doubts now that you truly were?"

Finch: "Yes, I think it was around 1953 for the first time that I began to have serious doubts."

Whichello: "And that was after the birth of your child, Raymond, Jr. Because of her 'frigidity,' you told us, she was afraid to have relations because of a—I think you said—'fear' of childbirth?"

Finch: "I would say we had a reasonably satisfactory marriage up until after the time or a little before Raymond was born. Until then, we were very much in love. We had only the average personality problems that come up in a marriage, after the honeymoon was over."

Whichello: "There was a honeymoon, then?"

Finch: "Yes. We were married in Las Vegas, and we stayed out there for a little while. It was the second marriage for us both. It was for a few days; I don't recall how many."

Whichello: "And then you moved into your home on Larkhill Street?"

Finch: "No, the home wasn't finished at that time. Actually, I stayed at my former apartment where my telephone arrangements were. Barbara Jean and Patti stayed at their apartment in Covina where they had been living."

Whichello: "You occasionally stayed overnight?"

Finch: "No, never. It would have been inconvenient. The apartment had only one bedroom with two small beds, one for Patti and the other for Barbara Jean. I continued living at my apartment until July of 1953, when our home was finished. It was then we all lived together."

Then the prosecutor asked about Barbara Jean's frigidity and inquired why a woman who would have caesarean sections would be afraid of childbirth.

Whichello: "Was Raymond, Jr., born by caesarean section?"

Finch: "Yes. I assisted another doctor, an obstetrician, in doing the operation."

Whichello: "And was the previous child, Patti, born by C-section as well?" Finch had delivered Patti when Barbara Jean was his patient at the Magan Clinic.

Finch: "No, I don't know."

Whichello: "Well, once there has been a caesarean, it is necessary to have a caesarean with all subsequent pregnancies, isn't it?"

Finch: "Well, not always. It depends."

Whichello: "I see." Whichello had his head tilted back. "Well, why would a woman be afraid of childbirth if she were going to have C-sections all the time, Doctor?"

Finch: "I would say she had a, uh, more of a fear of childbirth than of the C-sections."

Fred waited a moment, checking his notes.

Whichello: "Of course, psychiatry was a part of your training as a doctor?"

Finch: "A very small part, unfortunately. Most doctors," he was looking at the jury, lecturing, "after they are in practice for awhile, begin to realize that many of their patients have overlying emotional problems. All of us as individuals do."

Fred was checking his notes to get the name of the psychologist Finch had mentioned in his direct examination.

Whichello: "I have here the name of a Dr. Miller, a Doctor Vernon Miller, a psychiatrist, I believe. You had talked to him about Barbara?"

Finch: "Yes, not directly about Barbara and I. It was more in the abstract that the subject came up. You see, Barbara's father, Walter, was an alcoholic, and I had asked Vernon to take care of him. I had had Walter in the West Covina Hospital several times. He would dry out and then go on to drink after he got out. I thought maybe Vernon could do some good for him, so we admitted him to a sanitarium in San Gabriel. It was during our discussions about Walter's case that we talked of how Barbara, being a member of his family, might have been affected."

Whichello: "Well, in any event, you had decided that fear of childbirth and this other problem with alcoholism, both of these might have been a factor in her frigidity?"

Finch: "Yes, more or less."

Whichello: "Wouldn't a woman, who had been feeling sexually inadequate," Fred was walking around his table to the jury box rail now, "who, say, had a husband who was being unfaithful, be likely to not want to have relations with him because she was disgusted with him and not want anything to do with him?"

Finch: "Either that or the opposite way; she might want to prove to herself that she was not inadequate."

Whichello: "You, Doctor Finch, were you unfaithful to Mrs. Finch during the years 1953 to 1954?"

Finch: "Oh, yes, I went out with others."

There were several quiet gasps in the courtroom.

Whichello: "When you say 'went out,' you don't mean you went to the theater, or dancing, or to movies do you? You mean you had sexual relations, don't you?" For the first time Fred was at the witness box. Standing to the witness's right, he could look at Dr. Finch when he spoke, then to the jury during an answer or explanation.

Finch: "Yes, I did all of that."

More of a stir rustled through the courtroom, Evans had to quiet the noise with a smack of his gavel. In his initial examination by Cooper, Finch had told of affairs beginning in 1956. Today he was revealing an infidelity almost from the beginning of his marriage; it was the story of Mrs. X and Mrs. Y.

Whichello: "During the years 1953 and 1954 you had such an affair with a lady employed at the Medical Center, didn't you, as early as 1953?"

Finch: "Yes, I did." He showed no guilt, answering in a straightforward manner.

Cooper was on his feet. "Now, wait a minute. We should put the questions being asked in the proper perspective. On direct examination my client testified he did go out with some other girls. We said that already."

Whichello: "Yes, but that was stated as being after 1956. We're talking about 1953 here."

Cooper: "Your Honor, we did have a conversation in chambers in which it was agreed that for the sake of protecting the names of these ladies, we would use names other than their true names and that we would give you their true names. These women are 'Mrs. X' and 'Mrs. Y.'"

The feisty Eagan joined with an opportunity to distance his client from Finch. "You will also recall, Your Honor, that we have objected to this. The Tregoff team had not agreed to the anonymity understanding. It is not admissible in any way, shape, or form to enter evidence in such a secretive fashion, and we would remind the court that this evidence is inadmissible in any way, shape, or form against Miss Tregoff."

Evans had his palms facing the attorneys, nodding his head. "The women will be referred to as indicated by Mr. Cooper and their existence is offered only as to defendant Finch."

Whichello raised his voice for the next question. He was looking directly at Finch.

Whichello: "Well, was that lady, whoever she was, married or not?"

Finch: "Yes."

Whichello: "And how often did you see her—once a day, once a year?"

Finch: "I don't have any figures on that. It wasn't once a day, and it wasn't once a year either."

Whichello: "And where did you meet? In an apartment, or a hotel?"

Finch: "No, usually in the automobiles. We would go to no particular place as I recall, usually lonely roads up in the mountains."

Finch had been observed having romantic interludes in broad daylight on some of the city's streets.

CONVERSATION WITH LOUISA
WEST COVINA RESIDENT

"It was perfectly obvious what they were doing out there. They weren't private about it at all. They stopped on Astelle street in front of my house all the time, usually about lunch time."

Fred had returned to his desk; he was checking the notes from the interview with Mrs. X.

Whichello: "Did you ever meet her anywhere else?" He moved around so that he was standing on Finch's left, so that when Finch talked to him he would have to face the jury. Fred was holding his notes in his left hand, and with his right hand he held a fountain pen, with which he would point to one item or another, prompting himself. He spoke more slowly, almost singing the rest of his question: "Say, in San Francisco?"

Finch: "Well, there was this one occasion when I went to a convention in San Francisco. I got a room and arranged for her to come up, and I saw her at that time."

Whichello: "And...?" He waited. "Well, did sexual relations take place?"

Finch: "Yes." His lips pursed slightly.

Whichello: "Did Mrs. Finch ever discuss that relationship with you?"

Finch: "I believe she did."

Whichello: "And you told her about it, you admitted to her that it had occurred?"

Finch: "No, I don't think I did." He was speaking very slowly, measuring his words.

Whichello: "Did you gain an impression that she knew an employee of the clinic was involved?"

Finch: "Yes."

Fred walked back to his desk and picked up another piece of paper. He turned and asked his next question.

Whichello: "There was another employee, who was getting divorced, with whom a similar affair occurred, was there not?"

Finch: "There was this nurse I went out with from, well, mostly in 1956 and 1957."

Whichello: "Ah, but it was many months prior to 1956. Wasn't it?" He walked quickly back to the stand. "Many months prior to the so-called armistice agreement, wasn't it, that you saw Mrs. Y?"

Finch: "She was divorced. I saw *Miss* Y prior to that time. She had her own apartment, and I would meet her over there. I believe most of the events with Miss Y were over there."

Whichello: "Isn't it true that some of these 'events,' as you call them, took place while she was still married, before she had her own apartment?" He lifted up his heavy glasses and held the paper six inches from his face, looking for the exact dates. The interview with Mrs. Y had been very productive.

Finch: "I don't recall."

Whichello: "She had gone to Mrs. Finch and told her of the affair you two were having. Isn't that true, Doctor?"

Finch: "Yes, there was a time in 1957 when I started going with Carole that Miss Y became disturbed with me. Then in May she talked to Barbara, maybe in July, somewhere in there. She told Barbara she had been going out with me, and she told Barbara about Carole, also."

Whichello: "You told both of these women, Mrs. X and Mrs. Y, that you loved them. Isn't that true?"

Finch: "That would be pretty much routine, I suppose. Under these circumstances I wouldn't doubt that I told them that."

Most journalists recorded a smile on Carole's face at this point.

Whichello: "Now, Mrs. Finch knew both of these women?"

Finch: "Yes, she was an officer in some of the corporations of the clinic. She would visit the clinic occasionally and talk with the employees. Mrs. X had been up to the house on a couple of occasions to get some books out of the library, and Mrs. Y had been up there before with her husband and child to swim in our pool."

Whichello: "And she knew what had been going on with these employees. Isn't that true, Dr. Finch?"

Finch: "Well, I..." He squirmed in his chair and took a deep breath. "I think that she knew what was going on. Yes, I would say so."

Whichello: "And do you think that these affairs had any effect on her being frigid with you?"

Finch: "No, I don't think so." He looked away, to his right, at the exhibit table.

Whichello: "When did this affair with Mrs. X actually start?" He was within inches of Finch; his voice was raised.

Finch: "I believe it started at the Christmas party we had for the office in 1953. It was shortly after the birth of Raymond, Jr."

Quiet buzzes from the crowd would follow most of his answers at this point of his testimony.

Whichello: "And there were other women, weren't there, before then? Isn't that true, Dr. Finch?" He was looking at his notes again.

281

Finch: "I don't recall them." He was still looking at the exhibit table, a scowl having moved onto his face.

Whichello: "Wouldn't that be the sort of thing that would register in someone's mind?"

Finch: "Yes, of course. I meant, I don't think there were any others."

Whichello: "You don't remember them?"

Finch: "Yes, I remember them. I mean there weren't any."

Whichello: "Did Barbara Jean ever say to you, 'I don't want anything to do with you because you are carrying on with other women?'"

Finch: "No."

The courtroom buzzed louder. Evans did nothing; his attention was fixed on the witness. The doctor was glaring at Whichello.

Whichello: "Well, you mean she approved of these affairs? Certainly you are not telling us that she approved of these activities?"

Finch: "Well, after 1956 she did."

Whichello: "What about before that, before 1956? When she knew about Mrs. Y and Mrs. X and the others you weren't able to remember?"

Cooper's objection was sustained.

Whichello: "Well, when was the first time you two talked about these infidelities?"

Finch: "I believe it was in 1956, that was the first time I admitted to her about these activities. She had come to me to talk about Carole."

Whichello: "This was actually before the so-called armistice agreement?"

Finch: "It was like this, I think pretty much it was like this. She would hear of these things and ask me about them, and I would say there was nothing to it, and that would be all that would be said about it."

Whichello: "And then with this armistice agreement you would say that she approved of your infidelities?"

Finch: "Yes, she expected it."

Whichello: "She approved of your unfaithfulness. She expected your unfaithfulness?"

Finch: "Yes, because of her attitude toward me. As I told you before, the problem with Barbara and me was our incompatibility, and it spread into other realms of our marriage. She approved and expected me to have affairs with her stamp of approval on the armistice agreement."

Fred walked away from the witness stand. He turned and stood in front of his table again, ready with his next point.

Whichello: "How old was Miss Tregoff when you began your affair with her?"

Finch: "She was nineteen."

Whichello: "Barbara Jean was thirty-three at that time, in 1956?"

Finch: "Yes."

Whichello: "And you were forty years old, doctor?" His eyebrows were raised.

Finch: "I was thirty-nine."

Whichello: "You don't think the fact that Carole was so much younger than Barbara Jean upset her somewhat?"

Finch: "What do you mean?"

Whichello: "Well, let me put it this way. Didn't your wife ever question you about how young Miss Tregoff was to be your medical secretary?"

Finch: "She may have."

Whichello: "Before this armistice agreement, did your wife ever question you as to your possible relationship with Miss Tregoff?"

Finch: "No, never. Not at all." He seemed more confident now. "Not until she saw us at the grocery store together, as

I had mentioned to you, after the armistice agreement had been reached."

Whichello: "Yes, and you still denied the relationship?"

Finch: "Yes, I told you, Carole did not have such an agreement with Jimmy Pappa, and I didn't want to flaunt the relationship in front of her."

Whichello: "So you lied to your wife?"

Finch: "Yes."

Then Fred detailed a series of deceptions engineered by the witness, including those connected with the renting of apartments.

Whichello: "It became necessary for you to tell untruths to Barbara Jean about your affairs?"

Finch: "Yes."

Whichello: "And you admitted that you told lies to the apartment managers about who you were? You said you were Mr. and Mrs. George Evans?"

Finch: "Well, yes."

Whichello: "And you lied when you said to them you were a salesman?"

Finch: "Well, I was, in a way, I guess."

There was a sprinkle of laughter. Evans, unamused, quickly gaveled.

Whichello: "And you have told us that you affirmatively misrepresented the facts in the reconciliation matter, that you said you wanted to reconcile just to buy time while you built your hospital?"

Finch: "I would say I was insincere in my efforts at reconciliation."

Whichello: "You also affirmatively misrepresented the facts to your marriage counselor. You really did not want to reconcile."

Finch: "That would be true, I suppose."

Whichello: "You also lied to your partner, Dr. Gordon, telling him your marriage would be all right, that he could go ahead and invest with you?"

Finch: "No, he knew what was going on. I didn't have to tell him anything."

It was 4:30 and Evans adjourned court. Whichello had more, but it would wait. Most observers thought the jury was thinking it was Finch's infidelities that led to Barbara Jean's disgust with husband and her so-called frigidity.

TUESDAY, FEBRUARY 9, 1960

As the jury filed into their seats, they noticed Fred Whichello and Grant Cooper were engaged in animated discussion. Cooper, holding his suit's left lapel with his left hand, was pointing at something on it with his right index finger.

The two were discussing William B. McKesson, the District Attorney. McKesson would make frequent appearances at the trial.

"You get him to take it off somehow," Cooper was saying.

"He's my boss," Fred was holding his hands palms up and shaking his head back and forth. "You want me to tell my boss that he can't wear his Shriner's pin in court?"

"Two of the jury are Shriners and his wearing the pin might influence them." Cooper was still jabbing his right index finger at his lapel.

"It's an election year." The morning papers had noted McKesson's announcement he would seek election as District Attorney in November. "He's going to end up wearing a lot of pins, Grant."

"Well, if he doesn't take it off, I'm going to wear mine." Cooper and McKesson were members of the same Shriner's temple.

Judge Evans entered late. He had been on the phone with Los Angeles County Superior Court Presiding Judge Louis H. Burke. Burke thought that the photographic coverage of the trial was getting out of hand. "Photographs of the witnesses as they are giving testimony detracts from the dignity and decorum of the proceedings," he had told the visiting judge from Mono Lake.

"I must ask," Evans began, "that no photographs be taken while court is in session."

The ah's and oh no's were heard over disapointed mumbling. "The press has a right—," someone in the back began.

"It's to preserve decorum. I have no choice," the judge continued. "However, photographs can still be taken in court. You know, when we're not in session."

The disgruntled noises continued until court was convened.

R. Bernard Finch was back on the stand.

Whichello: "As we were recessing yesterday, I believe we were at the point of discussing how you deceived various people—your wife, the landlords of the two apartments you rented, the reconciliation court when you said you wanted to reconcile with your wife, and some of your business partners. May we assume you also deceived your other business associates in the West Covina Hospital and the bank from which you obtained the loan? You gave them the impression that you had a normal and stable marriage?"

Finch: "I kept up the appearance of a normal marriage, yes, sir."

Whichello: "So, is it a fair statement that you are no different from Jack Cody?"

Finch looked confused.

Whichello: "I mean, that the two of you, you know, lied for money, that you would lie for money?"

Finch: "I don't believe so. I believe there was deception on Barbara's part and on my part for financial rewards as well as social and other kinds."

Fred next asked about the marriage plans of Finch and Tregoff.

Whichello: "Could you tell us roughly when the subject first came up?"

Finch: "I can't, I'm afraid. It was sometime after we rented our first apartment and before we rented the second one."

Whichello: "And this was when Miss Tregoff was still married to James Pappa?"

The Pappas were separated eighteen months after the first apartment was rented.

Finch: "Yes. We had a target date of about 1961 to get married, set in our own minds, and we thought things would be worked out so it would be better for everybody concerned."

Whichello: "Was she still having sexual relations with Mr. Pappa during this time?"

Eagan objected and was overruled.

Finch: "I don't think so. She was not. I think she didn't feel that way toward him."

Whichello: "So you are saying that they shared the same house together for a year and a half and didn't have any sexual relations?"

Eagan: "My client's sexual habits are not relevant, Your Honor. The prosecutor is asking these questions as a way to personally attack Miss Tregoff. We object."

Evans: "I think I'll allow it."

Whichello: "You may answer now, Doctor."

Finch: "No, she just didn't feel that way toward him."

Whichello: "And I take it you knew that *she* wasn't frigid?"

Finch: "Yes." He was white, his face was drawn.

Bringgold and Eagan stiffened, sitting straighter. Carole Tregoff fixed her eyes on some papers before her.

Whichello: "Now, you told her that your wife was frigid, did you not?"

Finch: "Certainly."

Whichello: "Did she ever tell you that Jimmy Pappa was frigid?"

Eagan: "I object again, Your Honor. This is hearsay evidence."

Evans: "Overruled."

Whichello: "Well, did she?"

Finch: "No." He glared at the prosecutor.

Fred walked in a circle, from the witness box, to the jury rail, and back. He had tried to show Finch a liar, and Carole a harlot. Now to paint them both as shameless adulterers.

Whichello: "As you were renting this apartment and discussing your marriage plans, did either of you ever suggest that adultery was wrong, and that you might use some self-control and wait until you both had divorces before you had sexual relations?"

Finch: "No."

Whichello: "Were you so desperately in love..." He was facing the jury now; his arms were out straight out to the side, palms up. His head was tilted back. "...that it overcame your feeling in that regard, your moral views?"

Finch: "Partly, that is true. I didn't feel restrained by any moral views at that time. I was perfectly free to come and go as I chose."

Whichello: "You are a religious man?" He was back at the witness box, leaning into it. "Is it your understanding that a wife is free to permit her husband to commit adultery and that makes it all right? You mean it's not adultery if the wife doesn't object?"

Finch: "Yes."

Whichello: "How often would you and Carole meet at the Monterey Park apartment?"

Finch: "Just about every day. We would go there during lunch and meet there sometimes at night."

Whichello: "And yet when Barbara saw you and Carole in front of the grocery store, you denied you were seeing Carole."

Finch: "Yes, I explained that. I didn't want—"

Whichello: "And James Pappa went to Barbara Jean and told him you two were seeing each other. What did you say to Barbara at that time?"

Finch: "That was in September of 1958, a few days after Carole had left Jimmy. She told me to be sure and be discreet if I was going with Carole, according to our agreement."

Whichello: "So you didn't deny it at this time?"

Finch: "She was afraid I was going to leave her the same way Carole had left Jimmy. I told her, I tried to reassure her, that I was not going to leave her like that, just because Carole had."

As part of his attack on Finch's character, Whichello would try to show him as an incompetent physician.

Whichello: "Let's change the subject for a moment. You say you wanted to build the West Covina Hospital because it would be convenient for the patients, that the area needed a hospital. Isn't it true that you were not on any other hospitals' medical staffs, that you needed a place to practice?"

Finch: "Not at all. I was on staff at three other hospitals during the construction of the hospital, and I was Chief of Surgery at Monrovia Hospital."

Whichello appeared confused. He walked to his desk, read from a legal pad, then turned, ready for a different line of questions.

Whichello: "You had told us that at one point you thought you had been being followed by detectives and you asked Barbara about it. At first she had said, 'Could be,' and then later she had actually confirmed that you were being followed?"

Finch: "Yes. She told me she had hired detectives and was having me followed to get information on me and that she might use it some time in the future. She was not definite as to how and when she was going to use it. I did not know that she had seen Mr. Forno and had some discussions with him about a divorce."

Whichello: "Didn't she say that they had learned 'a great deal?'"

Finch: "I don't recall her saying it like that."

Whichello: "In your direct examination by Mr. Cooper you said that she indicated they had learned 'a great deal.'"

Finch: "Well, I think it was something like that, that they had gotten quite a lot of information. I told her that according to the armistice agreement, that's not the way things were supposed to work."

Fred had some questions about the $3,000 check Finch had said his wife had "cried" on after signing it. It was a chance to show the witness was also a forger.

Whichello: "You say she cried on this first check and spoiled it. What was she upset about? Did you ask her?"

Finch: "This was the same day we signed our divorce papers. She was crying all day. She cried on the way back from signing the papers, and she cried when she was signing the papers."

Whichello: "You didn't ask her why she was crying?"

Finch: "No."

Whichello: "She never indicated once why she was crying, she was just crying?"

Finch: "No, she didn't. I think it was just the whole marital situation, it being up in the air. She cried on the first check and spoiled it, so I went and typed out another one and gave that one to her to sign."

Whichello: "Did anybody see her sign it?"

Finch: "There was a girl who worked in the medical center going in and out, but whether she was actually there at the time or not, I don't know."

Whichello: "Have you asked her since as to whether she remembered the incident, this employee?"

Finch: "Mr. Whichello, I have not been able to get out of here to question her." It was the loudest laughter the court had heard so far. It took Evans more than the usual amount of time to get things back to order. "I suggest you ask her. All I know is that she signed the check, and I got it cashed."

WEDNESDAY, FEBRUARY 10, 1960

Fred would continue to pick away at Finch's credibility. There would be a new twist added to the conversations Finch had held in Las Vegas. He would say that he did use the word 'murder' and that he must have been misunderstood. Several times today Finch would be noted with his hands behind his head, leaning back in his chair as though waiting for Whichello to catch up. Occasionally, he would play with the prosecutor, asking if he should repeat an answer so that Fred would understand his meaning.

Whichello: "Why did you think that Carole would be qualified to pick out someone to follow your wife around and gather evidence?"

Finch: "She was as qualified as I was, and I knew there was a market for these kinds of characters in Las Vegas."

Whichello: "You didn't tell your attorney that you were planning this, or that you thought that someone could be found in Las Vegas?"

Finch: "No, I don't believe that I did."

Whichello: "This proposal to find someone with less scruples who might be willing to engage in misconduct himself, you did not tell your attorney that?"

Finch: "I am sure I didn't. There was one other factor in this situation regarding Carole, Mr. Whichello. I did not feel that she would be alone in this matter. I felt she would talk to Don Williams and his brother, Jimmy. You see, Don was like a brother to her, and Jimmy was like a father to them both. Jimmy had worked around town for some time, I think in some hotels, I forget in what capacity, and Don had worked around town as a bellboy at some hotels. They both knew a lot of people."

Whichello: "So you knew them, you had seen them before?"

Finch: "Well, no, I hadn't, but I knew that Don was like a brother to Carole."

Whichello: "Then you subsequently met with Don Williams and gave him a picture of Barbara Jean?"

Finch: "Yes."

Whichello: "And was Williams instructed to give the picture to Cody at that time?"

Finch: "No. I think the possibility of a man to do this job was mentioned, but I don't think the name Cody was mentioned at that time."

Whichello: "Did you ask Williams at one point whether Cody was capable of murder?"

Finch: "Not quite that way. I think the word was mentioned, however. I was concerned about Carole. She was having quite a few contacts with Cody, and I was a little concerned for her sake. I wanted to be sure this type of man wasn't dangerous to that extent. I knew he had a questionable reputation and was not beyond acting as a gigolo if necessary."

Whichello: "Not so fast, Doctor. Let's back up a bit. You said the word 'murder' was used then?"

Finch: "I said I thought I asked Williams what kind of a character is this Cody. Is he a gangster, murderer, or what kind of morals has the man?"

Whichello: "Then you did ask if he was capable of murder?"

Finch: "No. I think Don immediately assured me he wasn't that way at all, that he was just what he pretended to be."

Whichello: "You first met Cody on July 8?"

Finch: "Yes."

Whichello: "And what was your impression of him?"

Finch: "I thought he was capable of exactly what I had hired him for. I had no doubts about his ability to do this. He convinced me he was a ladies' man and had been working on a case similar to mine."

Whichello: "You actually think that this two-bit hood-lum could actually pick up your wife and actually have sexual relations with her?"

Finch: "Yes, my feeling was I thought Barbara was having an affair with someone else. Just because she was frigid toward me doesn't mean she was frigid toward everybody else in the world."

Whichello: "What made you think she would even talk to this sort of man?"

Finch: "I don't know whether she would have or not."

Whichello: "And you were going to use this man as your witness in a divorce case?"

Finch: "I wasn't considering him so much as a person; I just wanted the facts he was going to gather for me."

Whichello: "And you never once heard Carole say that she would be glad when Mrs. Finch was 'out of the way.'"

Finch: "No, never."

Whichello walked to the exhibit table and looked at the attaché case with its items, the "murder kit."

Whichello: "This emergency kit you told us about, it was sort of an innovation in your line, was it not, a novel idea?"

Finch: "Yes."

Whichello: "You got along just fine for sixteen years without one."

Finch: "It was...I hadn't used this before, no. It was to be a convenience."

Whichello: "Do you know any other doctor who has such an emergency kit separate from his regular bag?"

Finch: "Yes. I think several regular doctors carry special surgical bags. This was to be a combination of a surgical bag and the emergency kit for poisoning."

Whichello: "This was a new idea. You hadn't heard of it specifically before?"

Finch: "I wasn't copying anyone, from any others I had seen."

Whichello: "Well, what I don't quite understand," he was walking back to the witness box now, "is this carrying the case around in your car as you accumulated articles in it. Why was it not left in the medical center and articles put in it from time to time?"

Finch: "I was parking my car right back of the center, and had it centrally located where it would be easy to throw things in it. Also, it wasn't ready to use, and if I left it around someplace, people would take things out of it, and it just wouldn't get assembled."

Whichello then began leading up to the night of the murder, first by asking about the reasons the two had for going to West Covina.

Whichello: "Now as you were talking to Mrs. Pappa in Las Vegas, before you two drove back to West Covina, you came up with this plan for talking Barbara Jean into a divorce?"

Finch: "Yes, the plan of going back to West Covina and for Carole to talk to Barbara Jean and convince her to come to Las Vegas and get a six-week divorce. We discussed it at the Sands Friday night."

Whichello: "So this plan of convincing Barbara Jean to come and get a six-week divorce, that was specifically discussed by both of you?"

Finch: "Yes. We were going to try to convince Barbara that was the right thing to do."

Whichello: "Why did you need Mrs. Pappa to be there?"

Finch: "So there wouldn't be any false accusations. My attorney, Glen Martineau, told me not to go near Barbara without anyone with me after the incident when I tried to trade the cars. That wasn't the only reason. Carole thought that she could persuade Barbara she would be better off if she would quit heckling me and get a property settlement made out of court."

Whichello: "And you thought Mrs. Pappa would be the logical person to be this persuader?"

Finch: "Yes. I suppose there might have been others more logical, but they were not present, and we wanted to do it that weekend."

Whichello: "You had to do it that weekend, you didn't want to wait until Monday?"

Finch: "No, I wanted to come back to Las Vegas and get a place for Barbara, to establish her residence."

Whichello: "Now, when you telephoned Mrs. Finch, Saturday morning, before you drove down, you told her you and Carole wanted to talk to her about this new plan you two had?"

Finch: "Yes."

Whichello: "Did she say, 'Oh that's very fine. I'll be happy to see Carole?'"

Finch: "I don't recall her saying that."

Whichello: "Or did she act the opposite way, seem a little cool?"

Finch: "She, as I recall, was a little indefinite about whether she wanted to see us or not at all. She said that if I wanted, I could call her back."

Whichello: "Now by this time, Mrs. Finch knew of your affair with Mrs. Pappa, and you thought that had no bearing on the tact or tactlessness of bringing her along to discuss these matters?"

Finch: "Yes, I thought she would be more likely to talk to Carole and me than to just me alone."

Whichello: "So you left on this six-hundred-mile round trip without really knowing for sure if Barbara Jean would talk with you or not?"

Finch: "Yes."

Whichello: "And when you got there, you waited for Mrs. Finch to return home?"

Finch: "We didn't just wait; all sorts of little things happened. I walked up the hill after telling Carole to wait in the car and was returning when I saw her coming up after me carrying the attaché case. I started to do other little things. We played with the dog for a little bit. I got some rope out of the garage to use for my boat a little later. We were going to go into the house, but these other things just happened. Our intention was not to wait outside for her."

Whichello: "You expected Marie Anne to just let you in so that you could come in and wait. Is that what you are saying?"

Finch: "Certainly."

Whichello: "But you never did go in." Finch: "No."

Whichello: "Why didn't you just drive up your own driveway and park there? Why did you park in the parking lot of the South Hills Country Club?"

Finch: "We had tried that once before, to talk to her, and she just turned around and drove away. We were afraid that she would see us and just drive away."

Whichello: "Or the driveway of your father's house—you could have parked there, couldn't you?"

Finch: "I didn't want to disturb my Dad, he's seventy-seven-years old you know, and my mother is ill, too."

Whichello: "And you told us that when Mrs. Finch drove up the driveway, you were still playing with the dog?"

Finch: "Yes, I had blown up one of the rubber gloves and the dog had torn it up. I was in the process of blowing up the other one when Barbara came home. We were standing on the edge of the blacktop."

Whichello: "And then what did you do?"

Finch: "I helped Carole stand up. She had been sitting on the attaché case; we started walking into the garage."

Whichello: "Did it occur to either of you that your appearance at this hour, shortly before midnight, might startle Mrs. Finch?"

Finch: "Oh, no. I knew she would see me. Where I was standing was brightly lighted."

Whichello: "And then you said to Barbara, 'We want to talk to you?'"

Finch: "Yes, and she said, 'Well I don't want to talk to you.' That's when she reached into the car, and I looked at Carole like 'What's our next move?'"

Whichello: "And that's when she unzipped the shaving-kit and took out the gun?"

Finch: "No, actually I think she had the gun in her purse. It was a large, white purse."

Whichello: "And you told us you saw Barbara with the gun and lunged into her. I believe you demonstrated that on Mr. Cooper?"

Finch: "Yes."

Whichello: "And about that time you reached in and got the shaving-kit?"

Finch: "Yes."

Whichello: "What occasioned you to look into the car at a time like that?"

Finch: "I don't know; I just saw it. My face was about at the level of the floor of the car. I had the gun held up with one hand and I reached in the car to grab the shaving-kit. I thought there might have been another gun in it. I jiggled it around and something was in it and I just picked it up. I wanted to find out what was in it."

Whichello: "You wanted to find out what was in it and at the same time you were frightened it was a gun?"

Finch: "Yes, I wanted to find out what was in it."

Whichello: "Even if it were another gun, did you think Mrs. Finch could get at it?"

Finch: "Not then, but perhaps later. If she had pulled one gun on me, why not another?"

Whichello: "So then you threw it to Mrs. Pappa?"

Finch: "Yes, she was about an arm's length away. I threw it to her while I was still holding Barbara with the force of my body against the car."

Whichello: "Was she struggling?"

Finch: "Probably she was, but she was not very successful. My body weight was pinning her against the car. I stepped back so that I could get both hands on the gun. I tried to talk to her. I said, 'Barbara, please, please put down the gun.' She was trying to bite my arm and to stomp my feet with her heels, and all the time she was trying to pull the gun up into my face. Then she tried to hit me with her knee, so I turned sideways so she couldn't do that. I just lost my balance about then and fell backwards. I jerked the gun up to get it away as I was falling, and that's what made her hit her head against the wall."

Whichello: "Did this occur near the door of the car?"

Finch: "This was happening near the little passageway near the door to the garage. We were weaving around. I suppose that she could have hit her head against the car door. Then I was able to jerk the gun away from her."

Whichello: "Where was she when you jerked the gun away from her?"

Finch: "She was in a half-sitting position on the floor."

Whichello: "Once you had the gun, surely you could have kept it away from her without resorting to breaking her skull?"

Finch: "It was a case of keeping Barbara out of the scene of the fight so that I would not have two people to contend with. I heard footsteps, remember, and knew that somebody was coming."

Whichello: "Why didn't you just throw the gun out of the garage, through the door."

Finch: "I threw it to the floor—!" His voice was rising, half shouting.

Whichello: "That was after you hit her. Why didn't you throw it out the door right away?"

Finch: "Because Barbara could have got up and gone over and picked it up."

Fred appeared to have lost his place in the questioning. He walked to his desk and checked some notes. Ryan and Crail helped him.

Whichello: "Would you say that the blow with the gun butt was the blow that broke her skull?"

Finch: "Are you asking me?" He was pointing to himself with his left index finger. "You want my opinion? Well, yes, I think the one with the gun handle fractured her skull. The other injuries were against the wall or the floor."

Whichello: "Now, you hit her because you thought Marie Anne was coming into the garage with a rifle, is that right?"

Finch: "Yes."

Whichello: "You didn't really think that Marie Anne would shoot you with the rifle once she saw you, once she knew it was you, did you?"

Finch: "Certainly. She might if she saw me standing there with a gun in my hand."

Whichello: "But you had dropped the gun."

Finch: "No, I hadn't. I was standing above Barbara and I hit her with the gun. And if I was standing there when Marie

Anne came in with the rifle, I would have had to take a shot at Marie Anne. So I dropped the gun so I could disarm her."

Whichello: "Didn't you want to wait and see if she had a gun or not before you attacked her?"

Finch: "No. I didn't."

Whichello: "You slammed Marie Anne's head into the wall instead of making an effort to divert a long, clumsy rifle?"

Finch: "Yes. I didn't want to give her time to fire it. I just grabbed her by the arms to pin them down."

Whichello: "Marie Anne says that you grabbed her by the head."

Finch: "I have only the recollection that I grabbed her by the arms. I think Marie Anne phrased it well when she said that everything happened very fast."

Whichello: "She also phrased it well when she said you hit her head against the wall several times."

Finch: "Her head only hit the wall once. I don't think she knew much of anything because she began to fall down."

Whichello: "And she said you turned the light switch off."

Finch: "I may have hit it with my elbows during the struggle. That's possible."

The afternoon papers were full of reports that Finch was "on top" of the cross-examination and that Whichello appeared to be confused many times, asking inappropriate questions and failing to follow up with questions that many thought might have cornered the witness or caught him in a lie.

At the end of the day, a strategy meeting took place at the defense table. Cooper had moved his chair so that he was sitting facing Finch. Rexford Eagan had his back to the prosecutors. He was standing, leaning into the huddle, as was Bringgold, who stood behind Finch. Carole stayed in her chair, talking to her stepmother.

In addition to other things, the group continued their discussions of whether Carole should take the stand.

THURSDAY, FEBRUARY 11, 1960

Clifford Crail, Fred Whichello, and William Ryan were having their usual morning strategy session. On the table in front of them: the morning's *L. A. Times*, critical of Fred's "hesitant, kid gloves" approach to Finch. Many wondered why he hadn't followed up on the discrepancies between Finch's story and the physical evidence. For instance, the smeared blood stains on the passenger side of the roof would have indicated that he had carried Barbara Jean around the back of the car, as Marie Anne observed. Also, if the surgeon's gloves had been used to play with the family dog, why was the package of powder, used to make putting on the gloves easier, opened? And how did a torn latex finger tip get inside Barbara Jean's car?

Fred would harden. His surprise weapon for the day, next to the *Times* edition, was a single reel of recording tape.

Grant Cooper noticed the reel. He looked at it, then at the men talking, then back at the reel, then over to his client, who was studying a photograph with a magnifying glass. Others noticing the tape thought it may have been one made by detectives working for Barbara Jean Finch, and that it might contain recordings of conversations between the two defendants; it was not.

Whichello: "Dr. Finch, I had asked you why you didn't throw the gun away when you heard footsteps and your wife was becoming unconscious. Why did you drop it to the floor where it would be again available to your wife as she regained consciousness?"

Finch: "I just dropped it on the way to Marie Anne."

Whichello: "You could have stuck it in your belt or your pocket, or you could have hurled it out the door. And if you dropped it, as you say you did, did it not occur to you that it might go off?"

Finch: "No, I just dropped it to get rid of it. It would slow me down; I just dropped it to the floor."

Whichello: "Now, Marie Anne said that when she came into the garage, Mrs. Finch was lying on her back, face up, with her head about even with the car door, her head was pointed east, toward the house, and her feet were toward the garage door. Do you agree with that?" He was pointing to the diagram of the house and grounds that he had picked up from the exhibit table.

Finch: "Yes, I would say so."

Whichello: "What was your opinion of how badly Mrs. Finch was injured at this time?"

Finch: "I didn't think she was hurt very badly. There was no sign of a cut on her head. She didn't get completely unconscious; I just thought she was stunned."

Whichello: "Well, why didn't you just get out of there right then and there?"

Finch: "I don't know what you mean."

Whichello: "Well, both women were out of the picture, as you say. The gun was away from both of them. You could have simply left." Fred was at the witness box, leaning in. "I mean, why didn't you leave?"

Finch: "No, it didn't enter into my mind to leave at that point. Marie Anne was still dazed. She might have needed medical attention, so I went over and examined her."

Whichello: "From your knowledge of the blow you struck on your wife, didn't you have an opinion she would require some medical attention?"

Finch: "I didn't know."

Whichello: "You weren't staying there to give her any medical attention." He leaned into the box again. "So I ask you again. Why didn't you just leave?"

Finch: "I had no reason to leave."

Whichello: "You had no reason to leave?" He walked over to the jury box. "Well then, tell us, what reason did you have to stay?"

Finch: "Just the original reason."

Whichello: "Did you think after all this that your wife was coming to and would discuss the divorce case?"

Finch: "Once these events started to happen, there wasn't much time to think about anything."

Whichello: "Is your answer that you think you could have gone on and discussed the divorce?"

Finch: "I didn't think. I did not have a closed mind one way or the other."

Whichello: "Well, weren't you," he was looking at the jury as he spoke, "trying to avoid further difficulties?"

Finch: "Yes, of course."

Whichello: "Well, why didn't you just leave?"

Finch: "I didn't have time to sit down and think this over. Things were just going too fast."

Whichello: "When you went over to help Marie Anne, you picked up the gun. Why did you do that?"

Finch: "I told you. I went over to help Marie Anne, to check her for any injuries. I wanted to put her in the back seat of the car where it would be more comfortable. I picked up the gun on the way over to keep it out of circulation, to keep it in my possession."

Whichello: "For what purpose? For any particular purpose?"

Finch: "Just to keep it out of circulation, that's all."

Whichello: "Wouldn't that have been a good time to put it in your belt or pocket, or to have thrown it out the door?"

Finch: "I didn't want to."

Whichello: "You wanted to keep it in your hand? For what?"

Finch: "No particular purpose. I just picked it up to keep Barbara Jean from getting her hands on it again."

Whichello: "But she tried to grab it from you anyway?"

Finch: "Yes, just as Marie Anne and I reached the car. As I recall, Marie Anne was just pushing the door open and starting to get in when Barbara Jean grabbed me. I jerked my hand away and the gun went off."

Whichello: "Was the gun pointed out the door? There were no bullet holes inside the garage so it must have been pointed out the door."

Finch: "I don't know. My first thought was to check Barbara and see if there was a hole in her. I looked at her, and she had fallen back down. She was looking at me and didn't say anything, so I didn't think she was shot."

Whichello: "Then you helped Barbara get to her feet."

Finch: "Yes. I looked back at Barbara. That's when I saw blood coming from her ear. I called to Carole for help. She didn't answer, so I walked to the garage door and called again. Then I went back to Barbara and told her to get into the car. She sat up, but her legs wouldn't work, so I helped her down in the driver's side of the front seat. She slid over to the other side. I called for Carole again—still no answer."

Whichello: "She never stopped behind the steering wheel?"

Finch: "No, she just slid over and put her purse in her lap."

Whichello: "Again, you had another chance to throw the gun outside the door?"

Finch: "It didn't occur to me to do that." His voice was raised.

Whichello: "Ah, so instead it occurred to you to put it on the seat between you and Barbara Jean?" He spoke in sarcastic tones.

Finch: "Well, I had to do something with it. I had to grab ahold of her wrists to keep her under control, so I just put the gun on the seat between us."

Whichello: "So, you say she fought like a tiger when you got it away from her before, and you put it down right next to her. Is that what you are saying? Could you have put it on the other side of you, or on the floor?"

Finch: "Well, I suppose so."

Whichello: "Then you got the key?"

Finch: "I grabbed Barbara Jean by the wrist and held it tight. I asked her for the key. Then I turned and called for Carole, one last time. When I looked back, Barbara wasn't making any motion toward getting the key."

Whichello: "Why did you want that key?"

Finch: "So I could drive to the hospital and get help for them."

Whichello: "You didn't want the key for any other purpose? To, say, prevent anyone from escaping in the car?"

Finch: "No, of course not! Absolutely not!"

Whichello: "Then you saw the key in the ignition?"

Finch: "Yes. I let go of her wrist to take hold of the key. It wouldn't come out of the switch, so I leaned over to see which way it was turned. That's when Barbara got the gun and was gone out of the car."

Whichello: "You couldn't prevent her from getting the gun?"

Finch: "No. By the time I realized what had happened, she was at the back of the car. I wanted to get the car in between Barbara and me, so I got out and went to the front of the car. That's when she was jumping up and down pointing the gun at me."

Whichello: "She was pretty thoroughly recovered from the head injury at that time. She had at least one skull fracture at that time, is that true?"

Finch: "That is true."

305

Whichello: "Then she went out."

Finch: "Yes. About the time Marie Anne sat up in the car, Barbara took off. I was worried about Carole so I followed her out."

Whichello: "Then you say you saw Barbara Jean with the gun pointed at you again?"

Finch: "Yes. I went down the driveway and saw her pointing the gun back up the driveway. She was holding it with both hands. I ran over to her and she saw me and started to point the gun at me again. I lunged for the gun and knocked it out of her hands."

Whichello: "Then you said she tried to get the gun back? You said you were a couple of feet ahead of her. Why didn't you just scoop the gun away? You could have scooped it and had it go down this hill toward your father's house?" He was pointing on the drawing of the house again.

Finch: "I didn't think to do that. I didn't make any particular choice; I just did what came naturally."

Whichello: "And it came naturally to you to pick it up and throw it back-handed, as you have demonstrated for us, and that's when the gun went off. Is that correct?"

Finch: "Yes."

Whichello: "Didn't you wonder if Barbara Jean had been hit? Surely you wondered if she had been shot?"

Finch: "I don't remember."

Whichello: "You don't remember. Well, did she fall at that time. Do you remember that?"

Finch: "Yes. She didn't fall at that time. I just remember walking over to the edge of the garage to see if Carole was down there. I saw a white dress out of the corner of my eye, moving down the steps to my Dad's house."

Whichello: "Then you saw her fall?"

Finch: "I saw the white dress crumple. She fell just as I was at the head of the steps; that's when I went down to her."

Whichello: "You didn't know she was shot at this time?"

Finch: "No, I didn't."

Whichello: "Then as I understand it, you talked with your wife and after she had died you had this, this panic start up. But this panic didn't set in for some time, did it? You went back up to the car and picked up some of her things. Can you tell the rest of us the reason you left her there. Is there any reason you didn't pick her up and carry her to one of the houses, instead of just leaving her there like a dead animal?"

Cooper's objection was overruled. By now Finch was pale and shaken. He was speaking quickly now, no longer relaxed as he had been for the previous four days.

Finch: "I didn't think of that; I wasn't thinking."

Whichello: "So then," he was back at his desk, reading from the transcripts of the direct examination by Cooper, "You went back to the garage and got her purse and put her things into it. Why did you do that?"

Finch: "I don't know, just automatic. No reason."

Whichello: "And when you re-checked her and determined that she was dead, that was when you panicked and you ran. It seems that after this second check of her, your memory sort of shuts off, sort of like an electric current, doesn't it?"

Whichello was at the side of his desk, looking down at the eight-inch reel of magnetic tape. Dr. Finch looked at the tape, then back at the prosecutor.

Finch: "Yes."

Whichello: "Now, you hadn't done anything wrong at this point? According to you, there had merely been an unfortunate accident."

Finch: "No."

Whichello: "Then please tell us what in the world panicked you about an unfortunate accident. What were you afraid of?"

307

Finch: "Just a complete block of all thinking. I was not thinking from then on. I was completely unaware. I don't know. I can't remember anything for about six hours."

Whichello: "You remember nothing until the next day in Las Vegas? A complete block. Except that you think you must have been the person who stole all those cars."

Finch: "Yes."

The prosecutor walked over to the jury and looked at them as he asked his next question.

Whichello: "You made up this whole touching death scene in order to avoid the implication that you willfully murdered and left a dying woman on the lawn. Isn't that the case?"

Finch: "No, sir," he was yelling now, half-standing, "that's not the case. It's not true. That's absolutely false—every word of it."

The noon recess was called after Cooper strenuously objected to what he thought was the badgering of his client. Court was reconvened at 1:00 P.M.

Whichello: "Dr. Finch, you told us before the recess about this little conversation you and Mrs. Finch had as you watched her die, when she told you she was sorry and a few other things. Is that still your testimony?"

Finch: "Yes." He was watching Whichello walk back to his desk. Fred picked up the reel of tape, set it on an inch-thick stack of bound paper. Then he carried both items, slowly, to the witness box.

Whichello: "Well in that case I'd like to ask you some questions about the statements you made to Clark County sheriff's deputies and to Captain Ryan and Chief Allen Sill on the day you were arrested. I have here the tape recording made of those conversations, and a typed and certified transcript."

Finch: "Those..." His eyes were wide, his face ashen. "Those were taken without my knowledge." Whichello was walking to Evans, exhibits held high.

Cooper was already on his way to inspect the evidence. "That's hitting below the belt. We didn't know they—"

There was no "discovery" at the time. Prosecutors could gather evidence, telling the defense what they had as it was entered at trial. The transcript of the tape recording was allowed into evidence.

"I have a copy for you here, Grant." Whichello was at his desk again, handing Cooper his copy. The murmur in the courtroom was loud; Evans slammed his gavel several times.

Cooper said nothing as he took it. As a defense attorney, his sense of fair play was violated. He was to be President of the County Chapter of the State Trial Lawyers' Association the following year and would work to institute new legal canons to prevent such—as he saw it, unfair—tactics

Whichello: "Well, let's see." He stood straighter, his eyebrows raised in an ah-hah expression. "First I would like, Your Honor, to read some of the defendant's statements. You do," he was looking at Finch, "remember talking to the detectives that day and night, don't you, Doctor?"

Finch: "Yes." He spoke softly, looking at Cooper.

Whichello: "I would like to read into the record this series of questions, Your Honor:

> 'Question: Are you aware of how your wife died?
> Answer: I only know she died in a scuffle; I know that for sure.
> Question: How did you know she was dead?
> Answer: I didn't know it until I got here.
> Question: In other words, the only indication you have that she died is what you have heard since you have been here?
> Answer: I knew she was dead when I got here, at the station.

Question: Before that, before you got to Las Vegas, you didn't know that she was dead?

Answer: No.

Question: Do you know, have you heard, how she died? Do you know by what means she died?

Answer: No, she had been shot. I heard over the radio that she had been shot.

Question: Did you know that she had been shot, before?

Answer: Well, I think they did say that over the radio. The last twenty-four hours I just don't remember. Pieces seem to come through to me about everything. I am beginning to recollect things as they happened. I promise you, I will talk to you as soon as my lawyer says it is okay.'"

Whichello looked up suddenly.

Whichello: "You didn't know she was dead until after you returned to Las Vegas, did you?"

Finch: "I didn't know much of anything then; I was completely confused. I didn't remember anything when I got to Las Vegas."

Whichello: "Isn't it true that, as you told the officers, you didn't know your wife was dead, that you made up the whole death scene, with its touching words?"

Finch: "I told you, 'No.' I didn't make it up!" He was yelling; his face red, angry.

Whichello: "Just a couple of more items in here." He was slowly reading from his transcript again.

"'Question: You don't want Carole to get mixed up in this, do you? Too deeply mixed up in this if we can keep her out of it?

Answer: No, of course not.

310

Question: I mean she can sit in a bad light. She was quite nice with us and by the same token we are trying to be as nice as we possibly can and I don't think we want to put her in the middle of this.

Answer: No, we don't want her in the middle of this, but she is capable of facing up to questions, to anything you might ask her. I can't say any more about her part in this. I did hear something on the radio, something that she said to the police.'

"Now this radio that you heard some news on, was that a radio in the car, or a radio in jail?"

Finch: "I recall it was a radio in the jail and that Carole told somebody that we went to West Covina to talk about a divorce."

Whichello: "Do you feel," he was at the witness box, leaning in, "that you have an ethical regard for the truth?" He paused, then continued; his eyes were locked with Finch's. It was the last series of questions he would ever ask the defendant. "And for telling the truth?"

Finch: "Mr. Whichello." His confidence seemed to have returned, he looked his nemesis in the eye as he spoke. After a deep breath: "I am up here fighting for my life and liberty. I know this also, maybe Carole's also. The only armament I have is the truth, God willing. I hope that may assure that I am not convicted. I was and am telling you the truth on this witness stand."

Whichello: "Are you still in love with Miss Tregoff?"

Finch: "Yes."

Whichello: "And if the result of this trial permits it, and if her divorce is final, do you plan to marry her immediately?"

Carole leaned forward, her right hand at her chin.

Finch: "Well, some time in the future, if Carole will have me." He looked at her until Fred spoke.

Whichello: "Is that your answer?"

311

Finch: "I have answered the question."

Whichello: "Would you shade or distort the truth to help her or yourself in anyway?"

Finch: "I haven't done that, and I would not dare."

Bernard Finch was through with his testimony and cross-examination. Another sensational item, the "secret tapes," would be added to the litany in the afternoon papers and newscasts.

Whichello seemed, to some, to have been trying to show the doctor had no knowledge of his wife's death until he had returned to Las Vegas, hearing about it on the radio while in custody; he also would have learned Marie Anne remembered seeing him. The death scene story, then, would have been fabricated as part of his defense. More believable to others: he had known she was dead, even methodically determined death, taking her jewelry, then calmly returning to get her purse from the car, simulating a burglary.

There were still some unanswered questions for those convinced of Finch's guilt. For instance, did he think Marie Anne would, as a result of her head injury, forget seeing him? Or did he think she never recognized him?

Finch returned to his seat next to Cooper. He had been on the witness stand for eight days, looked haggard, and was slouching noticeably. He and Cooper began looking over the transcript of the Las Vegas interrogation. Evans announced court would not be in session the next day. Lincoln's Birthday was an official county holiday.

Robert Neeb had come to court after the noon recess. He had been asked by Don Bringgold to meet with the group. Whether or not Carole would take the stand in her own defense would have to be decided by Monday, when Cooper's defense was expected to conclude. It was arranged that the jury room of the courthouse would be available to them the following day. They would meet there and decide.

Neeb was trying to get around the dozen or so reporters who blocked his way from the courtroom.

"Is she going to?" one asked. "Is Carole going to take the stand?"

"We haven't decided," he announced. He gave up trying to get past the crowd and decided to answer some questions. "It is a very serious decision that an attorney must make as to whether his client would be best served by their testifying."

"Finch testified for himself. Shouldn't Carole?" another posed.

"He is a seasoned witness, having testified in numerous medical cases as a medical expert. Our client, on the other hand is innocent, innocent of legal affairs."

"Isn't she the only one who can support Bernie's story that they went to West Covina to discuss a divorce?" a reporter in the back asked.

Neeb was trying to get by them again. "We'll have an answer for you by Monday, as well as some other witnesses we have yet to announce. And no," he knew their next question, "I'm not going to tell you who they are, except that there are three of them and they're flying in from Las Vegas to testify on Monday."

The weekend news was full of references to the "three mystery witnesses" coming from Las Vegas.

ten

Witnesses for the Defense of Carole Anne Tregoff

MONDAY, FEBRUARY 15

THE USUAL GROUP of reporters was waiting at the front of the courtroom's center aisle. No attorneys or defendants had arrived.

"I think," said one, "Whichello figures that Finch never knew she was dead until he got back to Las Vegas; you know, he just took a shot at her and ran for it. Me, I figure it like this: he did know she was dead. I mean if he was calm enough to take her watch and ring and go back and get her purse, then he would have been calm enough to check her to see if she was dead. Then he hoped it would look like a burglary."

"Well, why didn't he find Carole and go back with her? That's what I don't understand," another asked.

"I figure he may have been trying," he answered, pointing his pen at the questioner, "but when Marie Anne came back out with his stepdaughter, Patti, well that's when he drew the line, that's when he just plain ran for it. Figuring later he could just say Marie Anne had it out for him, you know that she was making it up that he was there, or hoping she might have amnesia from her head wounds or something, or maybe even that she didn't recognize him in the dark. But when Carole blew his story in Las Vegas by saying she had driven him to West Covina, well, that was it, no more it-must-have-been-a-burglary story."

"I think," said the first reporter, "he was probably going to kill them both—the maid, too—till Patti came outside. That way no witnesses at all to worry about."

They then seminared on the topic for the day: Who were the mystery witnesses and would Carole Tregoff take the stand?

The reporter from West Covina spotted a familiar face on the right side of the courtroom. Sitting in an aisle seat, four rows back, was a muscular man, about five feet, ten inches tall, with thick, dark, short hair. His right leg was crossed over his left, and his left hand hid part of his face. The sleeve of his suit jacket fell partway down a thick, hairy forearm. And his gaze was fixed on the still vacant chairs behind the defense table.

"Hey." The reporter whispered loudly as he turned to walk. Two others followed him.

"Are you going to be a witness, Jimmy?" the West Covina newsman asked.

"No, not that I know of. I'm just here as a spectator. And I'm wondering how they're going to react when they see me here." He was looking at the empty chairs behind the defense table. Jimmy Pappa was a construction worker, famous locally as a body builder. It was his first appearance at the trial.

The reporters glanced quickly at each other. "Do you still have feelings for Carole, Jimmy?"

"No, of course not." He looked off to his right and then back at the chairs. "I'm just a spectator here. I washed my hands of Carole a long time ago."

The reporter farthest from Jimmy shuffled back a half step, then spoke as he wrote in his notebook. "Is it true that you and Carole had, uh, well, you know, no marriage in, uh, fact, when she was seeing Dr. Finch? You know what I mean."

He glanced at the reporter for only a moment, then back to the front of the courtroom. "I'd rather wait, uh, I'd rather not say right now."

"Are you planning to be a witness for Whichello, Jimmy?" The newspaper man from West Covina was talking again. "Has the prosecution asked you to testify?"

Judge Evans was calling the court to order. Jimmy did not answer the question. He would watch court this morning with little emotion in his face. Most of the time he was watching Carole. At the midmorning recess Fred Whichello would call him up to the prosecutor's desk and talk to him with Clifford Crail and William Ryan.

Robert Neeb, senior counsel for Miss Tregoff, would be in charge of her defense today. Only two of the "mystery witnesses" were called to the stand.

A bartender from the Sands hotel, Robert Trousdale, said he had known Dr. Finch for quite some time, and that in early June was introduced by him to a man named Jack Cody.

"He just walked right up, ordered a Scotch for this guy, and told me his name was Cody, Jack Cody. Didn't appear they were hiding anything to me."

Terry Kent was a cocktail waitress at the Sands Hotel and lived in the same apartment building as did Carole, on Desert Inn Drive.

"I had a bunch of my friends over one night in June for cocktails and dinner. Dr. Finch and Carole came. They introduced me to this weird-looking guy named Cody. They said he was doing some work for them, something about Mrs. Finch."

eleven

Testimony of Carole Anne Tregoff

Evans was watching Neeb, Bringgold, and Eagan, huddled; as he watched, a hush fell upon the room.

"Any more witnesses for you, Mr. Neeb?" he said after the men appeared to have finished.

Jerry Giesler also gave young lawyers advice concerning when to have clients take the stand in their own defense: "I wait till the last minute, to see what kind of case the prosecution has. If I think we might lose and that he has a case that may stand up during appeal, I put the defendant on the stand."

Neeb leaned down and whispered something to Carole Tregoff. She took a deep breath and nodded, looking all the time at the desk in front of her. Finch was sitting up straight, looking at Evans.

"Yes, Your Honor, we call Carole Anne Tregoff." The room filled with oh's and ah's as she walked to the stand. She was wearing her usual checkered dress and a plain white sweater.

Crail and Whichello studied her as she stood, being sworn. As experienced prosecutors, they were used to noticing every twitch, facial expression and body movement for clues to the strengths or weaknesses of a witness. Carole's expressive face would make it all the easier.

Tall and well-proportioned, she had been moderately successful as a local model. Many photographers sought her for her photogenic face. During the trial she would oblige most requests for a pose. Every photograph of her, whether from a modeling job or the trial, shows a different emotion, a different face, always something; Carole Tregoff had no "masks." Her fears and hopes and disappointments were written on her face.

As she lowered into the chair, it was noticed her face was pale and drawn. The sides of her mouth turned down; the cords in her neck were just visible. She looked at Finch, who was smiling and nodding at her. Her parents were in their usual place, two rows back on the right, behind her three attorneys who were having a last-minute conference.

She would be directly examined only by Neeb. His questioning would be brief. His chief objective was to corroborate the story of the two defendants' intention only to talk to the victim about an "amicable divorce."

He walked up to the witness stand with a tight smile on his face. His client's mouth was drawn back slightly more; her eyes seemed to draw together. He spoke slowly.

Neeb: "Miss Tregoff, did you at any time in the month of July, or did you at any other time, enter into any understanding with Raymond Bernard Finch or Jack Cody or any other person to kill Mrs. Raymond Bernard Finch?"

Tregoff: "Absolutely not!" She cleared her throat.

Neeb: "Did you on any occasions have conversations in Las Vegas, conversations with one Jack Cody?"

Tregoff: "Yes, sir."

Neeb: "I am referring now just to conversations in Nevada with this person you know as Jack Cody, you understand?"

Tregoff: "Yes, I understand."

Neeb: "Did you at any time have any conversations with Jack Cody in which you asked him to come to Los Angeles to kill Mrs. Barbara Finch or to do her any physical harm or violence?"

Tregoff: "I did not."

Neeb: "I will direct your attention to the date of July 18, 1959, and will ask you this. Did you on or about July 18 kill Mrs. Bernard Finch?"

Tregoff: "No, sir."

Neeb: "Miss Tregoff, you have seen the diagrams here and you know the location that has been referred to as the Finch home. On July 18 did you accompany Dr. Finch and go to Larkhill Drive in West Covina?"

Tregoff: "Yes."

Neeb: "Now, did you on the occasion that I have just referred to, on or about the eighteenth of July, go with Dr. Finch to the address that I have already indicated with any intent in mind or thought in mind to do any physical violence or any injury to Mrs. Finch or to any other person?"

Tregoff: "Absolutely not!" Her chin was lifted slightly, her voice sounded more secure now.

Then, questions concerning an event from the defendant's childhood.

Neeb: "Did you ever, in your childhood, have occasion to run and hide from anything unusual and frightening?"

Tregoff: "Yes. Once, when I was living with my mother and stepfather..." She looked away, then breathed deeply.

Neeb: "Please go on, Miss Tregoff."

Tregoff: "They didn't get along very well, sometimes fighting. One day I heard them shouting and I ran into the kitchen; my mother was trying to stab him with a long butcher knife. I was terrified. I ran into my bedroom closet and hid."

Neeb: "How long did you hide?'

Tregoff: "For hours. Until the next morning. Until they found me."

Neeb: "I have no further questions, Your Honor." He was walking back to his seat.

Clifford Crail would cross-examine. To him, as he would later tell the jury, Tregoff was the "Lady Macbeth," who had planned the whole conspiracy with Cody, fueling the engine of intrigue.

Crail: "Miss Tregoff, you were here in court during the entire examination of Dr. Finch, were you not?"

Tregoff: "Yes."

Crail: "And you heard him relate in some detail his association, his relationship with you. Do you want to add or take anything away from that?"

Tregoff: "No."

Crail: "So what he testified to is in accordance with what you remember?"

Tregoff: "Yes."

He slowly walked in a circle in front of her, going to his left, passing in front of Whichello.

Crail: "Now on July 17 you drove your car to the airport and met defendant Finch at about 11:30 P.M., after which you went to the Sands Hotel, to get something to eat in the Garden Room of the Sands Hotel. Is that right?"

Tregoff: "Yes."

Crail: "During the conversation you had there, did the subject of a Nevada divorce come up?"

Tregoff: "Yes."

Crail: "Who brought the topic up?"

Tregoff: "Dr. Finch."

Crail: "And the topic of going to West Covina the next night—who brought that up?"

Tregoff: "Dr. Finch. However, I believe I am the one who mentioned the time, to do it the next day."

Crail: "You had had discussions before, with Dr. Finch, about your possibly talking to Barbara Jean about the Nevada divorce?"

Tregoff: "Yes."

Crail: "Why were you in Las Vegas in the first place?"

Tregoff: "Dr. Finch advised it, for fear that I might be called in Mrs. Finch's divorce action as a corespondent."

Crail: "Did he tell you what information she had about you? Did you know what she knew about you?"

Tregoff: "To this day, I don't know."

Crail: "What made you think that she would talk to you?"

Tregoff: "Well, she had always been friendly to me."

Crail: "Friendly up to what time? When did you see her last?"

Tregoff: "I believe it was on the fifteenth of May, about 4:00 in the afternoon. She came to the West Covina Medical Center. I said 'Hello' to her and she said 'Hello' to me."

Crail: "Did she talk to you?"

Tregoff: "She said 'Hello.'"

Crail: "Did she talk to you?"

Tregoff: "No, she didn't really talk to me."

Crail: "So you thought she would talk to you even though you were about to be named as a corespondent in her divorce action?"

Tregoff: "I didn't know if she was going to name me or not."

Crail: "But you moved to Las Vegas because you thought she was going to name you."

Tregoff: "I thought it was a possibility."

Crail: "Now you believed she no longer loved Dr. Finch and that you did love Dr. Finch. Is that correct?"

Tregoff: "Yes."

Crail: "Well, why didn't you just pick up the telephone and try to talk to her about things?"

Tregoff: "I didn't believe it was my proper place to do that sort of thing." The cords in her neck were standing up more; her eyes squeezed smaller.

Crail walked to the exhibit table. He picked up the attaché case and walked back to the witness box, placing it on the rail in front of her. He spoke quietly and slowly, the box between his palms.

Crail: "Who took this case up the hill that night?"

Tregoff: "I did."

Crail: "You remember that distinctly, do you?"

Tregoff: "Yes."

Crail: "But when you gave your statement to the authorities in Las Vegas, you didn't. You actually forgot about the bag. Why didn't you tell them about it?"

Tregoff: "When I gave my first statement? It wasn't important."

Crail: "And when the bag was actually shown to you by West Covina police, later in West Covina, you said you had not had the case up on the hill, didn't you?" He leaned closer to her. "Why did you say that?"

Tregoff: "Because I didn't remember it."

Crail: "When you arrived in West Covina, you parked your car in the parking lot of South Hills Country Club, didn't you?"

Tregoff: "Yes."

Crail: "How long were you there before you got out of the car?"

Tregoff: "Just a few minutes."

Crail: "And when you got out, you took this bag with you. There has never been any doubt in your mind?"

Tregoff: "Since I remembered it, no."

Crail: "However, there was a time when you did not remember it?"

Tregoff: "Well, it was not important."

Crail: "You thought it had no significance?"

Tregoff: "No."

Crail: "And when the bag was shown to you on July 22 at the West Covina police station, at that time you did not remember if the bag was up on the hill."

Tregoff: "Yes I did. I did not remember it. It was not important. May I explain something to you?" She was leaning forward, more strain in her face.

Crail: "And yet ten days later, when you testified, you had no difficulty in remembering the bag and all the items that were in it."

Tregoff: "Not every item. I recalled some things about it."

Crail: "Now when you were testifying at Dr. Finch's preliminary hearing—"

"Objection!" Cooper and Neeb said at the same time. Both were standing.

"We request," Neeb spoke for the two of them, "a conference in chambers."

Crail had strayed into Exhibit 60, Carole's testimony at Finch's preliminary hearing. In chambers he was told not to ask any questions about it. Evans did say he would allow him to ask questions about Finch's testimony regarding the same events and he could ask questions about her statements to Las Vegas and West Covina police.

Crail was at the witness box with the attaché case again.

Crail: "Do you recall a day when Sergeant Ray Hopkinson and Captain William Ryan took a statement from you at West Covina police headquarters?"

Tregoff: "Yes."

Crail: "And that it was there you were shown this attaché case, state's Exhibit 40?"

Tregoff: "I cannot say where I was shown it."

Crail: "Well, do you remember that during your questioning it was shown to you?"

Tregoff: "Yes. I think it was."

Crail: "And you said you had no idea that the case was with you at the time you went up the hill to the Finch residence?"

Tregoff: "Sir, at that time I was telling the truth."

Crail: "Did you say that or not?" He was yelling at her, leaning into the witness box. She jerked away from him.

323

Tregoff: "I am not sure. I am telling you to the best of my recollection."

Crail: "Well, what is your best recollection as to whether Exhibit 40 was shown to you in the West Covina police station?"

Tregoff: "It was shown to me; I am not sure when."

Crail: "And what questions were asked of you about Exhibit 40?"

Tregoff: "I really cannot remember."

Crail: "You told the officers you didn't have the bag with you up there on that night, didn't you?"

Tregoff: "I probably did, since I didn't remember about it until later. At that time I didn't recall the bag at all, Mr. Crail."

Crail: "Did you tell them anything about a flashlight?"

Tregoff: "No, I don't believe so."

Crail: "But now you remember that you walked halfway up the hill and took the flashlight out of the bag?"

Tregoff: "I walked partly up the hill. I don't remember if I took it out of the bag or not."

Crail: "When was it taken out of the bag?"

Tregoff: "On the hill somewhere. I don't remember exactly where. It was before we sat down on the grass, near the steps between the two houses."

Crail: "So in any event, you were up there on the hill, and you waited about five minutes before Mrs. Finch arrived."

Tregoff: "It was a very short time, but it was more than five minutes."

Crail: "I notice, Miss Tregoff," he was standing at the end of the rail in front of the jury box, "that you have told a great deal more about these episodes than on previous occasions when you were questioned by the police."

Tregoff: "After this tragic occurrence I was very upset and I—"

Crail: "I don't suppose that Dr. Finch has been of any assistance in this regard, has he?" He was looking right at Finch who was beginning to slouch back in his chair.

Tregoff: "No." She cleared her throat.

Crail: "You mean, you have not talked these things over with him at any time?"

Tregoff: "Well, uh, we discussed some points a little bit. I don't know how many times."

Finch had his left palm over his mouth; he was slouching even more.

Crail: "Oh, 'some points, a little bit.' I see. Isn't it a fact that you discussed these things with him as late as last Friday, right here in this courtroom?"

Tregoff: "No, that is not true."

Crail: "You didn't see him here in this courtroom?"

Tregoff: "Yes, of course, but—"

Crail: "Didn't you discuss these facts with Dr. Finch as far back as the morning of July 19 when you saw him in the sheriff's station at Las Vegas?"

Tregoff: "No. I was with him no more than five minutes."

Crail: "And on the morning of July 19, when you found him at your apartment in Las Vegas? You arrived at 9:00 A.M. and didn't leave for work until 10:00 A.M. Surely you discussed with him what had happened?"

Tregoff: "Yes."

Crail: "And when the actual indictment against both of you was going on, you had many conversations with him, isn't that true?"

Tregoff: "I think mostly recently," she was looking down at her knees, her voice quivering slightly. "Not as much back then."

Crail: "I see. Now let's talk about the night of July 18, 1959. I know you were here when defendant Finch testified about his memory of the events that night."

Tregoff: "Yes." She was looking directly at Crail now. Her head was tilted slightly to the side. She was gripping the arms of the chair tightly.

Crail: "What were the first words spoken there by anyone, after you two went into the garage?"

Tregoff: "Dr. Finch asked Mrs. Finch something to the effect that we would like to talk to her. She was out of the car, standing with the door open."

Crail: "Were the lights off, on the car? Do you recall her turning the lights off on the car?"

Tregoff: "I don't recall anything about the lights."

Crail: "What did Mrs. Finch say?"

Tregoff: "She said she didn't want to talk to us or something like that. I don't recall her exact words. The next thing was that she had a gun. She just reached in and when she turned around she had the gun." She cried for a few moments. Crail waited.

Crail: "Then, at that moment Dr. Finch made a lunge toward her?"

Tregoff: "Yes, the next thing he threw something at me; that case came at me in that same instant." She was leaning forward, talking faster.

Crail: "Oh yes, the case. You didn't mention anything about the case, the shaving bag with the bullets in it. You forgot about that until you were on the witness stand for Dr. Finch, didn't you? You forgot about it when you were talking to Las Vegas police and the West Covina police, didn't you?"

Tregoff: "Mr. Crail, I didn't remember it until then." She was shouting at him.

Crail: "Well, what made you remember about it?"

Tregoff: "Well," she was looking at her knees again, "after I gave my statement to Sergeant Hopkinson and Captain Ryan on July 22, it just wasn't important. I didn't think it was important; I didn't remember it. After that I was asked to wait in Captain Ryan's office and someone was putting something into the bag and I saw the shaving-kit in the bag. It rang a bell, but I was not exactly sure what it was. Then I began recalling more and more about it."

Crail: "So you didn't recall the attaché case or the shaving-kit bag at that time?"

Tregoff: "I didn't think it was important."

Crail: "Had you ever seen this kit," he was at the exhibits table, holding up the shaving bag, "before the night of July 18, 1959?"

Tregoff: "No."

Crail: "Dr. Finch told us that he gave you the bag and to 'get out of there.'"

Tregoff: "Yes."

Crail: "And you put the shaving-kit into the attaché case?"

Tregoff: "Yes."

Crail: "When?"

Tregoff: "I don't know when for sure-shortly after I ran out of the garage. I just don't know how long, perhaps a few seconds."

Crail: "You were trying to get away from Mrs. Finch who had a gun"–he was in front of her again; she was looking down; her lips were quivering–"and you stopped to put the kit in the attaché case?"

Tregoff: "Well I was out of the garage, I was headed away from Mrs. Finch. She could not see me."

Crail: "Why didn't you throw the shaving-kit away?"

Tregoff: "I was, I was just completely upset."

Crail: "You were upset, so you stopped, opened the attaché case, and put the shaving-kit into it, closed up the case and then ran away?"

Tregoff: "Yes."

Crail: "And you told Las Vegas police, in your statement to them, that you ran into some bushes to hide."

Tregoff: "Yes."

Crail: "The same with the West Covina police. You told them that you ran into some bushes to hide after she pulled a gun on you?"

Tregoff: "Yes."

Crail: "But you told no one about defendant Finch throwing a shaving-kit at you?"

Tregoff: "No."

Crail: "And why not?" He was half singing, his tone sarcastic; he knew her answer, everybody knew her answer. "Tell us why you didn't tell them."

Tregoff: "I didn't remember it at that time. I saw the bag later after I had talked with Captain Ryan. I saw it and that started me to remembering it."

Crail: "Now, I'd like to read part of your statement to Captain Ryan, if I may, Your Honor." He made a quick bow to Evans before going to his desk. He stood there, reading.

> '"When we got to the garage Dr. Finch mentioned that we had come to talk to her and we would appreciate it if she would. And she hollered and said 'no.' Then she said she wasn't going to. Then she hollered and screamed or something and then she reached back with this gun and that is when I left.
>
> Question: How far away from Mrs. Finch were you?
>
> Answer: About five feet.
>
> Question: Did she say anything?
>
> Answer: I don't remember. When I saw the gun I got panicky and scared, and left.
>
> Question: Did you see Dr. Finch do anything?
>
> Answer: I saw him jump for the gun.
>
> Question: Did he get the gun?
>
> Answer: I don't know. I didn't see any more.'

"It seems you told nothing about the shaving-kit?"

Tregoff: "I told you, I didn't remember it at the time."

Crail: "Will you explain, then, why he was four or five feet from Mrs. Finch at the time you started running, explain how he could get the kit and give it to you after you were already out of the garage?"

Tregoff: "I'm sorry, I don't know. I have no answer." She was crying as she talked. "I know I was trying to tell the truth. I was just trying—"

Crail: "In fact, you never did see him reach into that car, did you? In fact, you were not telling the truth when you made this statement to the officers. In fact, you didn't mention anything to anybody about that kit until Dr. Finch's preliminary hearing, after you had had a chance to talk to him several times. Aren't these the real facts, Miss Tregoff?"

Tregoff: "I think I have already explained all that. I've tried to explain." Still crying, her palms battered at the arms of the chair.

Caril waited for her to calm.

Crail: "You had, at that time, talked to Finch several times. Is that true or not?"

Tregoff: "Yes, it's true."

Crail: "And it was after you had talked to West Covina police and seen that they had discovered this kit—only then did you start to, as you say, remember about it. Isn't that true?"

Tregoff: "Yes."

Crail: "It was at that point that you realized that you and Dr. Finch would have to think of a way to account for the possession of that kit up there, didn't you?"

Tregoff: "No, that wasn't important. I didn't think of that."

He waited a few moments until she stopped crying. He was getting ready for his next series of questions.

Crail: "I will read further from the statement that you gave to the Las Vegas police.

> 'Question: During the time that you lived in Las Vegas and during these visits to Las Vegas made by Dr. Finch, did he discuss his wife Barbara? Answer: No.'"

He eased slowly toward her, speaking quietly again.

Crail: "Did you make that statement?"

Tregoff: "Yes."

Crail: "It wasn't a true statement, was it?"

Tregoff: "I wasn't intentionally misleading anyone." She sounded like she was going to start crying again. "It didn't seem like we had discussed Mrs. Finch very much."

Crail: "Why did you tell the police that if it wasn't true, Miss Tregoff." Still speaking softly. "Are you telling us now that you didn't discuss Mrs. Finch?"

Tregoff: "Not very much at any time."

Crail: "Why have you just said, 'Not very much at any time?'"

Tregoff: "I don't understand you." She was yelling.

Crail: "Is that the best answer you can give?" he yelled back at her.

Both and Cooper and Neeb objected, and were sustained.

Crail: "You also told Las Vegas police that he only had one bag when he arrived in Las Vegas, didn't you? It's here on the second page, I believe. Oh, yes.

> 'Question: Was Dr. Finch driving his car when he came to Las Vegas?
> Answer: No, I picked him up at the airport.
> Question: Did he have any luggage with him?
> Answer: One bag.'

"One bag." He walked back to her. He tried to lock eyes with her, but she was looked down at her knees, her lower lip quivered again. "At that time, when you made this statement, you didn't know the police had found Exhibit 40 on the hill, did you?"

Tregoff: "I hadn't thought of that. I mean—"

Crail: "That came later in the statement, didn't it?"

Tregoff: "I don't understand."

Crail: "The police brought it to your attention later in the statement, didn't they?"

Tregoff: "I don't recall when they brought it to my attention."

She sobbed for a few seconds, then regained her composure.

Crail: "Now, when you talked to West Covina police, you said you had no plan about what you were going to say to Mrs. Finch—that you, if I could read from your statement, 'didn't have a plan as to what you were going to say.' And yet now you are telling us that you and Dr. Finch had planned to talk to her about a Nevada divorce. You had planned that in Las Vegas."

Tregoff: "I did mention something about a divorce when I talked to them. I did."

Crail: "As a matter of fact, you had no plan at all about what you were going to talk to her about because you didn't plan to talk to her. Isn't that true?"

Tregoff: "No, that is not true. I just, I had no plan about what I was going to say exactly. I was just going to say what I felt."

Crail: "You didn't tell them about the dog, either—about playing with the dog."

Tregoff: "That didn't seem very important, either."

Crail: "It wasn't until after you had found out they found fragments of rubber gloves around there you mentioned anything about playing with this dog, isn't that a fact?"

331

Tregoff: "I told you about it after I remembered it. That's all I can tell you, Mr. Crail."

Crail: "You were just trying to account for their presence, when you were asked about them at Dr. Finch's preliminary hearing, weren't you?"

Tregoff: "If I could, of course."

Crail: "Just like you were trying to account for a number of other things, weren't you?" He slammed the rail in front of her with his palm.

Cooper: "He's upsetting the witness by pounding on things, Your Honor!"

Evans, calmly: "You may not pound on things, Mr. Crail."

Tregoff: "Mr. Crail, I am trying to tell the truth."

Crail: "Very well." He walked away from her, then turned, standing in front of Cooper. "Tell us the truth about this then, Miss Tregoff. When you left the garage, after, you say, Barbara Jean Finch pointed a gun at you, did you hear any sounds?"

Tregoff: "Yes, sir."

Crail: "Oh." His voice rang with feigned surprise. He was standing in front of the jury now, his hands on the rail, eyebrows raised as far as they would go. "Well, tell us what you heard."

Tregoff: "I heard scuffling noises and what I now know was a gunshot. Then I heard Dr. Finch say, 'Please, Barbara,' or something like that."

Crail: "So, you heard no one screaming?"

Tregoff: "Yes, I think I did, yes. It was Mrs. Finch."

Crail: "You're sure it wasn't Dr. Finch?"

Tregoff: "No, sir, it was Mrs. Finch."

Crail: "You didn't hear him screaming for help at any time, did you?"

Tregoff: "No, sir." She glanced at Finch. He had slouched down in his chair as far as he could, his left palm over his mouth again. He was looking down, to his left.

Crail: "And while you heard this commotion you made no attempt to get away?"

Tregoff: "No, sir."

Crail: "You didn't try to find out what was going on? I mean, by now, you must have known there was serious trouble afoot."

Tregoff: "I did try."

Crail: "What did you do?"

Tregoff: "I walked back toward the garage and then I noticed Dr. Finch's hat and picked that up, and when I picked up the hat, I looked up and Mrs. Finch was standing facing toward the back of the garage. At the same instant she turned around, and I know she had a gun in her hand, and I ran."

Crail: "The first and most important thing you could think to do when you went in the garage was to pick up the hat?"

Tregoff: "Yes."

Crail: "You saw her with a gun, did you? When you went back this second time, she still had the gun?"

Tregoff: "Yes." She was still looking at him.

Crail: "As I recall, you never said at any time to the police, in any of your statements, that you went back into the garage."

Tregoff: "Yes, sir. I didn't remember going back to the garage until later."

Crail: "The first time you ever said that you went back to the garage was when you took the witness stand at the preliminary examination in the Finch case, correct?"

Tregoff: "Yes, sir."

Crail: "You never told the officers, did you?"

Tregoff: "No."

Crail: "Didn't you think–well, you know–wasn't it important for them to know whether or not Mrs. Finch had a gun at that time, when you went back to the garage? I mean, you told them about seeing the gun when you first went up to the garage?"

Tregoff: "I was scared. I forgot about it. The whole thing was just such a nightmare." She clenched her fists and held them over her ears.

Crail: "But you saw her with the gun, here behind the car, after you had heard the shot, earlier." He was pointing at the diagram of the Finch property. "You were standing where you had picked up the hat?"

Tregoff: "Yes."

Crail: "Did you see her run from the garage?"

Tregoff: "No. I had turned and run to the bushes at that time. I saw nobody leave the garage."

Crail: "Were the floodlights on?"

Tregoff: "Yes, I believe so." She cleared her throat.

Crail then pointed to the corner of the Finch home where Carole claimed she hid, behind a bougainvillea.

Crail: "And the next thing you saw, from your place here in the bushes, was the police cruisers arriving?"

Tregoff: "Yes."

Crail: "You saw no one else?"

Tregoff: "I've been thinking, yes, I did see someone else. I saw Patti and another girl with her, standing on the blacktop."

Crail: "Oh, now something else you remembered! This is the first time," his hands were literally up in the air, "in your life you remembered that, isn't it–right here, right now?"

Tregoff: "That is true. I only remembered it about a month ago."

Crail: "So you saw these two girls, and then the police arrived and you knew Mrs. Finch had a gun somewhere on the property."

Tregoff: "Yes, sir."

Crail: "Well, why didn't you go out to where the police cars were and find out why they were there?"

Tregoff: "I was scared."

Crail: "There were officers there at that time, weren't there?"

Tregoff: "Yes."

Crail: "You were afraid of them? Why would you be afraid of them?"

Neeb: "He's putting words into her mouth!"

Crail: "Okay, were you afraid of them?"

Tregoff: "I don't know what I thought."

Crail: "Were you scared of the officers or not, Miss Tregoff?" he was yelling.

Tregoff: "I was just scared. I don't know, Mr. Crail."

Crail: "You're telling us, are you trying to tell us, that now you do not know whether you were scared of the officers or not?"

"I object, Your Honor." Cooper was on his feet. "She answered the question."

"Objection is sustained." Evans looked at Crail, then at Carole.

Crail: "Well, let's put it this way. What was it about the presence of the officers that scared you?"

Neeb: "She never said she was afraid of the officers. Your Honor, he's putting words in her mouth again!"

Tregoff: "I don't know, Mr. Crail. I was just completely horrified." She was yelling back.

Evans: "I think we've gone far enough on this one, Mr. Crail."

Crail: "Very well. Weren't you, Miss Tregoff, curious as to what had happened to defendant Finch at that time?"

Tregoff: "I don't think I thought of Dr. Finch at that time."

Crail: "You didn't wonder whether or not he had been shot?"

Tregoff: "I don't think so."

Crail: "Why not?"

Tregoff: "I don't know." She heaved as she spoke, tears running down her cheeks now; she was wiping them with a handkerchief. "I was frightened."

Crail: "You were madly in love with him at that time, weren't you?"

Tregoff: "I was in love with him."

Crail: "So using the word 'madly' was carrying it a bit too far, was it?"

Neeb's objection was sustained.

Crail: "Okay, let's put it this way." He lowered his voice, speaking more slowly. "You felt at that time that you were more in love with him than with any other man in your life. Is that correct?"

Tregoff: "At that time, after what I had seen, I wasn't thinking whether I was in love with anyone."

Crail: "But he was the most important thing in your life at that moment, wasn't he?"

Tregoff: "Apparently not, if I didn't think of him."

Crail: "And you didn't think of him?"

Tregoff: "I don't recall." She seemed in control now. "I don't recall thinking of him."

He walked back to his table, standing behind it, next to Whichello. It would be his last few questions.

Crail: "How much did you pay John Patrick Cody?"

Tregoff: "$1,020, in total."

Crail: "In cash?"

Tregoff: "Yes."

Crail: "Why in cash?"

Tregoff: "I did not have a checking account in Las Vegas. I got the money out of my safety deposit box."

Crail: "And you didn't ask him for a receipt? Why not?"

Tregoff: "I don't know; I wish I had."

Crail: "You had nothing at all to show that you had paid him all that money, is that correct?"

Tregoff: "That is true."

Crail: "And you had been a secretary for Dr. Finch and had some business experience. Why didn't you ask Cody for a receipt?"

Tregoff: "I don't know."

Crail: "Your Honor," his arms were at right angles to his body, palms up, he shook his head from side to side slightly, "I have no further questions."

Carole Tregoff was crying as she stepped down; she was met by Bringgold who helped her to her chair.

Court was over for the day. Carole had been on the stand for two days.

Bernard Finch was sitting at the defense table; his attorney was conferring with Robert Neeb. He stared blankly at the desk top. Noticing the day's *Los Angeles Times* sticking out from under a stack of Cooper's papers, he pulled it out, scanning the headlines. One caught his eye immediately.

"High Court Rejects Chessman's Appeal," the paper yelled. The U.S. Supreme Court had rejected another of Caryl Chessman's attempts to avoid the gas chamber. The kidnapper-rapist was scheduled to be executed in two days. Finch tried to read another story on the front page, one about Queen Elizabeth expecting another child. He read part of the first paragraph, then buried the newspaper back under the stack of briefs, transcripts, and statements.

twelve
Final Witnesses
Summation of Clifford Crail

FRIDAY, FEBRUARY 19

FOR THE REST of the trial a parade of policemen from Minneapolis would offer their judgments of James Patrick Cody's credibility. Cooper had found three officers who thought he would lie, even under oath; Whichello and Crail had found three that thought he would tell the truth under oath.

Marie Anne Lidholm would be the last witness, once more saying Dr. Finch had grabbed her head and not her arms, and that he had not assisted her into the back seat. She said she was quite sure Barbara Jean Finch was forced into the passenger side of the car and not the driver's side, as Finch had testified.

Before the attorneys made their closing arguments, they frequently met in chambers, discussing the instructions to be given to the jury.

Evans, as presiding judge, would have the discretion of telling the jury if they could find the defendants guilty of lesser offenses, like manslaughter.

Governor Edmund Brown, an acknowledged opponent of the death penalty, had ordered a sixty-day stay in Caryl Chessman's execution. "You know, President Eisenhower is going to South America soon, on his tour, and I was afraid that an execution in the United States might provoke demonstrations during his trip. In fact, I have a cable from the State Department saying that demonstrations against him are expected," he announced during a Sacramento press conference.

"That's a bunch of malarkey." Whichello berated the governor's decision during a meeting in Evans's chambers the following day. "We checked with that Haggerty guy, you know the press secretary at the White House, and you know what, they send routine cables to all of the governors that there might be some sort of demonstrations. They were worried about Uruguay. And they never said anything about Chessman being executed."

All attorneys were present and were soon to make their motions regarding jury instructions.

"Well, he was elected governor, Fred." Neeb was leaning forward, looking down the long line of suits. "And if he's opposed to the death penalty, it's to be expected he would do things like this. Besides, it's a good case to take a stand. Chessman was never convicted of murder, just kidnapping and rape. In fact—"

"He was convicted and sentenced to die by due process. And I can tell you our office is pretty upset." Fred looked back at Evans. "It's a pretty sad day when a bunch of Communists down in South America can shake up the administration of justice in California."

Evans waited until Fred finished ventilating. "I think this Chessman decision could affect the jury adversely, gentlemen. I'm going to recess court for the rest of the day." The men were all looking at him now. "And I've decided to sequester the jury until they reach a verdict."

"Good, we don't need those Communists influencing the jury on this case. I—"

"I'm going to cut off all contact with their families, including phone calls, except for emergencies, of course. And I'll instruct the bailiffs to screen all newspapers and television shows." He looked at the attorneys in front of him. Most were nodding their approval; he had expected little dissent.

"Now," he continued, "I understand from reading the *Los Angeles Times* that I am leaning toward instructing the jury that they can find for second-degree murder also. What are you gentlemen planning on asking me to do? What about the state?" He looked at Whichello, who was thumbing through some papers.

Crail spoke first. "We still intend to ask for the death penalty, Your Honor, for both counts, murder and conspiracy."

"Yes, well, as far as the other possible counts go," Fred spoke, still shuffling papers, "we think it appropriate that they find for just the charges that were filed by the grand jury, should the court so find, of course. We move for no possibility of lesser charges."

"All right," Evans was writing on a yellow legal pad as he spoke, "no other counts. Mr. Cooper? Can you give me an indication of what you are thinking at this point?"

"I'll probably ask that the jury be given as much discretion as the law allows, Your Honor. This is a very complex case and they should be able to find also for simple assault, assault with intent to murder, assault with a deadly weapon, as well as the ones mentioned by Mr. Whichello." Cooper's remarks came as no surprise to Evans. He nodded slowly, still writing on the pad.

"Mr. Neeb?" He asked the senior counsel for Carole Tregoff.

"We want total acquittal or a verdict of guilty on the existing counts. Nothing more, nothing less." Neeb leaned forward slightly as he spoke. Whichello and Crail looked at him eyebrows raised.

"Just the existing counts or acquittal?" Evans was trying to not sound surprised.

"Yes, Your Honor." Neeb was nodding his head.

Evans finished writing, then excused the attorneys for the rest of the week. Closing arguments would begin Tuesday, since Monday would be Washington's Birthday.

The weekend newspapers would put chances for a conviction at "50-50." The final arguments were predicted to be a major determinant of the jury's verdict.

SATURDAY, FEBRUARY 20, 1960

Bernard Finch had consented to give a brief interview at the visitors' desks of the County Jail. There were about twenty reporters present when he came in. He did not sit down, but stood behind a small desk; the reporters were standing, also. He had not given an interview for some time. Cooper had advised against it until the trial was over. The questions asked him by the reporters during recesses in court were increasingly sarcastic, almost accusatory, and the doctor did not appear as self-assured as in previous interviews.

He had not exercised nor been outside since his arrest eight months before, and was pale, looking tired to the reporters, who recorded bloodshot eyes and more gray hair.

"I am confident of an acquittal." He began what appeared to be a prepared statement. His voice was hoarse. "after the jury—"

"A little louder, please, Doctor. We can't hear you back here." A short, rotund reporter in the back spoke, right hand cupped to his ear.

"I said," Finch was speaking louder, his chin raised up slightly, "I am confident that the jury will acquit myself and Miss Tregoff after they complete their deliberations, which we hope will start this week. We've got the best lawyers in the country, and we're not guilty, and that's the truth."

"What's it like, the routine in jail?" A reporter from the *Herald* asked.

"It's been rough. It's still overcrowded in here and there's still the cockroaches. For the last two nights some poor man's been yelling for the whole night. I don't think anyone got any sleep."

"What are your plans for the future?" It was Ed Kessler, a reporter from the *San Gabriel Valley Tribune*, the daily afternoon paper of West Covina.

"I don't know." Finch glanced at the floor, then back up. "Undoubtedly, the publicity has hurt my practice in West Covina. I still have my license to practice, as far as I know. I mean I haven't been convicted of anything, so I think I still have it."

"You didn't mention Carole, Doctor," the *Trib* reporter pressed him. "As I recall, during the trial you said you would still marry her."

"Well, you'd have to ask her about that." Then he glared at the reporter, as though just remembering something. "You know, Kessler, you ought to get out of the newspaper business. You and your paper have never reported this fairly."

"Really?" Kessler lowered his notebook to the side and looked at Finch intently. The other reporters stopped writing and began glancing back and forth at the two.

"Yeah, really!" Finch had his right index finger raised up in front of him, jabbing it down to the floor. "There was and still continues to be a lot of yakking going on about this. It's ridiculous. My attorney is unhappy about it, too. How can I get a fair trial with the kind of stories you guys put out?"

Kessler did not answer; the two stared at each other for a few moments. The reporter in the back asked, "Where do you think the gun is, Doctor, and your wife's purse and jewelry?"

"I don't know where it is." He was yelling louder. "You guys keep asking me the same questions, all the time, the same stuff."

"Well, did you toss them out of the car on the way to Las Vegas?" another asked.

"Or did you bury it somewhere on the golf course?" It was the rotund reporter again.

Finch turned quickly, walking to the door that would take him back to his cell. "Let's get out of here," he was muttering to the guard. Just as he got to the door, Ed Kessler hurled one last question.

"What's your opinion about the reprieve granted to Caryl Chessman by Governor Brown?"

He stopped and looked back, eyes wide, eyebrows raised high. His teeth were set, and his lips opened slightly. Then he appeared to calm. "I have no comment." He wasn't yelling; his voice was quieter. He turned and left.

"Wow, talk about looks that could—" One reporter was talking to Ed Kessler. He was cut off by another.

"Well, I still think he buried the stuff somewhere on the golf course. You know, they're always doing something out there. I talked to one of the maintenance guys. Especially on the back nine, which they just opened up a couple of years ago. There's always a hole or a ditch somewhere."

"No way," the shorter man said, "would he risk having it be found; his fingerprints were all over everything. He dumped it in the desert."

"Big deal," the tall one retorted, "It's his gun, so what if his prints are on it. I think he buried it there because he didn't want to get caught with the murder weapon as he was making a run for it, so he ditched it there. If they found it on the golf course, he could say somebody else put it there."

As they left, the debate continued.

"Desert," said the one, "desert for sure!"

"Back nine, back nine." Their voices echoed in the now empty room.

TUESDAY, FEBRUARY 23, 1960

Fred Whichello was driving to court on the new San Bernardino freeway from his home in San Gabriel. His car was buffeted by blustery Santa Ana winds. Coming through one of the last turns before his exit, he noticed something swinging from the Soto street overpass. Nearer, he squinted and leaned forward. Suddenly it was obvious.

"My God, it's a body!"

Then he noticed the wind lifted and knocked the figure with unexpected ease. It was a stuffed effigy of Governor Brown. A sign around its neck said, "Hang Brown and Chessman both."

The state was debating the fate of Caryl Chessman. State Attorney General Stanley Mosk was quoted in the *Los Angeles Times* as saying Chessman would go to the gas chamber as planned, "as soon as the reprieves run out—and they will run out."

At the courthouse Clifford Crail arrived early carrying two briefcases, both stuffed so they would not close completely. He was wearing a heavy overcoat; it was quite cold this early in the morning, and the Santa Ana winds would chill quickly. He was the first person in the courtroom.

Methodically, he began arranging the papers on the large defense table. There were six thousand pages of transcript so far. He had them organized by day and he laid them out in order, the first day on the upper left corner, then a row down, then over for a new column. The arrangement would take up the entire desk top, except for a little square on the bottom right part, which he saved for Whichello. Today Crail would be sitting in the chair closest to the center aisle.

He had persuaded Whichello to let him give the first closing statement to the jury. And he would give it today, frequently walking to the neat rows of transcripts to refer to certain testimony.

Evans was late to court, and looked worried, having just spoken to his bailiff in charge of sequestering the jury. First news of friction among certain jurors had reached him; racial conflicts were rumored.

Crail first talked of Barbara Jean Finch's state of mind the night she died.

"The first question I want to ask you, members of the jury, is in regard to the victim's state of mind as she was driving up the hill to her home that night. We know from the testimony of other witnesses that she had wanted nothing to do with him. That she had turned and walked away from him at the Los Angeles Tennis Club just a few weeks before, without talking to him.

"We know that she hired a bodyguard to be with her on certain occasions to protect her from the defendant. We know from the testimony of Miss Lidholm that she was in fear of her life, that she was convinced that the defendant would take her away some weekend and murder her on the desert or try to make it look like a car accident. And we know from defendant Finch's own testimony that once she had driven up the driveway in broad daylight, seen the defendant, and turned around and driven away.

"Let me ask you this, ladies and gentlemen. If you believe the defendant's testimony he called Barbara Jean and told her he was coming there Saturday, do you think for a minute she would have driven up the hill all by herself? Of course not!

"Let's assume that she didn't know he was going to be there, and that she drove into the garage. Let's remember

345

that Marie Anne said there was an interval of time where she heard nothing, long enough so she became uneasy about it. What was going on in that garage during that interval of time? How did the blood stains get on the steering wheel, and on the left side of the seat, and on the top of the left side of the car? It wasn't when she got into the car. Miss Lidholm has said that the victim got in on the right side of the car. She also told us that the door was closed when she came into the garage, that she herself opened the door to get in. I ask you again, how did that blood get all over the left side of the car?

"If Mrs. Finch was aware of their presence when she drove into the garage while she was still in the car, she would have immediately backed out of the garage. If she had become aware of them after she had time to get out of the car, she would have fled. But she didn't. Why?

"Because something detained her in there, for those few moments of silence when Marie Anne heard nothing. And when the blood was spilled on the left side of the car.

"I would ask you to remember what it's like to get out of one of these new automobiles. You have to duck your head down, because the tops are lower than they used to be. Remember from the coroner's report that the only wounds she sustained that resulted in any bleeding were on the right side of her head. Ladies and gentlemen, she was grabbed and the right side of her head was pounded against the automobile as she was exiting the car. That's how the blood got on the top of the car and on the steering wheel and seat.

"This explains the interval of time noticed by Marie Anne. She was dazed and incapable of calling for help. But then she came to enough to scream, with a scream such as Marie Anne had never heard before."

He then talked about Dr. Finch's attack on Marie Anne.

"Marie Anne told us that when she got to the garage door, it was partway open, and that she came in and turned on the lights, and that when the lights came on, she saw the defendant coming toward her, in her direction. When she came to, the lights were off again.

"What would be the first thing he would do if he were trying to protect himself from her, if he thought she had a rifle, like he says. Would he turn off the lights to avoid detection? Would he grab her by the head? Of course not. He knew she didn't have a rifle. That's why he didn't try, as Miss Lidholm testified he didn't, to pin her arms down to her sides.

"This is the first of many points where you will have to decide, as you deliberate, whether you are going to believe Marie Anne Lidholm or," he turned and pointed to Finch and Tregoff, "these defendants.

"Another point has to do with the firing of the first shot. Marie Anne has testified that he fired the shot while she was leaning up next to the wall, in an effort to scare her into getting into the car. What's his story? He tries to make us believe that he is helping Marie Anne getting into the car and he is then jumped by the victim as the two walk by, therefore making the gun go off. He is cutting the cloth to fit the pattern, ladies and gentlemen. If she had come to, as the defendant states, she would have run for the safety of her father-in-law's house. She wouldn't have attacked him in an effort to get the gun. Can you believe a 125-pound woman would have attacked a man, a well-developed athlete of the tennis courts, to try to wrestle a gun from him? Of course not!

"She tells us that Mrs. Finch got into the passenger side of the car, that her feet were still dangling out, ready to run. He says he put her into the driver's side. Why? To explain the blood stains on that side of the car. Another cloth cut to fit the pattern.

"Then he tells us his reason for following Barbara Jean down the hill, that Barbara grabbed the gun while he was looking for the keys and ran down the hill. He says he went out to protect his co-defendant from harm, and that he saw her point the gun in his direction. How strange that a woman in fear for her life, who had, as he says, armed herself with a gun, would not use it. There is no evidence anywhere that she fired the gun. In truth, she never had the gun.

"Little Marie Anne next runs back into the house to call the police. In five minutes the police cars are there. In the meantime she does a very foolish thing. She came out of the house with little Patti and the two of them walked around that area of the driveway. She didn't see anybody out there. Not a soul. The lights were on. No one was in sight. Where was everybody? Where had they gone?

"Defendant Finch tells you that he came back into the garage, and I haven't any doubt that he did go back into the garage. And, ladies and gentlemen, he came back for a very specific reason. He wanted to see if Marie Anne was still in there. And if she had been, she wouldn't have testified from this witness stand. What do you think would have happened if she had stayed in the car? She would have been the next victim. But instead, the defendant saw her with little Patti and decided to flee.

"And what about the children in the house? He is asking you to believe that he is taking these two women to the hospital to care for them. Wouldn't this have been the time to say to Marie Anne, 'You go call an ambulance while I stay here?' Wouldn't this have been the time to let the children in the house know where they were going? Of course, but there is no mention of that in any of the testimony.

"Let's look at the differences between the testimony of Miss Lidholm and defendant Finch.

"One, turning off the lights in the garage. Finch's final conclusion was that the lights may have been turned off when he attacked Marie Anne. I don't see how that could have happened with the location of the switches, but that's what he says, and she says the only way they could have been turned off was if he simply turned them off after he hit her head against the wall.

"Two, grabbing Miss Lidholm by the arms. She says he grabbed her head.

"Three, number of times he banged her head against the wall. He says once; she says twice, maybe more.

"Four, he claims he felt the back of her head to check for bruises. This she denies.

"Five, he claims he told her that she 'did not know what had been going on in the garage.' She denies this.

"Six, he said he helped her into the car, by grabbing her arm. She says she got in on her own.

"Seven, he says Mrs. Finch got up and grabbed for the gun, causing it to discharge. She denied seeing this, too.

"Eight, he said Mrs. Finch got into the car on the left side. She says she got in on the right.

"Nine, he says she never said 'Please don't kill me.'

"Ten, he claims he never said he would kill or shoot Mrs. Finch if she did not give him the keys, only that he would slug her.

"Eleven, he said Miss Lidholm lay down in the back seat of the car. Remember him saying that, that she lay down? He is trying to get her down so that she cannot see what is going on. She says she saw everything.

"Twelve, Marie Anne says he did not get out of the car and go to the front of it and stop, bobbing up and down to escape Mrs. Finch's aim, as he says.

"Thirteen, Miss Lidholm says that at no time did he call out for Carole. Why didn't he call, ladies and gentlemen?

Because he knew where she was, outside on the lawn waiting with her little murder kit for the right time to come in.

"Fourteen, Miss Lidholm says he did not say anything about going to the hospital.

"These are things that he cannot agree with her on, things that he must dispute or else he has no hope of reconciling the conduct she has described with innocent actions on his part.

"This gets us up to the testimony of Patti Daugherty. She said she heard mad, angry, and loud sounds, sounds of someone being thrown around in the garage. Defendant Finch has the temerity to tell you he did not use such words. He tells us that a twelve-year-old girl is not qualified to discern an angry voice. I ask you, what is the very first thing a little toddler learns? To distinguish between an angry voice and one of approbation. Even a little puppy learns to respond to an angry voice.

"Then they say they are wanting to hire a detective to gather evidence against Mrs. Finch, that they are not hiring a murderer. What's one of the first things that they do? They go down to the airport and buy an airplane ticket to Phoenix. If they were sending a detective to Los Angeles, why would he buy a ticket to Phoenix? Because they were sending a murderer to Phoenix, so that he could take a bus to Los Angeles, and cover his trail. That's why.

"Then they pay him a large lump sum. Defendant Tregoff says she paid him $1,020 and Finch says it was $1,350. Looks like somebody got shortchanged to me, but that's not important now. He was not getting paid his fifty dollars a day plus expenses, which was the going rate for detectives. Why did they pay a lump sum? Why didn't they get a receipt? Because they had not hired a gigolo. They had hired a murderer, and they didn't want to leave a trail.

"Donald Williams says that his lifelong friend Carole Tregoff asked him to help her hire somebody who could get Mrs. Finch out of the picture permanently. I don't know how you could have put her out of the picture any more permanently than they did."

THURSDAY, FEBRUARY 25, 1960

Crail would continue his methodical dissection of the defense's version of events. He would highlight a list of things that just "seemed to happen" to the defendants, first talking about the attaché case, referring to it with the traditional word, "grip."

"Do you recall the items in this grip, that some have referred to as the 'murder kit'?" He turned and looked at Finch.

"There was no rubber tube in it, by the way, which would have been necessary had it been intended as a 'poison kit.' In fact, is there anything in it that could have been used as a surgical kit? No. Go over in your mind the items in there, and see if you can find any reason to believe that they were designed for any minor surgical purpose. What occurred to me was that if he was getting this kit together to use in surgical cases and in poison cases, why doesn't he assemble the things that are ordinarily used for that purpose? Why these make-shift instruments? For instance, wouldn't you expect to find cotton balls, wound dressings, adhesive bandages, surgical tape, or things of that nature there?"

"And what reason did he give us for carrying the case all over town with him? That he, a big owner in a big business such as a hospital, is carrying it and assembling it gradually. We all know that he could have sat down and dictated to a secretary, in ten minutes, the items that should be in there.

"That bag was never intended to cure anyone. It was intended to destroy life, and that is why he was up there on that hill that night.

351

"And then, what reason does he give us for taking the bag to Las Vegas? Inside are some Seconal tablets and an ace bandage for defendant Pappa. So he takes the whole bag? Wouldn't it have been simpler to just put the items in his pocket and take them that way?

"Now, then we have a succession of things that I like to call, 'things that just happened.' In fact, I have taken the time to number them for us.

"One, he just happened to have the bag in the front seat of his car, with no reason for carrying it around.

"Two, he just happened to have put the articles for defendant Tregoff into the grip.

"Three, he just happened to leave it in defendant Tregoff's car after she picks him up at the airport. After bringing these things all the way from Los Angeles, he forgets and leaves it in the car?

"Four, he just happened to put a flashlight, knife, and hammer in the bag. Some items he had bought for defendant Tregoff to use around the house.

"Five, the bag just happened to be locked, so that defendant Tregoff had to bring the whole bag up the hill instead of just the flashlight.

"Six, the two just happen to think of blowing up some rubber gloves to play with the dog. They had never done that before, but they decide to do it at 11:30 at night, and one of the gloves breaks and leaves these fragments on the driveway. And let these fine defense lawyers tell you how the finger from one of the gloves ended up on the floor of the car, on the driver's side.

"Seven, he just happened to go into the garage and find some rope that he decided he needed for his boat.

"I want you to take this murder kit with you when you go into chambers to decide your verdict. I want you to note that the packages for the gloves have been opened and that the empty packages were put back into the case. Why? So nobody would know that rubber gloves had been opened there that night. And listen to this! In each sack containing the gloves is a little package of powder to be put on the hands so that the gloves will be easier to put on. You will find that one of the little packages has been torn open. Why? Because he put them on his hands, that's why.

"I urge you not to believe any story that these two come in here and tell us. It has to be a reasonable story, one that goes along with reason, such as we would encounter in everyday experience. I would say this. If I were to choose between Cody, for instance, and defendant Finch, knowing that Cody's is a record of drunkenness and disorderly conduct, and comparing it with the things this fellow Finch told you about his personal life of deception and deceit, I would believe Cody.

"Remember how precise defendant Finch was with certain parts of his testimony? How precise he was in telling us about arriving at his house, his altercation with his wife and Marie Anne? Up to the point of his picking the gun up off of the asphalt, after the third scuffle for the gun began. Then things get pretty vague. Why? Did his memory suddenly fail him? I think it's because even after seven months it is pretty difficult to come up with a story that will satisfactorily explain why you shot a woman in the back at close range when she was running away from you. That's why he is so vague and indefinite. All he remembers is how he picked up the gun and threw it away. Remember how he told us he threw it away, backhand? Is that the way you would throw a gun away? Of course not. He had to tell you he threw it that way to fit the evidence.

"And he can't think of a reason to tell you why he took her purse, nor her wristwatch. Could it be that he wanted to make it look like a robbery, like Cody said he had planned?

"And what of defendant Tregoff? The judge will instruct you that a person who aids and abets in the commission of

353

a crime is as guilty as the principal, whether that person actually commits the crime or not. I have discussed her efforts to find a man who would kill for money in Las Vegas. Cody, realizing that she is sincere in her wish to kill the woman, tries to talk her out of it. What does she tell him? 'If you don't do it, Dr. Finch will, and if he doesn't do it, I will do it myself.'

"I will ask you to remember that she stayed in those bushes after she heard two shots fired, and she remained there even after the police arrived. How many women would not have gone out and tried to determine what had happened to the man they loved? Why didn't she? Because she knew he was all right. She knew that he had shot his wife. Because she is holding the murder kit that just a few moments before had held the murder weapon.

"And if she had a perfectly innocent reason for having the murder kit up on the hill, why did she not tell the police about it? Wouldn't you have? She didn't because she had no innocent reason for having it, that's why. She only had a story to account for it after she knew it had been found, and after she had had time to talk to defendant Finch about it.

"What part did she take in deciding to go to West Covina that night? I will read from her own testimony. 'From what I recall, Dr. Finch talked about seeing her and talking to her about some things and I suggested going down there the following night.' It was all her idea. And she must have known about the planned murder, or else she would not have been in the car.

"And finally, let's look at the motives these two had to bring about the death of Barbara Jean Finch. Dr. Finch's partner, Dr. Gordon, said he would not tolerate another Finch divorce. It would impair Finch's credit and would bring a property division. Goodness knows on the evidence Mrs. Finch could have presented in court it is not difficult to see how much of that property would have gone to her. A great deal, if not all of it, not including alimony.

"But one shot in the back could have taken care of all of that. And it could have prevented the divorce, and the delay in their own marriage. Let's not forget the $25,000 from the insurance company for her life insurance policy also.

"Murder is the deliberate killing of a human being with malice aforethought. If it is willful, deliberate, premeditated, and planned, as this murder was, then it is murder in the first degree, and it could not be anything else. I say to you, ladies and gentlemen, by overwhelming evidence in this case. I believe we have established beyond even a possible doubt the guilt of these two defendants on both counts contained in the indictment, first-degree murder and conspiracy to commit murder. Thank you."

thirteen
Defense Summation for
Carole Anne Tregoff

DURING A BRIEF recess, Robert Neeb talked with Carole at the defense table, occasionally giving her a reassuring pat on the top of her forearm. He would be the first defense attorney to address the jury. Photographs show him customarily pensive and brooding, sometimes scowling at the prosecutors. His bushy, expressive eyebrows could arch slightly on one side with suspicion, or lift high on both with an insight. His address would sometimes be didactic; other times, spirited and eloquent. It was the veteran defense attorney's last chance to persuade the jury his client had been victimized by police and prosecutors, and to a certain extent by her lover.

"I have not been at all of the trial, but I have studied the transcripts, and I have studied them very carefully and gone back over them many times. And I cannot find one single, one single solitary particle of evidence that Carole Tregoff on the night of July 18 caused injury to anyone, struck anyone, or caused harm to any human being, certainly not Barbara Jean Finch. So the prosecution, as you heard, has to fall back on 'aiding and abetting' to get a conviction. What does 'aiding and abetting' mean?

"The law has a particular reason for saying 'aiding and abetting,' and not 'aiding or abetting.' Anyone might aid or assist in committing a crime, yet not be guilty of a crime. You could not be brought into court if you had no knowledge-ful participation. Abetting means that you do something with full knowledge of what the other person is going to do. You take an active participation, either when the event is happening or immediately before it happens. You have placed yourself right in the picture as an active participant to the crime that you in your own mind knew was going to be committed.

"For instance, suppose a friend of mine is having trouble with, say, a tenant. And he asks me to drive him over to the house, and he's carrying a paper bag with him. Suppose when we get to the house he has an altercation with the tenant and pulls the gun out and kills him. Am I guilty of murder? No, of course not, because I did not have knowledgeful intention of participating in the shooting.

"Unless you jurors, in your own minds, think that while defendant Tregoff, while she was driving across the desert at night, that during that ride Carole Tregoff had in her mind an intention to kill, she is entitled to an acquittal on the charge of murder. You have to be convinced beyond reasonable certainty that while that car was going through the night, this young woman was proceeding mile by mile with intention to kill. Or else you have to acquit her.

"Now what about the charge of conspiracy? Who is it that puts the twist of criminal intent on every conversation Miss Tregoff has with Mr. Cody? Why, it's Cody. There is no evidence, no corroboration, except the twist he puts to those conversations. Just because they were talking together does not constitute conspiracy to commit the crime that is charged here. Corroborative evidence must be evidence which stands alone and not merely a set of circumstances to which someone gives a corrupt twist.

"If Cody has an occupation it is that of a professional liar, and I suppose we should compliment him that having chosen such a field of activity he has certainly succeeded.

"I think that the fact that Carole voluntarily surrendered herself when asked to do so was an affirmation of her innocence, and so was her decision to take the witness stand and leave herself open to any questions which the prosecutor might throw at her.

"As I listened to the prosecution's cross-examination, I began to be aware that the prosecution was not looking for the truth, they were seeking only a confession. And if that is what they were looking for, and if that was the only way they could get a conviction, then they must not have had many facts to begin with. As I read their cross-examination, I became aware that they were not looking for the truth; they were looking for a confession."

Evans refused to let Neeb finish. Court was adjourned.

THURSDAY, FEBRUARY 24

Spectators settling into their seats immediately sensed something different; jurors were leaving the courtroom through their side door—except for Eddie Lindsey, the black postal worker, who was walking through the swing gate, following a bailiff. Lindsey was holding his right cheek with his hand, rubbing his palm back and forth; his face was swollen on that side. It was obvious he was in pain.

At the bench all attorneys were standing, looking up at Evans.

"Your Honor," Neeb was agitated, "I'm at a critical point in my address to the jury. A delay at this point could confuse the jury. It's already been overnight and I'm almost through. May I finish before—"

"I've ruled that he must see the dentist today, Mr. Neeb. They already made the appointment for 10:00. I'll see all you gentlemen tomorrow."

Dr. Roy C. Johnson examined Lindsey, took some x-rays, and decided not to extract the tooth. He started his patient on antibiotics and returned him to jury duty.

FRIDAY, FEBRUARY 27, 1960

Neeb would take little time to finish his address.

"I think it would be helpful to remember what I asked Carole when she took the stand in her own defense. Remember that under the rules she can only be asked questions by the prosecution that are related to what she answers in our direct examination. We asked her if she entered in an agreement with Cody to harm or kill Mrs. Finch. She said 'No.' We asked her if she went to West Covina with Dr. Finch with any intent of physical violence or any injury to Mrs. Finch. She said 'No' again. I don't know how lawyers could possibly and purposefully open the door to cross-examination any more completely than we did in that regard. Why? Because we had nothing to hide. Our client is innocent.

"The prosecution tries to make something evil about the fact that at first she did not remember having the briefcase up on the hill that night. How many of us have forgotten and it later comes back to us. I was recently in an automobile accident and would have to testify that I can't remember all the things that happened, and yet when I was able to get back to court, little flecks of that accident would come back and little things fall into place. The mind is affected greatly by emotional shock, as well as it is by some kind of accident.

"If Carole Tregoff would have had any criminal intent with regard to that bag, do you think she would have simply left it there in the yard to be found? If she were guilty, would she just run off and leave it? Of course not.

"And remember that none of the prosecution witnesses ever placed Miss Tregoff at the scene that night. She did.

If she had any thought in mind of having participated in any kind of a crime, would she, the very next morning, tell Las Vegas police that she had been there? Of course not. And remember her statement to the officers in Las Vegas. She tried to answer every question made to her, never once refusing to answer. Is this something someone guilty of a crime would do? No.

"Let's remember Cody's testimony. There was one thing about his testimony I would have you question. If Cody in truth was engaged in Nevada in a diabolical plan to take a human life, the highest crime there is, and he, being wanted for bad checks, being an escapee at the time, knowing that one day the hourglass would run out and he would be apprehended for these things—would he have something that would connect him with the person with whom he would have engaged in such a terrible agreement? This picture? No.

"But did he? Yes. It is very interesting. They went through his belongings and they found a picture of Carole. Would he be carrying her picture if he had engaged with her in the worst kind of conspiracy? No.

"He has testified to his ability to drink the liquor and that he has a habit of getting drunk and not knowing what is going on. This is the witness on whom the prosecution is basing its case of conspiracy to take a human life. I believe Cody is a pathological liar. It is a form of paranoia, perhaps insanity. He says he lies to suit his purpose, and it depends upon whom he is dealing with. Again, this is the man by which the prosecution seeks to rest their case so far as conspiracy is concerned.

"And let me suggest, do you think the prosecution would have brought into this court this sort of person unless they needed him? If they had a case without him, would they bring him here, knowing how he would appear? No, they wouldn't have, unless it was an absolute necessity. Without it, they would have no case. This is their principal witness for my client's conspiracy charges.

"Now, there are some points that have occurred to me. Do persons who enter into a conspiracy, which is a very secretive thing, a partnership to commit a crime—do they go about together socially? Of course not. Yet my client appeared with Cody at a cocktail party. Would you go to a cocktail party with a person you just conspired with to commit murder? I don't think so.

"I am going to say this to you and I mean it very sincerely. The transcript speaks for itself. The prosecution has no evidence on the record that on the night of the eighteenth Miss Tregoff took part in any violence or did any harm to anyone. And there is no evidence of any corrupt agreement to commit any terrible crime except on the testimony of the witness Cody. And I say that in analyzing this record, it is apparent that the prosecution, knowing they don't have evidence, have based their contention against her upon what I often call the 'little four S's' of a desperate and weak prosecution: speculation, supposition, surmise, and suspicion.

"And none of these are evidence in any courtroom in the United States of America. I hope and I pray they never will be raised to the dignity of being evidence. Because mark you this: if ever that time should come when people could be accused, let alone convicted, of serious crimes upon such things—after that we might as well fold up our courts, because there would be only an empty shell remaining.

"I respectfully submit from all this evidence here presented that this lady is entitled to an acquittal of both of these monstrous charges, both as to count one and count two, because she is innocent and there is nothing in this courtroom that matters except the truth."

The handsome, clean-cut Bringgold, only a few years older than Carole, was next.

"I can add little to the eloquent address you just heard from Mr. Neeb. I would only like to say that the credibility of the witnesses in this case is in your hands and your hands alone. An attorney can only present a case to you, but it is your own common sense which should tell you whether or not a witness speaks with the ring of truth.

"Mr. Cody has told us a rather fantastic tale, in my opinion—one replete with inconsistency after inconsistency. Mr. Neeb rightly described it as something that read like a ten-cent novel. He had a motive for his testimony, which you must look to when you consider his testimony. This is the man whom sworn police officers from Minnesota told you they would not believe under oath. His is the only testimony, the sole testimony, that the prosecution can offer to us that Carole is guilty of conspiracy to commit murder. I join with Mr. Neeb in urging you to acquit on both counts."

Rexford Eagan had been characterized by the press as the badger of the three defense attorneys for Carole. He had been the bluntest, seeming to enjoy a scrap with the prosecutors, or even with Cooper at times. The short, muscular ex-Marine who had served in the Pacific theater had also played college football. He was not to disappoint anyone. He would take longer than anticipated.

"I doubt that it has happened in your lives, as it has not happened in my life, that we were all faced with a responsibility as in this case. I want you to know one thing. When I sit down, no other voice can be heard again in defense of Carole Tregoff. So I want you to believe me when I tell you that if we have forgotten something the prosecution has brought, there is not a single thing we can do. Please put the blame on us, and not on our client.

"It is ridiculous to say that Carole Tregoff took any part in a murder, or in a conspiracy. And you will be told by His Honor that the penalty for conspiracy to commit a crime is the same as the crime itself.

"Do you remember that old nursery rhyme, 'Rub-a-dub-dub, three men in a tub'? Well we have our three men in a tub, too, and they were Jack Cody, Richard Keachie, and Donald Williams. You know what Williams reminds me of? He reminds me of a puppy dog who is torn between the little boy, the little girl, and the mother of the house. This is Williams. He grew up with Carole and then succumbed to the influence of Las Vegas and the influence of Richard Keachie.

"Williams, when he came to court, was torn like that puppy dog—between Cody on the one hand and Carole on the other.

"And let's not forget the immunity that Cody was granted for his testimony here, that gave him carte blanche as far as this case was concerned. I believe it was Mr. Crail who referred to him as a fighting Irishman, at one point. He is no fighting Irishman. His record is one of drunkenness and disorderly conduct. He is just plain bad.

"Do you for a moment think that he made a deal for immunity for this case alone? No, he made a package deal, and I want to ask you one thing about Cody. Do you think for a minute that five minutes after you convict Miss Tregoff, Cody will be in jail? I liken him to a coyote, preying on the bodies of women. I want you to remember Cody and then to look at my client. Is it worth it to let Cody walk the streets and kill this young girl? You convict her and five minutes after you do, Cody will again be putting the con on somebody in Minneapolis and soliciting young girls for immoral purposes. Can you believe such a man as this? I don't think you can.

"Would you hire such a man to commit a murder? Hire a drunk? Who would blab about it all over Las Vegas? And would you introduce him around town, as Carole and Dr. Finch did? Anyway, you would hire a man capable of violence, wouldn't you? Is this man capable of violence? He has no record of violence.

"I am going to tell you something. I have met Cody before. Yes I have seen him. I have seen him in the jungles of New Guinea, in a jungle swamp. He was a malaria-bearing mosquito and I should have slapped him when I had the chance.

"You must be getting tired of all the yak yak, I know. But I want to make this final point. If Carole had any guilty knowledge, wouldn't she have bundled up Dr. Finch and run him out of her apartment in Las Vegas? Of course. Would she have gone to work at the Sands, where she was eventually contacted by the police? Of course not. Would she have immediately told the officers where Finch was, like she did? No.

"The prosecution will tell you that it is not believable that Carole could have frozen in those bushes for six hours. But I ask you to consider this. Look at how she is sitting at the desk now. Look at that girl now. Notice how she sits with her arm on the table. You have been watching her for weeks and every time you look at her, that arm is in the same position. That is not something we told her to do; nobody has told her to do that. I tell you, this girl is capable of freezing for five or six hours, without her mental faculties. She is capable of doing that. Let's not forget what she told us about the night, when she was a young girl, her mother attacked her stepfather with a butcher knife. What did she do? She ran and hid, for hours, a frightened little girl.

"Carole is not guilty of murder, and she is not guilty of conspiracy to murder. If there is any blame attached to her, it is the age-old story of a young girl in love with a man. That is her only crime. If you in your hearts can call it a crime. Ladies and gentlemen, we put in your hands the destiny of Carole Tregoff. May God grant you take good care of it. Thank you."

fourteen
Summation of Grant B. Cooper

MONDAY, MARCH 2

THE DAY BEGAN with a preposterous, some thought, request.

"Your Honor, I need special permission to call a last-minute witness who became known to me only recently." The jury was present as Cooper loudly made an impassioned doomed-from-the-beginning request. "It will affect the case greatly and help to show certain weaknesses in the testimony of Mane Anne Lidholm." It was a masterful attempt to get the jury's attention, and to raise questions of credibility with the state's star witness.

Evans looked confused. "What? You want to call a witness. Now?"

"Yes, Your Honor," Cooper looked amazingly self-confident. "I want to call Connie Staes."

"The newspaper reporter?" The judge's eyebrows raised for one of the few times in the trial.

"Yes, Miss Lidholm made statements to her that—"

"That's enough," Whichello was on his feet. "Your Honor, it's another of his cheap Perry Mason tricks. It's the same old last-minute-surprise-witness maneuver. He does it all the time. I'm tiring of such things. Mr. Cooper cannot start telling us what he thinks this witness may testify to if she is allowed to."

All counsel went to the bench. Cooper continued his plea. He knew he had no chance whatsoever of calling a witness. He, like all counsel, had closed his case. Everyone would yell in a hoarse whisper. Some jurors cocked their heads to the side and leaned forward slowly.

"And I want to call Ray Hopkinson, too. The maid made statements the night of the murder that were inconsistent. She gave two different stories." Cooper persisted.

"Hoppi? You can't recall Hoppi Hopkinson. He was *my* witness!" Whichello had his right elbow on the judge's bench and his left fist pushed into his side. He turned to Evans. "Now he wants to start calling my witnesses back to the stand. Your Honor, he knows my witnesses can only be cross-examined after I call them."

Cooper spoke faster, knowing a ruling was coming. "That's not right. I reserved the right to recall Hopkinson. If the Court checks the record, we'll see—"

"Mr. Cooper," Evans began in a whisper loud enough for most to hear, "You know I can't allow you to do this. Now let's get on with your final address, if we may."

Grant Cooper would have the attention of an alert jury for his closing remarks. He took a moment to straighten the three piles of transcripts on his desk, standing in three-foot-high columns. He waited a few moments; the room quieted. A few moments more, then.

"You know, people of the jury, I have been watching you since this trial began, and I notice that some of you give your full attention to the prosecution when it is talking and that you sort of stare out into space when any of the defense lawyers speak. I am going to ask you for your full attention during my address because my client's life depends upon it.

"I also want to explain something to you. I thought, and most defense attorneys feel, that it is not in the best inter-ests of their clients to discuss the case before it properly be-gins in the courts. That is a reason that you only heard the prosecution's side of things in all the tremendous pretrial publicity this trial got. And believe me this trial got a lot of publicity, not only in this country but from overseas, too. I have gotten letters from all over the world with advice. I am going to ask you to push all that publicity from your mind as you listen to our final arguments, and as you deliberate the fates of the accused.

"I'd like to say that I have never heard a better, finer argument from a prosecutor than Mr. Crail expressed to you in his remarks. Of course, he's wrong and I don't agree with him. You have to understand that his point of view has been conditioned, and understandably so, by more than thirty years of being a prosecutor.

"I believe Mr. Crail started his discussion with the night of July 18, 1959, so I will, too. I will start with the time that the officers arrived and with what they found. And what did they find?

"You will recall that Marie Anne, after a harrowing experience that night, phoned the police. What she told them is beside the point now, but the police arrived promptly, and there at the point indicated, lying in the grass dead with a bullet in her back, was a human being, Barbara Jean Finch. There were no weapons found there. What other conclusion could the police come to at that time but that someone had murdered Mrs. Barbara Finch?

"Obviously, she couldn't have committed suicide. Certainly no one could shoot oneself in the back and then have the weapon disappear. So when Captain Ryan and his brother officers arrived on the scene, they immediately came to the conclusion that murder had been committed. And, I personally think they were justified in thinking that. Especially after Captain Ryan took a statement from Marie Anne about an hour and a half afterward.

"And I am sure that Marie Anne, having in mind the things that she had been told by Mrs. Finch, believed that

Dr. Finch had shot his wife in the back. So then the wheels of the law started in motion. And they have been continually in motion, grinding away ever since. And even before morning broke, news was flashed all over that Dr. Finch was wanted for murder. And the next day it was emblazoned in headlines in all of the newspapers, and on the radio and television, that Dr. Finch was wanted for murder.

"Then, of course, the next day he was arrested in Las Vegas. And the presses rolled, and the television cameras ground, and the radio put out all of that information. Again, Dr. Finch and his mistress were wanted for murder.

"Now let me take you back to the first days of the trial, ladies and gentlemen, when you were being questioned on had you read in the newspapers the day after Dr. Finch was arrested that Carole had broken his alibi. And some of you said you may have or didn't remember, but you know now, having heard all of the testimony in the case, that Dr. Finch never offered an alibi, so no alibi had been broken. There was no alibi.

"Then Dr. Finch called his attorney at the time, Mr. Martineau, and was advised by him not to make any statements to Captain Ryan and Chief Sill. Now some of you may wonder, 'Why does a lawyer advise his client not to make any statements to anyone if he is innocent?' It is very simple. Guilty or innocent, this is the advice of any experienced lawyer, for the simple reason that when things are repeated they can take on a different meaning. And you are faced with this when you are cross-examined. I will demonstrate this before I am through.

"Dr. Finch was following the advice of his lawyer; that's why he didn't make any statements at that time. He admitted nothing and said nothing. But again the presses continued to roll more and more headlines, all pointing to the guilt of Dr. Finch. Not one word up to this point was spoken in his defense. On July 27 and 28 in the city of West Covina, during the hot summer months, Dr. Finch's preliminary hearing was held. Again the press had a field day. It was a Roman holiday. And again all the evidence was aimed and directed to the guilt of the defendant.

"You will recall—it is evidence here—that Carole Tregoff was dramatically arrested during this period of time. Now, not only Dr. Finch, but his red-headed sweetheart were in the news. And still nothing from the doctor, nothing from his lawyer. And people naturally and understandably wondered why the defense doesn't get something going? Why doesn't Dr. Finch speak up in his own defense? But there wasn't a word.

"We continue to August and the preliminary examination of Carole Tregoff. Again, more newspaper news, more newsreels, more television, more radio, all directed to the one point—'guilty, guilty, guilty.' And yet the American public never stopped to consider one important point. 'Have we heard the other side of the story?' And they think to themselves, 'If he doesn't talk, he must be guilty.'

"Then in September, about the tenth or eleventh, we hear news of Keachie and Williams. Do you remember the newspapers from then? 'Murder for Hire. Dr. Finch Paid Killer.' If the public didn't think he was guilty before, they surely thought so now. Then my friend, and your friend, John Patrick Cody, was interviewed in a Minneapolis jail. And again, the headlines, television, the radio, all pouring out the news–'guilty, guilty, guilty, pound, pound, pound.' And still not a word from Finch, not a word from his lawyer, not a word from the lawyers for Carole Tregoff. Then in September the doctor and Miss Tregoff are indicted by the grand jury. Again, the presses roar, radio and television. The doctor and his mistress are indicted.

"Now, I suspect that some of you here are saying to yourselves, 'Well they were indicted by the grand jury, and the judge held them over for trial at their preliminary hearings; maybe they are guilty.' Let me suggest to you, ladies and gentlemen, that you have all taken an oath to uphold the law in your deliberations as jurors, and I believe that you will. A preliminary hearing and a grand jury hearing are the system we have for bringing people to trial. All that is necessary to hold a man to answer, or a woman to answer, is a strong suspicion, that is all.

"And I agree with the grand jury. A man flees, steals two cars, refuses to talk. I would have indicted him too, given the evidence. But let me advise you that before a grand jury a defendant is not compelled to be a witness unless he voluntarily asks to be heard. And let me advise you that if he does decide to testify, he does not have the right to have his lawyer present to advise him, but the district attorney can ask him questions.

"Any lawyer who would allow his client to go before the grand jury and testify, in my opinion, is a fool. And ladies and gentlemen, Grant B. Cooper is no fool. The judge will instruct you not to be biased by any of these facts that I have talked about so far. And he will forbid you to be governed by sentiment, conjecture, sympathy, passion, prejudice, public opinion, or public feeling. We have the right to expect you to conscientiously consider and weigh the evidence and define the law.

"I want each of you to ask yourselves if in the smallest way some of the pound, pound, pound of the news about this case didn't infiltrate into your mind, and if you had formed the slightest opinion of guilt of these two people. Now, where did this news come from? It didn't come from the defense, and it didn't come from me. It had to come from only one source, the police and the prosecuting authorities, and possibly some enterprising reporters. But remember this! When that came to you in the form of news, it was all slanted, it was all one way, because that is all of the news they got.

"You may ask me, 'Well Mr. Cooper, why didn't you speak out? If all these things were untrue, why didn't you say something?' Well, I think you have a right to know the answer to that question. Both the canons of ethics of the American Bar Association and the ethics of the American College of Trial Lawyers forbid it. We are bound by ethics not to talk about a case before it goes to trial. Because the law of the United States says that a defendant is innocent until proven guilty in a proper court of law.

"And that is why I have the right to believe, the right to rely upon you, that each and every one of you would presume that my client is innocent and that he has been innocent throughout the entire trial, even after you heard all the evidence from both sides, even after you hear our arguments, even after you hear your instructions from the judge, yea, until you go into the jury room to begin your deliberations. My client is innocent. That is what you told me you would do when I examined you before you became a juror. Do you remember? And that is what I expect from you now.

"Now, quite properly, because the burden of proof is on the people, Mr. Whichello made his opening statement in which he very clearly and lucidly told you what the people expected to prove. He told you a story of what he thought had happened. And it wasn't a very nice story either, was it? And he backed up his story with some witnesses, didn't he? And it must have been difficult to keep telling yourself that my client was innocent when he made his opening remarks and presented his witnesses. But I asked you to do it, and I have a right to expect you to have done it.

"Let's talk about 'reasonable doubt,' if we could. His Honor will tell you that if you find any reasonable doubt that my client is guilty, you must acquit him. Reasonable doubt is defined as follows. It is not a minimum possible doubt; it is that state of affairs which, after the entire comparison and consideration of all the evidence, leaves the minds of the jurors in that condition that they cannot say they feel an abiding conviction to a moral certainty of the truth of the charges.

"The law adds this: the law does not require demonstration for that degree of proof which, excluding all possibility of error, produces absolute certainty. Only that degree of proof is necessary which convinces the mind and directs the conscience of those who are bound to act conscientiously upon the facts.

"Now, I am concerned about some of you, about your ability to reason with me with an open mind. As I have sat through the trial, it has appeared to me that notes have only been made while the prosecution was talking, and not when the defense was talking. And I noticed that some of you seemed to be staring off into space when the defense was talking. I ask you to give me the courtesy and exercise your duty, and please listen and reason with me. Let's get to the facts.

"I believe that Marie Anne was trying to tell the truth, although I think I can demonstrate she cannot be relied upon. That doesn't make her a liar. Every lawyer who has tried cases knows that if you have a dozen witnesses you will have a dozen points of view. And I can't see why she would deliberately lie, either. But let me ask each of you this question: how would you have handled her as a witness if you had been me, if you had been representing a client and she took the stand against him.

"I tried to be as much of a gentleman as I could, first of all because I hope I am. But even if I were not, I realize that this fine-looking young lady, a fresh, wholesome young lady, who was here in a foreign country, was obviously trying to do the best she could. But I don't think any of us are free of prejudice completely. Take, for example, her testimony about May 16, which was the morning after the alleged altercation between my client and his wife in the master bedroom.

"I think it natural that she would take to the side of her employer and not have kindly feelings toward Dr. Finch after what was said to her. After all, Mrs. Finch was her employer, and the two had apparently unloaded their innocent thoughts upon each other and taken each other into their confidence. It would have been less than human for Marie Anne not to side with Barbara Jean. So it was with this background that she took the witness stand.

"I think you will all see that during the testimony she had no trouble at all understanding the questions and then answering them. You will remember that she at first denied that my client had called his wife on the morning of July 18 and then later finally admitted that he had, when I cross-examined her. Can you imagine if there had been no cross-examination? That was important because one doesn't call up a prospective murder victim and make an appointment with them and then lie in wait for them."

He glanced at the clock over the main door of the room. "I see the hour is late, Your Honor, I think it best that I continue in the morning. I have some transcripts to read. It is very dull business, but vitally important to show discrepancies in her testimony."

TUESDAY, FEBRUARY 3, 1960

"Let's talk about the discrepancies in the maid's story. I took the time to count all of the different versions of things she said in her statements to the police, her testimony at the preliminary hearings, and her testimony at this trial. I have counted eighteen different subjects upon which she told at least two and sometimes three different stories. Altogether, on these eighteen different subjects there are thirty-four different versions. Now the prosecution may say, 'Well, what difference does it make whether he grabbed her by the hair or the shoulders, or if he said this or that? These are little things.' But they are important, and I will tell you why.

"You will remember this, for instance. It was light in the garage and that the lights on the car were on, which would give plenty of light. You will recall Marie Anne testified that when she saw the gun, it was light in the garage, and then at another point she said my client had turned out the lights, so you see these things are important. Even though they are little things, they are important.

"Now when His Honor gives you his instructions, one of the things he will talk about is 'the credibility of a witness.' A witness who has been careless in his or her observations, and because of such has made statements inconsistent with his or her testimony, not necessarily willfully or in the intent to deceive, may be distrusted by you. You may reject in part or in whole the testimony of any such witness if you choose. And the weight you give such a witness is entirely up to you.

"And there is another instruction the court will give to you concerning the credibility of witnesses. It applies to witnesses who testify falsely, and the court will instruct you as follows. You are the sole and exclusive judges in the effect and value of the testimony presented by the witnesses. And the character of the witnesses must be taken into consideration when you are determining their credibility. You must scrutinize the manner of the witness when on the stand, and also their degree of intelligence. Although the witness is presumed to be truthful, this may be repelled by the manner in which he testifies, his interests in the case, his biases or prejudices, and the character of the witness.

"With regard to Miss Lidholm, I ask you first, have I not discussed her testimony fairly and objectively? And I put this question to you: if someone near and dear to you were on trial, sitting here as Dr. Finch is sitting at the present, would you be willing to have his life and liberty taken on the testimony of Marie Anne? As lovely a girl as she is, as sweet and wholesome as she is, would you honestly be willing to rely on that testimony?

"Now we come to another phase of the evidence, one that is a little difficult for laymen as opposed to lawyers. It has to do with the state of mind of Barbara Jean Finch on the evening of July 18 and for some of the days preceding it. This is very important. You remember that Mr. Crail analyzed the testimony of Marie Anne and Mark Stevens in his closing remarks, but he passed over very lightly the testimony of one very important witness, that of Mr. Joseph Forno, Mrs. Finch's attorney.

"Evidence has been offered by the prosecution and received in evidence that the deceased, Barbara, in her lifetime, allegedly made statements to these people that the defendant Finch had made threats against his wife. I believe the court will tell you, that you will recall, that on each such occasion the court has instructed you that such evidence was offered by the people and received solely for the purpose of attempting to prove the state of mind of the deceased, and that it was not intended as evidence to show that the doctor actually made those threats or did any of the acts contended in any of her statements. In other words, it does not mean the threats were actually made. You will be instructed to treat this evidence as though no threats were ever made, because there is no evidence that they were made.

"So when you get into the jury room and one of you says 'Hey, what about those threats,' I want one of you to act as a monitor and say, 'You are not following the law; those threats were never made.'

"Let's talk a little about her state of mind. Let's go back to April 15, 1959, when she and her husband made out their wills. In hers she says, 'I hereby appoint my said husband Raymond the guardian of the person and estate of our son Raymond Bernard Finch, Jr., and I hereby appoint my said husband the guardian of my said daughter, Patti Lee Daugherty.' So as late as April these were her feelings. She was willing to entrust those who were nearest and dearest to her, her son and daughter, to Dr. Finch.

"Let's get back to May 15, when she alleged to Marie Anne and then later to the police that her husband had hit her. You will recall that he said Barbara had been ill for several days and then had fallen. What kind of a situation, what state of mind, might she have been in at that time? Let's remember that she had, for a period of six months, been going to her lawyer, Mr. Forno. He testified that she had been in twenty-five or thirty times. She had detectives following Dr. Finch, and obviously had gotten the goods on him. And generally, with most women, when it gets down to getting a divorce, it is important to the women that they get their just deserts in dollars and cents. The wife generally wants money, and the husband doesn't want to give as much as the wife wants. Husbands always, you will find, complain they don't make as much as they used to, and wives will always say that their husband threatened to kill them.

"Mrs. Finch had been through a divorce case before. She was anxious to get as much money as she could. She needed to build up her case, that's why she hired the detectives, because it would put him over a barrel. And I think it is a fair inference that she was telling all of her friends these various stories because she thought her friends could later come and testify that they actually happened. They can't, because that is hearsay.

"You will recall there were some discrepancies in the testimony about the threats my client allegedly made to

Mrs. Finch. Mr. Forno testified that she told him Dr. Finch had hit her with a gun and was going to push her over a cliff in a car. But in the affidavit that she had signed in her divorce filing, she said nothing about a cliff. And in the original police report filed by Officer Handrahan, he said, 'Suspect owns a gun, but has not used it to threaten her, and she hasn't seen it on him.' See how this story changes?

"Do any of you think he hit her with a gun and then threatened to drive her off a cliff somewhere? Would any reasonable person, after that, get into a car and drive with him to the hospital where he could put in stitches? As she did? Let's think about things that are reasonable.

"And what about the alleged altercation on June 25 during the exchange of automobiles? Marie Anne testified that Mrs. Finch had told her that Dr. Finch was going to be coming to exchange some automobiles. I asked her, 'Did she tell you anything about the car?' And the maid answered, 'No, she just said that Dr. Finch took her car, and that his car was in poor condition so she had to get it down to the gasoline station.' Now, later I asked her something about whether the doctor had keys to the house, and she answered, 'I believe he had, because he was up once and stole Mrs. Finch's car and all the keys she had.'

"Now, was there anything about this incident that would justify exaggeration that he stole the car? So we have a lot of these kinds of stories. That he stole a car. We have Mark Stevens saying he sat on her chest for four hours. He wasn't even in the house for four hours; we know that from the maid's testimony. Mr. Forno was telling us that she was afraid of guns being used on her, and yet there is no mention of guns in her court filings against the doctor. Why is that?

"Why was she telling one thing to Marie Anne and another to Mr. Stevens, and then another to her attorney? Why, it was for the purpose of trying to lay the groundwork for a divorce.

"I am sure you heard Mark Stevens's testimony, after which you would have thought that my client beat his wife all the time. But remember that Marie Anne testified to hearing only one argument in all the time she was in the house. Either Mr. Stevens is a liar, or Mrs. Finch was not telling the truth.

"I am not going to spend much time on the $3,000 check the prosecution alleges my client forged. Mr. Mire, the handwriting expert, said he could not tell us for sure who signed it. If that is the case, then how could he have been so sure that Mrs. Finch did not sign it? She had just returned from a session with an attorney about her divorce. What woman would not be upset and sign her name differently?

"Let me ask you this. If you were going to forge a check, as they say my client did, would you send somebody else to cash it, and would you ask for one thousand dollar bills, as my client did? Why, you might as well put a neon sign over your head that says 'forger.'

"I'm not going to tell you that my client is perfect, or that he is above reprehensible behavior. There is no question that he cheated on his wife, violated a couple of the Ten Commandments, committed adultery, and lied to his wife and business partners. And Dr. Finch, I want to tell you that I think it is reprehensible that you hired Cody to follow and possibly compromise your wife.

"Ladies and gentlemen, I think it all started with the Garden of Eden. Dr. Finch was not the first man to make these mistakes, nor will he be the last. Sometimes people do funny and stupid things. But that does not mean he is guilty of murder.

"Let's get to the night of the eighteenth of July. I will ask you to remember my client's testimony about that night, about how his wife died in his arms. And then of his sheer panic as he fled. What he did in leaving the scene that night was consistent with guilt. But it is also consistent with innocence. People react and do funny things in times of stress.

"If Doctor Finch is a murderer, then he is the stupidest murderer that I have ever come in contact with. The prosecution says, 'One shot in the back takes care of all the defendants' problems. No divorce, no property settlement, no scandal, no alimony, plus they get $25,000 in life insurance.'

"Well, I say to you, I know that Dr. Finch would will that his wife were here, and so would I. If she had to be shot, then thank God it was an accident.

"Remember that when Dr. Finch went out of the garage to see what might have happened to Carole, he had already been seen by Marie Anne. No man with any amount of intelligence at all, after going to the pains that the prosecution suggests to kill his wife and cover up his tracks, and knowing he had been seen in the garage by Marie Anne, would ever dream of shooting his wife in the back for the purpose of getting out of alimony, or for a $25,000 insurance policy. It just doesn't make sense.

"And if he is a murderer, then he is also an accomplished actor. Dr. Finch, I say to you, if you have lied about this, you are as vile as they make them and you deserve to be convicted, but I can't believe a man could get up on this witness stand before twelve ladies and gentlemen and describe this scene unless it happened.

"Remember this, ladies and gentlemen! This case rests first on the testimony of Marie Anne, and it rests on the testimony of Cody and Williams, and the balance of the case, so far as what happened, is entirely circumstantial evidence.

"It is better that one hundred guilty men should go free than that one innocent man shall suffer. Remember this: you and you alone now know the facts. Having heard all of the evidence, having now heard both sides, can you say that you have within your hearts an abiding conviction to a moral certainty of the proof of the charge? If you have, you have to vote him guilty. But if you haven't, it is your duty to find him not guilty.

"At the outset of the case, when I talked to you before you were selected as jurors, I asked each one of you if you would give us the benefit of your individual attention, and I remind you of it now. Both the people and the defense are entitled to the individual opinion of each member of this jury. I ask you that you reason it out with your fellow jurors. Discuss it pro and con. Discuss the law. Discuss the bad, and discuss the good. We are entitled to your honest opinion."

He walked to his client and looked at him while he spoke.

"Dr. Finch, we have been together a long time. I am going to leave your case now to these twelve jurors. Ladies and gentlemen, I place the responsibility that has been on my shoulders, on your shoulders. Please guard it well. Thank you."

Bernard Finch, eyes red and tearful, rose to shake Cooper's hand. The two hugged.

"Thanks, Grant. You did a swell job."

fifteen
Summation of Fred Whichello

THURSDAY, MARCH 3, 1960

"JUST A COUPLE of more, Fred." A photographer was taking Whichello's picture, just minutes before he was to begin his summation. His face was serious and dour. He was holding two photographs. In his left hand was a picture of young, pretty Barbara Jean in her tennis outfit, holding a racket in the ready position. In his right hand: the one taken by Officer Frank Meehan in the early morning hours of July 19. Barbara Jean was sprawled on the lawn, face up, lifeless.

In his conferences with Crail, the two had decided to focus more on Carole's conspiracy charges. They felt Finch would be convicted and that Carole might evoke sympathy from the jury as an "innocent girl in love" and possibly be acquitted.

He began by showing the two photographs.

"We've heard all about two of the three people in this love triangle. I would ask that you not forget about the third person, Barbara Jean Finch. Here you see her alive and vibrant, and here cold and lifeless, left dead on the lawn of her father-in-law's house, like an animal. Let's not forget these two defendants would not be here were it not for the broken, butchered body of Barbara Jean Finch, the woman they sent to her grave.

"I will do most of my talking about Dr. Finch, but let's not forget this latter-day Lady Macbeth sitting at the end of the table. Carole is really the aggressor and instigator of this whole thing; Dr. Finch was the executioner of the plan.

"I agree with Mr. Cooper when he says that the police, when they arrived on the scene that night, had every reason to believe that a crime had been committed. And I think you will find that we still do have every reason to think so, and that as you form an opinion, and consider the evidence of the defense, you will find that the prosecution is better off now than it was at the beginning of the case.

"If a defense is to succeed, then it must do so by way of an explanation. And in this case the explanation is unsatisfactory beyond human experience and utterly unreasonable, so the prosecution is better off than when we started these proceedings. In fact, I wonder if your reaction to the defense was the same as mine—that there was a beautifully executed and beautifully detailed series of "grasping for straws," a hanging on to little, tiny, unimportant points; the stressing of so many little things because there wasn't anything better to work with.

"And I want to draw your attention to Mr. Cooper's abilities. He is the best there is. And he did the best he could do with the material with which he had to work.

"I note that the prosecution and the defense agree on a few points. No one questions that Dr. Finch fired the shot that killed his wife, that he fled from the scene, stealing two automobiles in his flight. And of course, no one can dispute the physical evidence at the scene: the blood stains, the rubber glove fragments, and the rest.

"And let's remember the things that weren't there. They are just as important. There was no watch, and no purse on the victim. And there is no question that Cody was hired to do something to Mrs. Finch. The issue is what was he hired to do. There is no question that Mrs. Finch had filed for divorce, or that there was a great deal of property at stake. There is no question that insurance existed, or that there was a will which gave defendant Finch all the property.

"A tremendous amount of this case is not in dispute. We claim the existence of the motives. To conclude that they existed is inescapable—the financial gain, the lack of a scandal, a quicker wedding for these two defendants. The problem the defense has is to explain and come somewhere near to making sense. And what do we find when they cannot explain away certain things? The oldest trick in the book: 'I can't remember.'

"Now, I think it would be logical to say that after you consider the issues that are now at issue, and if you believe Cody and Marie Anne, and when you decide that the defendants' actions after this occurrence are inconsistent with innocence, you find them guilty of murder in the first degree, as to each of the defendants. I think the question, 'Why would they run away?' will be the most convincing evidence you will consider. If any of you has any doubt to their guilt, the fact that they ran will convince you.

"The next most difficult thing for them to explain away, after the fact that they ran away, is this shot in the back, from high up, slanting downwards. In a sense, that is the strongest physical evidence against them. It completely eliminates self-defense. It is awfully difficult to account for things as an accident with this fact, and that's when things get awkward for the defense, in trying to explain this.

"Let me say I seem to be spending a lot of time talking about defendant Finch. It isn't because I am intending in any way to neglect our Lady Macbeth over there. The evidence against her is just as compelling. I believe that you will find that she was really an aggressor in this matter.

"Let's not forget, on the question of motive, that these two defendants are free to say anything they want to about poor Mrs. Finch, about what she did that night, because she cannot rise out of the grave and call them liars. They can say they had this armistice. And defendant Pappa, and don't for a moment forget that she was married at the time, can say she was friendly with Mrs. Finch. He seems to feel that this armistice seems to justify his acts with the co-defendant, like it made everything all right.

"He did not claim that he had any evidence whatsoever that Mrs. Finch had committed any improprieties, but he had to explain his actions with Cody—that Cody would be able to seduce her. I want you to examine Mrs. Finch's associates, those you saw here. Can you imagine Cody at the Los Angeles Tennis Club. What's he going to do? Walk up to Mrs. Finch and say, 'Hi ya,' babe?' How can any human being imagine Cody being allowed to do to Mrs. Finch what they said he claimed he could do?

"And do any of us believe this story of the armistice agreement? Do you think Mrs. Finch would have said, 'All right go out with anybody you want—I don't care—even the employees at the clinic?' Finch lied to you from the witness stand about that, and I don't often use that word, unless the lying is clear beyond any doubt. This armistice agreement simply didn't happen; it is contrary to human existence. As is the frigidity he made up. Don't you think that her alleged frigidity is really just a reaction of disgust to his loose activities?

"I think she was a lady, one who didn't want to share her husband with the other people at the medical clinic. Of course, he claims that her frigidity justified his actions and his love affairs. Remember he says these were just small love affairs in which it was standard procedure to tell the ladies you loved them. And I suppose in his weird, egocentric system of morals he would think his position was justified. But the rest of the world does not think that way.

"And I would like to know his authority for saying that if a wife or husband says it's okay, then there is nothing wrong with adultery. I have read a little philosophy and theology and I have never seen that before. The nearest thing I can remember that it comes close to is the 'nihilists' who say that there should be no laws at all.

"Incredulously, he tells us that he thinks his wife has it made. She has her armistice agreement which relieves her of any wifely duties, her Cadillac, and her modeling courses, and of course he never laid a hand on her, according to him—even though we know that she filed for a divorce and went to a doctor who examined her for her wounds after one altercation.

"I was not surprised that Mr. Cooper spoke unkindly about John Patrick Cody. He beat me to the punch when he said that Cody was a poor choice as a witness. I ask you to consider that he would be just as poor a choice of a witness in a divorce case. Picture yourself running around Las Vegas wanting to pick someone to follow Mrs. Finch, to find out if she is doing something wrong. If she is doing nothing wrong, a person would need to lure her into doing something wrong. So, you do need someone unscrupulous, I suppose. But do you want a criminal? Do you want a murderer? Do you find them by involving yourself with the criminal element of Las Vegas? Of course not. You hire somebody here, in Los Angeles, it's standard procedure in a divorce case, every divorce attorney knows who to call.

"But, ladies and gentlemen, if you are looking for a murderer, all that makes sense. And let's not forget that Finch did ask if Cody was capable of murder, saying that he was worried about Carole. The man is going to be in Los Angeles and he's worried about Carole? That doesn't make sense to me.

"Let's see what gain Cody got out of agreeing to testify for the prosecution. He talked to us in Minneapolis. He talked to his lawyer, and agreed to testify. And then he went into court, pleaded guilty to a bad checks charge, and was given the maximum sentence. What kind of a 'deal' would that be?

"I can see that His Honor is starting to feel the need for us to adjourn for the day. I will see you tomorrow, at which time I will, I am sure, conclude. Thank you."

THURSDAY, MARCH 3, 1960

Whichello could create his own excitement.

"You know I was thinking, over the night, that this case reminded me of a case from 1937 that I remember. I was a new prosecutor at that time, having been on the job just a few months." Whichello was well rested and seemed to bounce more when he walked.

Crail leaned forward. Whichello appeared to be on the verge of citing a previous case. There had been no cases cited during the trial, and the attorneys were prohibited from discussing case law in their summations. Evans glanced at the defense attorneys; none spoke.

"Two men bought a couple of rattlesnakes with the intention of murdering one of their wives. They put her feet into the sack and she was bitten, but she did not die. What were they to do? Well, they drowned her instead, and the bite marks were not noted at the autopsy. Later, however, their plan became known, and a second autopsy revealed the snakebite marks. They were convicted of first-degree murder, of premeditated murder, because they had thought ahead to bring the snakes. You see, even though they didn't kill her with their original plan, they had a plan all the same, and that's what constituted premeditation."

Crail was looking at the defense attorneys; still, all were silent.

"It's the same with our two defendants here. They planned to drive Mrs. Finch off of a cliff, plans went awry, and they ended up shooting her in the back instead. You must remember that in your deliberations."

"Your Honor,"—it was Neeb—"may I come forward."

All the attorneys went to the bench to talk about Fred's mentioning the well known Rattlesnake James case.

"I want a mistrial, Your Honor," Neeb's eyebrows were raised full up. "I am moving for a mistrial for both defendants. To talk about Rrattlesnake James and make an analogy with our clients is prejudicial. How can we get a fair trial now?"

"There is nothing wrong with quoting case law, Your Honor." Crail was speaking for the prosecution. "Rattlesnake James, we feel, is very instructive to the jury."

Evans wasted no time. "You can't bring up case law in a closing argument, Mr. Crail. However instructive it might have been, it happens to be my job and it will be stricken from the record. Motion for mistrial will be denied. I will instruct the jury to disregard Mr. Whichello's analogy."

Fred returned to the subject of Cody's credibility. Many noticed his voice was growing increasingly hoarse as the day went on.

"I am not holding Cody as an admirable character. However, if you believe he is substantially accurate, the evidence of guilt is overwhelmingly complete. Of course, a great deal of his testimony has been given a twist by the defendant Finch. But I would urge you to consider that the best corroboration of Cody's testimony comes not from the defendants' statements, but from their actions on the night of July 18. These were the actions of people who would have said what Cody said they said.

"I believe our two most challenging questions that we posed at the beginning of this case have not been answered adequately by the defense. The first is: Why would one drive six hundred miles in the middle of the night to settle a divorce case, bringing one's mistress along to talk about it in the garage? He explains this, or tries to, by saying that he has thought of something new, a new idea that just can't wait until Monday, when he was planning to be back in town anyway. So what is this new idea? That she abandon her position in Los Angeles, where she had an abundance of evidence of adultery against him, that she abandon all that and come rushing up to Las Vegas and live six weeks and get a quickie divorce. He gets so enthused with this idea he just has to drive six hundred miles and tell her right away.

"And Carole has said that she and Mrs. Finch got along fine, just fine. That's why she thought she would be able to talk to Mrs. Finch that night.

"Then he says that when they got there, he said to Barbara, 'We want to talk to you.' Now, Carole has said that there was nothing Mrs. Finch liked better than to have a cozy little chat with her at the old medical center, but what does Barbara Jean do on July 18? She comes out of the car and points a pistol at her! Surprise!

"The truth is that neither situation happened. They didn't get along and Mrs. Finch never pointed a gun at them. The defendants have changed their stories so much that the absurdities are glaring.

"An appointment to discuss a divorce matter at 11:00 at night! Sounds like an absurd time to me. But it sounds like a great time for an ambush and to kill her—a dandy time, in fact. They can't drag her out of the house and kill her because the children are inside. But they can ambush her and kill her as she comes home, can't they?

"Think of the situation these two defendants were in just the week before the murder happened. They had told witnesses that they were certain that Mrs. Finch had damaging evidence against them. It not only would be self-evident from the fact they were maintaining these apartments, which could be found out very quickly, but specifically, the defendant Finch told you his wife told him he had been followed and quite a bit had been found out. And they had no evidence against her; everything they had tried had failed.

"And let's not forget the circumstances of her restraining orders. She had him hemmed in: she had total control of his business affairs and income.

"Now, there was a very important fact, or so far as Mrs. Pappa was concerned, desire to not go the way of Mrs. X and Mrs. Y. She had known them both and seen them both come and go, and she wasn't about to see that happen to her. Carole wanted to stay up there on the gravy train. And I call your attention to the fact that she had taken the lead in hiring Cody. Now isn't that odd, on anybody's theory? A twenty-two-year-old girl taking the lead in important negotiations for a man twice her age, and with twice her experience!

"I think that's because she was the instigating force, the aggressive one of the two, the one who undertook the negotiations for the murder of Barbara Jean Finch. And we have seen that she did the hiring, and making the plans, and the plans being ratified by the defendant Finch. He comes into the picture a little later, and I don't want you to ever forget the statement by Mrs. Pappa. 'If you don't kill her, Dr. Finch will; and if he doesn't, I will.'

"Don't you think that it is a little absurd that the two defendants were sitting at the Sands Hotel in the early morning hours of July 18 discussing a new plan for an amicable divorce they were going to drive down and sell? Don't you think it is more reasonable to believe that with all that there was to be gained by killing her themselves, it was Mrs. Pappa who said, 'Cody has run out on us. Let's you and I go down and do it right.'

"And Dr. Finch starts adding his ideas, which have been brewing, no doubt, in his mind for some time, assembling a kit which will provide a flexible procedure—a number of means will be provided. There is a very convenient cliff right near the garage, and it wouldn't be unheard of for a car to go over that cliff. And it isn't impossible to hit someone with a gun knocking them unconscious, wrap them up with a rope, give them an injection of Seconal, then put them in the car. Then off with the ropes, back the car around, push it off the cliff, and they are gone. That is all his contribution to that little scheme of theirs.

"These fabulous stories that the two defendants have fabricated—they are so ridiculous that they act as enormous signposts that say 'Guilty, guilty, guilty.'

"One of the most blatant absurdities of the whole trial is the one about blowing up the rubber gloves to play with the dog. In cross-examination defendant Finch admitted that he had never done it before, and that he had never heard of anyone doing such a thing. But it was the best they could do to explain the rubber fragments in the driveway, and the fact that they stayed outside on the lawn when honest people on an honest errand would have gone into the house to wait for someone to come home.

"One thing that is certain about this is that the dog didn't play with the glove and get a finger of it on the inside of the car where detectives found it later. Now I ask you, did they play with the dog, or did they have the gloves on to avoid detection by fingerprints? Which sounds more reasonable to you? I suggest that they took out two pair of surgical gloves and put them on with the plan of executing a vile operation on Mrs. Finch.

"You saw the little piece of paper, the tiny envelope that holds the powder that they use to put on their hands just before they put on the gloves, to make putting them on easier. This is the answer to your whole case, this little piece of paper. You recollect my talk of signposts. Well, this is a big one that points the way to guilt.

"And I think that the evidence is overwhelming that as she stepped out of the car, he smashed her over the head with the pistol. She did not black out as quickly or as completely as they had hoped. A period of time elapsed, and then a struggle occurred in that garage. And not just a little blood, but a lot of blood. Blood on the garage floor. Blood on the top of the car. Blood on the right-hand side of it. As if the lady was struggling along, leaning against the side of the car.

"I do not believe for a moment that a small-statured woman like Mrs. Finch fought like a tigress to obtain control of the gun and shoot her athletic husband. We presented plenty of witnesses to show that she didn't know anything about guns and was, indeed, afraid of them. She wouldn't have grabbed for a gun; she would have fled.

"If you believe the gunshot wound sustained by Mrs. Finch was an accident, then you have to find them both innocent of both charges. Nothing else, I submit, meets the case.

"But let us look at the defendant's version of how the gun went off. First of all, would you pick up the gun and try to throw it backhand with your palm facing out, like he said he did? Or would you simply scoop it off the ground and throw it? He said he held the gun up high, before he threw it. You don't do that if you want it to go far. You start down low and throw up. He never threw the gun at all; he simply had to make his story fit the bullet wound in his wife's back.

"And the crowning absurdity to it all is his soap opera description of her death. Mr. Cooper has told us that the defendant Finch is either a murderer or a consummate actor. Well, I can tell you that he is neither. I think that he is a ham and that his performance was less than the worst class B movie. I think he is worse as a playwright and a writer of dialogue.

"It is inconceivable that a woman who has been smashed in the head, having suffered a fractured skull, and with a mass of blood from the hemorrhage pouring into her lungs, would say and do what he said she did and said. She could not.

"And there is one other fact that makes this story unbelievable. She was shot in the back, remember. She didn't know if it was an accident or not. As far as she knew, it could have been deliberate. Do you think for a minute that she would say what he says, that she was sorry and that she should have listened to him, and that he should take care of her children? That is absurd.

"This whole story has been imagined for your own consumption, deliberately and calculatedly, to appeal to your emotions. A doctor does not kneel beside a woman who has been shot and cry. I don't think a doctor acts that way, particularly a surgeon. A doctor rips off the person's clothes and tries to stop the bleeding.

"In fact, I don't believe that he ever went back down there to see whether his wife was shot or not. I think what he said in Las Vegas to the officers was correct. That he didn't know when he left there that his wife was dead. I think you are going to find that from the evidence.

"I don't believe that woman lying there on the lawn said anything. Her husband had shot her in the back as she was struggling down the steps. With a fractured skull, hobbling along with the heel of one shoe gone, going down the driveway seeking safety and a haven. And that is something to shed tears about, ladies and gentlemen, not this man's self-pity at his own second-rate soap opera.

"And then he ran away. That is what they have the most difficulty explaining. If he had done nothing wrong, why did he run away? A surgeon panics at the scene of an accidental, blameless death? I have never heard of a doctor panicking and running away from death. Especially a respected surgeon running away in such a panic that he steals a neighbor's car. I submit that he did not panic; he was in fear of being caught. It was fear that made him steal a car and drive off into the night.

"And what does he do after he steals the car? Does he drive east to Las Vegas? No, he drives west to La Puente. Pretty good idea for a man escaping from a murder scene, don't you think? And he has a good idea that the license number of this car is being broadcast, so he carefully effectuates a course of action. The first car was not abandoned. It was carefully driven into a garage out of sight and a Cadillac stolen. Are these the actions of an innocent man who has panicked?

"I submit to you that these actions are those of a man who has just planned and committed a murder. And I submit to you that both the defendants planned and committed this murder. This was no second-degree murder. There was certainly malice aforethought. I would ask you to remember Cody's statement that he was to say, 'Tell her this one's from Bernie.' They went there with a plan and with the tools to do it. And defendant Tregoff carried the tools up the hill.

"We are asking you to convict them of first-degree murder and conspiracy, if you convict them of anything. Second-degree murder can be intentional but not sufficiently planned, considered, weighed to amount to premeditation. But in this case, it is no problem at all. Because by any kind of a tough standard you might set up, if it happened at all, it was plotted, planned, and arranged for. And it is premeditated on anybody's theory.

"This could never be a second-degree murder. It is either a first-degree murder or an accident. And logically there can be no distinction between the defendants. They both played a part in the picture. The evidence in my opinion reflects beyond a shadow of a doubt the participation of both defendants equally. The conspiracy is there beyond any doubt.

"Now Mr. Eagan talked about the way that Miss Tregoff has a habit of sitting with her hand resting fixedly on the table. In fact, she is doing it now."

He walked to Carole's side. Her eyes were wide.

"This," his voice was loud, growling, and he was pointing to her left hand, still at her chin, "is the hand, ladies and gentlemen, that carried that murder kit up the hill that night. This is the hand that is stained with the blood of Barbara Jean Finch. And well may this woman say, as did another murderess, 'Out damned spot! Out I say! Here is the smell of the blood still and all the perfumes of Arabia will not sweeten this little hand,' as Lady Macbeth said.

"For thousands of years physicians have been bound by the Hippocratic oath to never do harm to anyone. They swear 'to be myself far from all intentional ill-doing.' The evidence clearly shows Dr. Finch violated that oath and the law of God and man, and you have the power—and it is an awesome thing, indeed—to commit this precious pair to walk up that aisle free as the air, hand in hand, congratulating themselves that they have gotten away with murder, if you so choose.

"I am asking you not to do that. I ask that you follow the only logical conclusion that can be drawn from this evidence beyond a reasonable doubt, that both are guilty of murder in the first degree and that both of them are guilty of the crime of conspiracy to commit murder."

He was through. Carole had broken down during his Lady Macbeth analogy. As she sobbed, Bernard slouched down in his chair, staring off and down to the right. Evans shuffled through his papers looking for the outline of his instructions to the jury.

Judge Evans gave the jury the usual instructions concerning how they could consider evidence, especially with regard to witnesses, and what to do if witnesses disagreed. He told them they should reach a verdict regardless of pity or compassion they may feel for the defendants. Then, the part all wanted to hear the most.

"I have decided that you can reach the following possible verdicts and sentences: Guilty of murder with premeditation, that is, first-degree murder, with a penalty of life imprisonment or execution; guilty of second degree murder, that is, without premeditation, penalty of five years to life; or you can find for an acquittal of the murder charges. You may find the defendants guilty of conspiracy to commit first-degree murder, with penalty of life imprisonment or execution, or acquittal of the conspiracy charge."

More than the usual number of people were waiting in the courthouse hallway this day—so many that the crowd backed into the adjacent parking lot where the yellow county bus used to transport the jurors was parked.

"Gas 'em both!" Some admonished the group as they went into the bus.

"Let the girl off. He made her do it," said others.

Fred Whichello was walking to his car when a small group of reporters spotted him.

"I just want to say we are confident of a conviction. I see no possibility of anything less than a first-degree murder conviction. It can't be second-degree murder. Either it was planned or it was an accident." He was at his car. "I also think the press coverage was fair and impartial, and I think we were all satisfied with how Judge Evans handled the case."

"How long before they reach a verdict, Fred?" one asked.

"Hard to say." He had started his car. "No sooner than Monday. I'd say for sure no sooner than Monday."

Later, at his home, he read the evening paper as his wife clanked and clattered in the kitchen. He shook his head from side to side, studying the story under the large front page headline. "Who would have ever thought?" he muttered. The headline: "Lucy Sues Desi for Divorce."

sixteen
Jury Deliberations

SATURDAY, MARCH 5

"Are you awake, Mr. Whichello? I asked you how soon before you could get here. I told His Honor it might take you an hour at the most." It was Mel La Valley, on the phone. And it was 8:00 A.M.

Fred was starting to wake up. "They have a verdict already?"

"No, they've asked to hear some of the testimony again. And they want to see the gun, and the rubber gloves, too." Mel had just gotten to court that day when Alfred Alm, the jury foreman, called saying they wanted to review some of the evidence. "They want to hear parts of Finch's examination, and of your cross-examination, the part about the death scene."

All of the day would be taken with Cooper reading his questions put to Finch. Monday, Whichello would read the prosecution's questions and Finch's answers.

MONDAY, MARCH 7

"We'd like to hear the tapes, too." Al Alm advised the judge. "The tapes of defendant Finch's questioning in Las Vegas."

Alm had asked to see the gun again. Cooper studied him as the tape machine was being set up. Alm showed the gun to the woman next to him. He was whispering to her, pointing to different parts of the revolver. Then he was holding it above his head with his left hand, palm facing up. Then he moved his arm, as though throwing.

The tapes were replayed. Then Whichello began droning the prosecution's cross-examination of Finch. There were only five or six spectators scattered about the courtroom. At one point Fred stopped reading and noticed one had fallen asleep.

"Your Honor, I ask that this man be asked to leave; he is detracting from the dignity of the court." The man was prodded, then asked to leave.

At another point a buzzing noise was heard from the section reserved for photographers.

"What's that?" The ever-vigilant Cooper was the first to speak.

"I'm sorry." A photographer wrestled with a watch on his wrist. "I just got it for my birthday; I don't know how to turn it off. You know, it's one of those watches with the alarm on it." The buzzing stopped with the help of a peer.

TUESDAY, MARCH 8

The group of seven women and five men was back in the jury room that adjoined Department Twelve. Finch and Carole had received permission from Evans to stay in the courtroom while the deliberations continued.

Above the door leading to the jury room was a buzzer, activated by a push-button switch inside. Deputy William Conroy had the job of monitoring the buzzer. "Three times and they've got a verdict," he explained to a reporter. Also in the courtroom was clerk Mel La Valley and the guards assigned to the defendants. Occasionally, Cooper or Bring-gold, having a case in a nearby court, would stop by, checking progress.

THURSDAY, MARCH, 10

The buzzer sounded three times. "Hey, come on," a photographer said to his colleague; they scrambled for a good position to photograph "the news."

Conroy opened the door slowly, taking a deep breath. Finch and Tregoff had straightened in their chairs. Mel La Valley fingered the telephone on the clerk's desk.

Conroy opened the door. "May I inform His Honor that you have reached a verdict?"

"No." It was Irene Fluhr. "You can get our pencils sharpened. Do you believe there is no pencil sharpener in here?"

A special guard had been appointed for a woman juror who reported getting two obscene notes from one of the men on the jury.

Most had expected a verdict by now. Rumors of a deadlock were beginning to circulate.

FRIDAY, MARCH 11

The jury and alternates said nothing as they marched into the deliberation room, this for the seventh day. One alternate brought a magazine and a scrabble board.

At noon the defendants were being taken back to the County Jail for lunch. The usual five or six photographers were waiting as they walked down the steep steps. Carole, looking haggard and tired, had not the slightest of smiles for the group. She tripped and was grabbed by her guard,

Iona Freer, but still skinned her knee. The manacled Finch came over and helped her get up.

As she got up, Carole glared at the group of reporters. "Oh please, just go away! I wish you all would just go away!"

SATURDAY, MARCH 12, 1960

As anticipation of a verdict grew, so did the crowd. Four hundred people waited outside in the corridor, some having to sit on the steps outside. On three or four occasions a reporter would go into the courtroom, rumors of a "verdict" would ripple through the mass, and all would shove to get inside. The bailiffs would announce there was no verdict, and the commotion would abate.

It was shortly after noon when the buzzer started sounding again. Conroy, was the only person in the courtroom; all others had gone for lunch. It was not the slow measured three buzzes of before. It was a staccato rush of buzzes, sounding repeatedly as he unlocked the door and looked inside. His eyes grew wide in disbelief. Then he stepped inside and quickly closed the door.

Geraldine Lang was shuffling around the large table. She was moving sideways, occasionally stopping to grab the back of a chair. She would move to keep the table directly between her and Dolores Jaimez. Gertrude Mann, a nutritionist, was standing next to the door, still pushing the button.

"Okay, I'm here. What? Stop pushing the button, Ma'am. I'm here!" For Conroy, it was a first. The two jurors continued to dance around the table as the others looked on.

"Can't you do something?" Mann yelled. "These two are going to kill each other! Do something!"

"Would you two please stop this!" Al Alm was pleading.

Jaimez took off his coat and threw it to the side. He spoke with a thick Hispanic accent. "Not until you listen, all of you; we're voting our consciences here. You people just—"

"We just want–" Lang interrupted him.

"You're not going to interrupt me any more. You know why? Because I'm going to jump over this table and throw you out of that window there. You hear me! I've had it." Jaimez was red-faced. By this time Conroy had him from behind, grabbing around the chest and under the arms, squeezing. Gradually, Jaimez, bluer, quieted. Lang was still crouched behind a chair, breathing heavily. The free-for-all concluded.

"Look," Jaimez said, still in the bailiff's hold. "We got a problem here. You better tell the judge that a lot of these people want to let the girl go and give him second-degree murder. Just because she's white and pretty, they want to let her go."

"If she were black," Gilbert Lindsey said loudly, the black postal employee, "I think we would have convicted her a long time ago."

"How can you say that!" Another woman yelling.

"Okay, look," Conroy had his hands up, palms facing forward, "I think we better let Judge Evans know that we have some problems here. Mr. Alm, would you please write a message to His Honor, and I'll have it delivered in a few minutes. In the meantime I need everyone to stay calm."

In Pasadena Walter Evans was enjoying his day off in the patio of his home. It was cloudy and a bit cool. Some scattered showers had been forecast, but there was enough sun shining through to make sitting outside pleasant. He was reading the morning paper's first reports of multiple arrests made in Hollywood the night before. Some stars had been caught with little or no clothes on, scampering about yelling "This will ruin us!" Marijuana had been found at the "wild showbiz party." Sadly, he read that William Talman, who played the district attorney on the Perry Mason show, was arrested also.

The doorbell rang. Soon after, his daughter ran onto the patio with an envelope. He opened it and read: "I am sorry to advise you that we appear to be deadlocked. We request instructions on what to do now."

He asked his daughter to tell the deputy who brought the message to come to the patio. He wrote on the back of Mr. Aim's note: "Mr. Foreman, keep trying."

Within half an hour the scene was repeated. His daughter brought a second envelope. This time the deputy waited at the patio door. "We are hopelessly deadlocked, Your Honor, on the following votes. For defendant Finch ten votes to two for guilty of first-degree murder, eight votes to four to acquit on conspiracy. For defendant Tregoff, eight votes to four to acquit on all counts."

Evans walked inside and called Mel La Valley, instructing that all counsel should be called. Court would convene at 2:00 P.M.

At 2:12 P.M. Evans slammed his gavel to convene the case's last session. It took a few moments for the excited crowd to quiet.

"Mr. Foreman, I understand that you have not arrived and cannot arrive at a verdict," Evans began.

"That is correct." Al Alm was standing. He had always had the second chair from the left, in the first row. Next to Genevieve Lang.

"Do you think, well, would it do any good to rest over the weekend and try again?" he posed.

"I don't think so, Your Honor." Alm appeared tired and defeated. He was looking down, shaking his head.

"I would ask for a poll of the jury to be sure." Evans knew it was no use. "Those of you who feel that resting over the weekend and giving it a fresh try on Monday would do no good, please raise your hand." All hands seemed to rise together within a second of his words.

"I thank you for your efforts and am sorry we could come to no consensus. The jury is admonished against talking to anyone, including the press, about your deliberations. I will meet with counsel in chambers. Court is adjourned and the jury is excused."

The press pushed in a wave to the defendants and their attorneys.

Carole said nothing; she was led away sobbing.

Cooper was the first to speak. "Well, boys, I can tell you that I'm very disappointed, very disappointed. We had thought we would get a complete acquittal on all counts."

"Will you represent Finch at the next trial?" one asked.

"Well, I would estimate the next trial could begin within a month. I do have other cases that have been stacking up." Cooper was putting his papers into a briefcase. "And of course, there's the matter of economics."

"Does that mean Dr. Finch is out of money?" His question was never answered. Cooper was watching his client speak with another group.

"We are disappointed; I am very disappointed. I felt the jury was going to acquit both me and Carole." Finch was looking down at the floor as he spoke. "I just hadn't thought I would have to go through this again."

"She'll have to go through this all over again." Carole's father was speaking. "I was sure they would let her off; we were so sure." His wife was at his side, crying into her handkerchief.

Whichello appeared angry. "These two are guilty of murder. We will try them again and they will be convicted."

"Fred?" Someone asked. "Is it true that you're being transferred back to Pomona, regardless. I mean we hear it's already been decided you won't be prosecuting if there's a retrial."

"That's simply not true; I am willing to try these two as long as it takes." Fred was on his way out.

He answered no more questions. He stepped outside into the chill and rain settling onto Los Angeles. It had been sunny and warm when he left his San Gabriel home and he had brought no umbrella or heavy coat. He walked to his car, buffetted by wind. In his left hand: his briefcase, stuffed too full of papers to close completely; with his right, he held the collar of his suit coat, closed at his throat.

Part III

Subsequent Trials and Other Places

one
The Second Trial

Soon after the first trial, Robert Neeb had a motion to dismiss Carole Tregoff's case denied. His basis: the eight-to-four vote to acquit showed a high probability another trial would be unsuccessful for the state. His motion for separate trials was also denied. He was, however, able to persuade Judge John Barnes to free his client on $25,000 bail. She had been in jail for five months.

On Saturday, April 2, Fred Whichello was giving another interview with TV newsman Baxter Ward. "I still say, Baxter, that these two are guilty of murder, of first-degree murder, and they will be convicted."

On Monday, April 4, a press release was quietly distributed, without comment, from District Attorney William McKesson's office. "Fred Whichello has requested to be returned to his duties at the Pomona Court in order to catch up on the backlog of cases that has grown since his involvement in the Finch-Tregoff case. The prosecution of the case will be handled jointly by Stephen D. Powers, who will be assisted by Clifford Crail."

The last news of Fred Whichello in connection with the Finch-Tregoff case came a few weeks later. Filing for a workman's compensation claim, he said he had developed a polyp on his vocal cords; according to his physicians it was the direct result of his marathon two-and-a-half day summation. His voice would always tire and hoarsen easily. It was a permanent disability.

Dr. Finch's malpractice cases continued to be litigated. On April 5 he gave a deposition in the case brought against him by James Pappa, who claimed he had been permanently disabled after an operation to remove a cyst in back of his right knee.

On April 7 Presiding Judge John Barnes announced that Leroy Dawson would preside at the second trial. Both defense teams were opposed to Dawson and planned to use an objection to get another judge. Cooper still was pursuing his plan to move the trial out of Los Angeles County.

The upcoming trial took a back seat to other news during this period. Gary Powers was shot down in his U-2 while flying over Russia, and a massive earthquake in Chile killed thousands, sending a huge tidal wave to Hawaii and Japan, killing more. The months to come would have news of the national conventions that were to nominate Richard Nixon and John Kennedy, and then the election. And much of the glamour and attention of the first trial just was not there. It was held in the old, dingy Hall of Justice, across the street from the new county courthouse of the first trial.

Judge Dawson ruled he would stay on the case, and that all defense counsel had exhausted their exceptions to selection of a judge during the first trial. An appeal to the California Supreme Court by Robert Neeb was eventually unsuccessful. He argued that since it was a new trial, counsel should be given more "exceptions" to use. At the first trial it was Cooper who had used the single objection allowed the defense. Neeb argued his client should have an objection also. It was still a new law that gave such powers to defense attorneys, and it was, for Neeb's purpose, to be interpreted against him by a vote of five to two by the State Court. He would appeal to U. S. Supreme Court Justice William O. Douglas. This, too, would be denied during the jury selection phase of the second trial.

Bernard Finch had petitioned the California Supreme Court, as well, to have a private conference with Carole. This was denied.

Pretrial motions betrayed a rift between the two defense teams, which would consist of the same attorneys as the first trial except for Eagan, who cited ill health as a reason for dropping out. Cooper spoke in opposition to separating the trials, as did Clifford Crail. Dawson ruled the two would be tried together. Cooper then moved for a change of venue, which in turn was opposed by Neeb and Crail.

Cooper and Neeb would each seek separate pretrial meetings with District Attorney McKesson. Rumors had it that Bernard Finch was interested in plea bargaining to manslaughter, and that Carole would turn state's evidence under certain circumstances. Both meetings were abruptly canceled by McKesson after reports leaked to the media.

Jury selection began on Monday, June 27, 1960. News coverage focused on the Democratic national convention being held at the sports arena. Carole was noted to be thinner, having lost fifteen pounds. She looked tan and healthy. And she did not talk with her co-defendant. In fact, she would avoid his gaze, sitting far to the left of him, as far as she possibly could. On one occasion Finch stared at her for thirty minutes as she struggled to avoid his eyes. Finally she cried, and Finch stopped his staring.

The new jury of eleven women and one man began hearing evidence on July 18, 1960, the first anniversary of the death of Barbara Jean Finch. They jury had been selected from a group of two hundred forty; most candidates were rejected due to their objection to the death penalty. And Stephen Powers made it clear the state was going to ask for it.

First day of the prosecution's case: Carole did not show. Instead, her stepmother, Gladys, had news for an unsympathetic Dawson. "Carole has the hives. She is ill and cannot attend."

The judge was furious, immediately issued a warrant for Carole's arrest, and sent the jail physician and a female deputy, Gabrielle Johnston, to the home of Carole's father on Oak Hill Drive in South Pasadena. Carole fought with the deputy, kicked her in the stomach, and tried to hit her in the face, before she was subdued. The physician found no evidence of hives. Bringgold tried desperately to keep Carole out of jail. Many surmised he had hoped to keep her under the stabilizing influence of her father and stepmother during the trial. Two of his own physicians would examine her. They found no hives, and Carole would remain in jail.

Leroy Dawson was a contrast to the placid Walter Evans, clashing with defense attorneys on many occasions and often duly noting "respectful objections" made to his "judicial misconduct."

James Patrick Cody was again a key prosecution witness. He had not been in jail when the trial began, having been paroled shortly after the first trial ended. He was arrested, in Chicago, during the jury selection phase of the second trial, for grand larceny and a bunco charge, and again was transferred to Los Angeles under guard.

The prosecution's case was a rerun. Another visit to the Larkhill home, testimony from Marie Anne, Cody, Williams, and Forno, Barbara Jean's civil attorney. A new witness: James Pappa testified he thought he had a normal marriage until early 1959, when Barbara Jean told him of the affair. Finch, according to Pappa, denied everything when confronted and threatened to sue him for slander. Pappa had then confronted Carole, who denied the affair also. During the argument that ensued, Pappa slapped her; the next day she moved out.

Crail accused Cooper of attempting to pay Keachie to change testimony, and Cooper claimed the prosecution had bought Cody's testimony, at the first trial, with a promise to shorten his two-year jail sentence.

Stephen Powers produced two "mystery witnesses." Chief Sill was one. He told his story of finding the two heavy-duty extension cords on the south side of the garage and how, with the ends reconnected, a floodlight lit up the area in front of the garage. A neighbor testified that the light was always on, every night. "This shows the defendants did not want to be seen," Powers would later tell the jury.

Gerald K. Ridge, the coroner, fine tuned his testimony. "It was the left pulmonary artery that was pierced by the bullet," he would describe. "This would fill the lung cavity with blood almost immediately; it would be very difficult to speak."

"Hard to make a tender death speech?" prosecutors would note.

Dawson allowed the Tregoff statements to Las Vegas and West Covina Police and Exhibit 60, her testimony at the Finch preliminary hearing. And the jury examined any and all discrepancies.

On Monday, August 29, the defense began its case. Finch and Carole testified again. Public interest in the case was at a low. Even jurors seem disinterested to some. The press would report daily how many were able to "doze off" without Dawson noticing.

It was Kennedy and Johnson versus Nixon and Lodge, and the battle over Medicare was raging in Congress. Dag Hammarskjold was trying to peaceably settle differences in the Congo between Patrice Lumumba, the Belgians, and a group of rebels. And Fidel Castro was making "incredible" charges that the United States was plotting to kill both him and his brother. Earl Long would entertain the press with his colorful language and his relationship with a stripper named "Blaze."

Bernard Finch described the death of his wife and her speech—this time without tears, it was noted. Two spectators were ejected for giggling during his testimony.

Robert Neeb, suffering from an exacerbation of tic douloureux—a painful condition of the facial nerves—kept a low profile during the entire trial, leaving the final summation to Donald Bringgold. "There is not one single shred of evidence that she injured or harmed anyone," he told the jury on October 5. He was emotional during his final summation, his voice breaking several times, his eyes tearful. "We have never denied the fact that Carole had a love affair with the doctor. Let me read you this from the Bible. 'He that is without sin among you, let him cast the first stone. And the Lord told the woman to go on her way and sin no more.'"

On Thursday, October 20, the jury began its deliberations. This trial was the longest in California history–seventeen weeks. Ninety-nine witnesses had taken the stand and one hundred fifty exhibits were displayed. Judge Leroy Dawson instructed the jury to find the defendants guilty or innocent of first-degree murder, second-degree murder, or conspiracy to commit first-degree murder. He also instructed them not to "overdo it." They would end deliberations every day at 4:30 P.M. and could meet only until noon on Saturdays, not at all on Sundays.

It was Wednesday, November 2. The jury had requested to hear 180 pages of Carole's testimony. Before returning to their deliberations, the foreman told Dawson that the jury wanted to ask him some questions.

"Your Honor, is a person to be considered an accomplice if, upon surmising that a crime might be committed, he does nothing to prevent that crime?" the foreman read from a note.

"My answer to that is 'No.'" Dawson advised.

"And what would the penalties be for each of the verdicts that we were given to consider and how much time off could they get for good behavior?" the foreman continued.

Dawson refused. "That is not a proper question for you to be considering. I have instructed all of you that penalty is not to be discussed at this proceeding." He glared at the foreman, "I would say also that I think that this is a case where you should be able to reach a verdict quickly."

Cooper objected. "Your Honor, the defendant Finch takes exception to Your Honor's peremptory instruction to the jury, in which Your Honor said this is a case in which they should be able to agree quickly." He cited Dawson for another, one of several so far, act of judicial misconduct.

Dawson snapped back, "Well, he can take all the exceptions he wants to. It's a fact and I believe it! I can instruct the jury in matters of fact. I have a right and a duty to do so."

Bringgold joined in. "I respectfully request Your Honor to instruct the jury to disregard your remark."

"I will not!" And court was abruptly adjourned.

Grant Cooper moved for a mistrial on the basis that since the jury had been deliberating for sixty hours they would not, in all probability, be able to reach a verdict. Dawson refused that motion as well as Cooper's next motion that the jury be polled.

At the end of the next day's deliberations the foreman advised Dawson of a deadlocked jury; it was a nine to three vote for conviction on first-degree murder for both defendants. The judge was furious, and he advised his clerk to convene court in the morning. He would make some startling remarks to the jury.

"I understand from your foreman that you are deadlocked in your deliberations. I can comment about certain aspects of the evidence and intend to do so."

Cooper: "Your Honor, we object—"

"It is my opinion that you should believe the testimony of John Patrick Cody, that he was hired to murder the doctor's wife, Barbara Jean, and that you should not believe the testimony of the defendants that they hired him to gather divorce evidence."

Defense counsel were flabberghasted. The judge was telling the jury who they should believe.

Bringgold: "This is irregular, Your Honor. We would ask—"

"It is also my opinion that Finch and Carole lied about their purpose in visiting Mrs. Finch's home on the night she was killed.

"I also believe that defendant Finch's story that his wife was killed accidentally was a concoction."

His words were like hammers beating on the defendants. Finch's face went to his palms as he slouched down in his chair; Carole began sobbing uncontrollably. Finch and Bringgold continued objecting that such remarks were unprecedented and grossly prejudicial to the jury.

Cooper, customarily more persistent, was twice cited for contempt.

"Counsel will remain silent while I instruct the jury. I am not instructing the jury to find for any particular verdict, but only am commenting on the evidence as the law and constitution of this state allows me to. I do, however, feel that the minority of you that are opposing the view of the majority ought seriously to consider changing your minds."

The next day set another record. The jury had deliberated sixty-three hours, the longest for any murder case in the state.

On Monday, November 7, the day before national election day, Dawson declared a mistrial. The jury could not come to a conclusion on either defendant. Interviews with jurors later revealed they had, on the first day of their deliberations, decided Finch was guilty, but were unable to decide on what degree. The vote: eleven to one to convict on first-degree murder.

"It's no use continuing," the sole holdout said. "I'm not going to change my mind."

"We told the judge we couldn't agree on the degree of guilt for Finch. And he sent us back a message saying that he wasn't going to accept that, and that we were supposed to continue our deliberations." One tired juror said later, "The next vote was nine to three to convict on first-degree murder, for both defendants, and that's where we stayed. We went on and on, and it stayed the same."

"I just did not believe that Cody witness, and Carole never did anything to harm Mrs. Finch. I thought she should get off," one woman juror said.

Manly Bowler, assistant to District Attorney William McKesson, gave an interview at the chief prosecutor's office.

California Penal Code: If a jury agrees on guilty but disagrees on the degree, a judgment for the lesser degree was to be automatic.

"We would have accepted a second-degree murder verdict against Finch or Tregoff, and according to California law, if a jury decides a defendant is guilty of murder but can't decide on the degree, a second-degree verdict is mandatory. However, since a mistrial was declared by Judge Dawson, we have no choice but to retry on the original charges."

two
The Third Trial

THE DATE FOR the third trial was tentatively set for January 3, 1961; the Finch-Tregoff case was stepping into its third calendar year.

On December 16, Finch's motion to have his charges dismissed was presented to Judge David Coleman, who would hear the third trial. It was argued that since the second jury had indeed found him guilty of murder, as evidenced by their affidavits, to retry him would constitute double jeopardy. The motion was denied. Finch was represented for the first time by Maxwell Keith, a former prosecutor who had joined Cooper's law firm as an associate four years before.

After this hearing it was announced Keith would represent Finch at the third trial; Grant B. Cooper took a bow.

"You know, boys, I have a backlog of cases at the office, and besides," Cooper explained to some pressmen, "I plan to appeal my contempt charge and that $500 fine Judge Dawson levied upon me." He would win his appeal to the State Supreme Court and, moreover, Dawson would be reprimanded by the court, both for his judgment and his behavior.

Stephen Powers would still be the prosecutor, assisted by Clifford Crail. Crail and Donald Bringgold were the only attorneys present for all three trials.

Jury selection began on Tuesday, January 3, 1961.

Bringgold's usual motion to have separate trials was denied, and Maxwell Keith made Finch's usual motion for a trial outside of Los Angeles County. It was also denied.

A young Los Angeles County Supervisor, Kenneth Hahn, had asked the District Attorney's office to advise him how much the trials had cost the taxpayers so far. He was told at the next supervisor's session by a representative from the D. A.'s office.

"Well the second trial cost more; it was the longest—$94,407. The first trial was only $75,189. The third trial, of course, will have to be seen." The small man, an aide from William McKesson's office, wearing wire-rimmed glasses, was reading from his notes.

"Well, what about the fourth, and the fifth. I'm not saying it's inappropriate to continue with these trials. I'm just saying some of these fancy private attorneys know how to really run up the tab." Hahn was sounding irritated. He had been getting complaints from his constituents.

"Oh, don't worry, Mr. Hahn. There won't be a fourth trial." The aide was smiling as he wrote something on the pad in front of him. Then he looked up, noting all were quietly studying him, some with mouths open. He cleared his throat. "Uh, under California law, if there are two hung juries, the state is prohibited from any future prosecution."

The first trial's had hung, the second trial had been a mistrial.

The group remained uncustomarily quiet for a moment, then went to the next item of business, approval for some items concerning construction of a stadium in Chavez Ravine, the recently approved home for the Dodgers.

The third trial had few surprises. Marie Anne Lidholm, now 20 years old, was flown back from Sweden at county expense, to give her testimony one more time. There would be two court sessions held at the Larkhill address; the first would start the trial, and the second would come at the end of the trial on March 10, 1961.

The Finch property had been sold to the Kearth family shortly after the second trial and the new family was living in it during both visits. Nonetheless, Bernard would inspect the gutters and the wood siding and comment on the need for some repairs. It had been a major asset, liquidated for massive legal expenses.

And the press would monitor Carole's weight with regularity, noting a thirty pound gain on the starchy jail diet. Photographs show a face ballooning gradually over the three-month trial.

News of the trial was seldom accorded front page coverage. Instead, there were daily reports of three to five paragraphs, usually on the second page. Public attention was on the new Kennedy inauguration and the exciting days that followed as he chose his cabinet.

This time things were noted to be a faster pace than before. Trial was being held again in the small courtroom on the eighth floor of the old Hall of Justice. Jury selection took just two weeks. This time it would be mostly men, starting with nine. Shortly after the trial began, one of the women excused herself after showing a doctor's report saying that she was suffering from emotional strain; her high blood pressure was affected. She was replaced by a male alternate. The verdict would be decided by ten men and two women. And they would listen as the Tregoff police statements and Exhibit 60 were read.

Carole Tregoff and Bernard Finch would again take the stand in their own defense.

Clifford Crail delivered the prosecution's opening address on Thursday, January 19. The last prosecution witness, on Tuesday, February 14, was none other than Judge Al Miller, who again maintained that, in his opinion, Carole was aware of her rights when she testified in his court. Final summations were completed on March 24.

TUESDAY, MARCH 28, 1961
3:55 P.M.

It was four days since jury deliberations had begun. Few observers were still in the small courtroom or the hall outside. Most had gone home for the day, thinking this panel would take at least as long as the first two, and they had only been deliberating twenty-one hours. This jury asked for the gun on Friday and kept it. They had also asked for a measuring tape. There were only a few reporters present in the Hall of Justice courtroom.

The buzzer above the door sounded once. The jury had been carefully instructed to sound the buzzer only once if there was a need for something or a question.

"We have a question." James Gyer was the jury's foreman. His regular job was to install telephones in the San Fernando Valley. "Does that mean everybody has to be called back?"

"Well, what kind of question is it?" The bailiff asked. "Do you, like, need something else or is it a question for the judge or—"

"We had some questions about the possible verdicts," Gyer interrupted.

Carole and Finch were brought to the room from their holding cells higher in the building. Each had changed into their jail uniforms and were told to switch back to street clothes. Bernard Finch had been smoking a pipe and reading when told the jury had a question. Carole Tregoff was working in the kitchen of the women's section. Both defense attorneys and the two prosecutors arrived within fifteen minutes.

Coleman had reviewed the jury's question before re-convening court. He would read it into the record. It had been scrawled on an eight- by twelve-inch, yellow legal pad.

"Would there be any legal conflict in," he read slowly, holding his glasses with his left hand and the legal pad in his right, "verdicts of second-degree murder against one defendant, first-degree against the other, and conspiracy against both?"

"My answer is 'No,'" answered Coleman. "You may so find, if that is your decision. Now, it's almost 4:30. Can I dismiss court for the day? I mean, you've been going at it all day. Are you tired? Would you like to quit for the day and come back tomorrow?"

"No." Gyer appeared bouyant. "We would like to continue for just a few more minutes."

Finch looked at Keith. The two spoke quietly. They, like all the others in the room, knew what the verdicts would be. And both defense attorneys knew they would soon be arguing to save the lives of Carole Tregoff and Bernard Finch.

At 5:14 P.M. the buzzer sounded three times. There were about thirty reporters and photographers present now. The jury filed in. Some avoided looking at the defendants. Many took a deep breath after they sat down. Others would lock eyes with Finch. Carole was looking down at the table, crying quietly.

"Have you reached a verdict?" Coleman knew the answer.

"Yes, Your Honor." Gyer slowly waved the papers held in his right hand.

Alice Mishikawa was the court clerk. She walked to Gyer and took four sheets of eight-inch by twelve-inch paper from him. The only sound in the courtroom was her footsteps, tiny quick clicks, as she walked back to Coleman. She was less than five feet tall, having to stretch from her toes to reach the judge. Coleman read, then handed her the papers.

"Would the clerk read the verdict into the record," he instructed her.

Mishikawa showed no emotion as she read, after first clearing her throat.

A loud "Shhhh" came from the back of the room.

"We, the jury, find the defendant, Raymond Bernard Finch, guilty of murder, and that the degree of murder is in the first degree."

Carole's crying could be heard now. Finch, also wiping away tears, was looking at Mishikawa.

"On the count of conspiracy to commit murder, we find him guilty." She slid the top paper away and began reading again.

"We find Carole Anne Tregoff guilty of murder, and that the degree of murder is in the second degree." Carole began to heave. Finch tried to reach for her with his left arm. Bringgold grabbed it and shoved it back. She quieted, listening for Mishikawa's next words, knowing that conspiracy to commit murder was punishable by death.

"On the count of conspiracy to commit murder, we find her guilty." Mishikawa was through. Bringgold was holding Carole up. Finch tried again to reach to her with his left hand and again Bringgold pushed it away. Then Bernard looked back at Mishikawa, who was walking to her small desk. He turned to the jury; one of the two female jurors, Mildred Brown, sitting in the front row second from the left, was staring coldly at him. He grabbed his face with both hands and began crying; then he slowly lowered onto the desk.

Coleman announced that the sentencing deliberations would begin the following Monday and that he was going to allow the jury to go to their homes until then. He also admonished them not to discuss the case.

Carole was still sobbing. Photographs captured the next dramatic moments. As she walked by Finch, he stood, pulling her toward him. His left arm was around her back as he stroked her hair with his right hand. Her face was buried in his left shoulder.

He whispered, loud enough for others to hear, "I love you, Carole; I'm sorry."

Suddenly she jerked away, pushing him with her left forearm. There was a flurry of flashbulbs popping. Bringgold was standing about three feet away. He was, as he had for the last twenty months, monitoring his client's every move. Dr. Finch reached for Carole again. Bringgold moved between them, his back to Finch. He had Carole's left elbow with his right hand and was leading her away.

Finch slouched and turned back to Keith, who was still sitting at the defense table. "My God," he told his attorney, "after all this time."

"This is what should have happened at the first trial!" the feisty Crail was telling a group of men surrounding him. "At last we got twelve intelligent people together."

Maxwell Keith had little to say. "I am very disappointed." And he quietly left the courthouse.

Bringgold appeared upset. After he helped Carole out of the courtroom, he went over to his wife, standing at the defense table. He threw some papers into his briefcase and gave his answer to the reporters for one last time.

"I told you," his voice was raised, his face contorted in anger, "I have no comment. No comment!" Then he took his wife's left elbow in his hand. "Come on, Jan, let's go."

Powers was talking to another group. They were quizzing the obviously happy prosecutor about the possible sentences. "We will ask for death for both defendants. Under California law Carole's verdict of conspiracy takes priority over the one for second-degree murder. So her possible sentences will be life in prison or the death penalty, just like for defendant Finch."

"What if there's a deadlock on a sentence?" A reporter anticipated.

"The Judge has the discretion to call another jury, or he can impose a sentence himself," Powers instructed. "But, he cannot impose the death sentence. That means all he could give them would be life. We will do everything we can to get the death penalty. We will ask the jury, 'If this case doesn't warrant the death penalty, then what case does?'"

Mildred Brown would later tell how the jury came to their decisions. "We re-enacted the whole struggle." She would explain. "I played the part of Barbara Jean, and Bill Macias played Finch because he was the same height, five feet, ten inches tall. We went over it time and time again, and each time we found that if Finch's story was true, she would have been shot below the waist line, instead of in the back."

She would give several interviews after the trial. "We also found it hard to believe that both defendants would black out at exactly the same time, and land back at the same destination. Things just didn't add up. We thought Carole should get second degree because she didn't handle the gun at all. None of us believed that she hid in those bushes for all that time."

"I would say that Dr. Finch and Carole were their own worst witnesses and convicted themselves," she would analyze. "We all believed Cody, mostly because he didn't seem like the type of person that anyone would think could seduce a woman like Mrs. Finch. And, of course, we all believed Marie Anne Lidholm, everything she said."

Marie Anne said, "I'm glad it's all over now. Now I can begin living my life again and continue with my plans to become an American citizen." She was working for a couple in Redondo Beach while she took her first art lessons at nearby El Camino College.

All newspapers put out "extra" editions that night. There would be no photographs of Bringgold grabbing Finch's arm during the reading of the verdicts as court was still in session. But there were many of him moving between the two defendants and leading Carole away. Some of the stories speculated whether Carole would be the fifth woman to die in California's gas chamber, joining others with names like "The Duchess," and "Bloody Babs" Graham, whose case was detailed in the movie *I Want to Live.*

James Pappa was quoted as saying, "I'm sorry I can't do anything about it. I wish they could have gotten off free. I don't think that what happened was deliberate."

MONDAY, APRIL 3, 1961

Judge Coleman instructed the jury to consider only two possible verdicts for each defendant, death or life in prison.

Powers was first to speak. "You may feel that these defendants have suffered enough, but when you consider their pain and suffering, consider the months of agony Mrs. Finch went through before she died. She knew exactly how she was going to die, and you heard Marie Anne Lidholm tell us that she was sure that she would die."

He spoke for only thirty minutes. "Finch is a severe man, an egomaniac if there ever was one. This man likes to hurt people and defendant Tregoff is just as guilty of the murder. She planned and masterminded the whole thing. If you have any tears to shed, don't shed them for these two. Save them for Barbara Jean Finch."

Maxwell Keith was next. "Most civilized countries have abandoned the death penalty; it is inhumane. My client has lost his career, his life investments, and has been through the mental torture of three lengthy murder trials. He should not be executed, but should go to prison instead." His remarks took less than thirty minutes also. "If you order Dr. Finch executed, you and I and everybody here will be with him in the gas chamber when they drop those gas pellets."

Bringgold made his last statement on behalf of Carole Tregoff. "My client was only eighteen when she met this man and became involved with him. She does not deserve to die. If one of you is against the death penalty and if you allow yourself to be talked into it, you are as much responsible for the dropping of the death pellets in San Quentin as the warden. My client did not kill anyone."

Crail was last. "Let's not forget that Carole shopped around Las Vegas to find a killer. She told Cody, 'If you don't do it, Dr. Finch will; and if he doesn't, I will.' I ask you: Who really pulled the trigger that night?"

The closing arguments of all attorneys would be completed before the day was out, lasting less than four hours.

On Wednesday afternoon, Coleman learned the jury was having trouble deciding on the penalty for Finch. They had agreed on life in prison for Carole. He sent them a message that he would impose sentence himself if they did not agree by the next day.

The crowds were gathering, lining the hall. World attention was focused, once more, on the trial. Mary Malone, representing the *London Times*, was there, as were reporters from Paris, Rome, and most other European countries. To pass the time and gather material for their stories, the reporters would interview each other about "opinion" in the home countries. Television and movie cameras were set up every day at 9:00 A.M. and taken down at 4:30.

Tregoff, Finch, Bringghold after verdict.

Bringghold blocks Finch. *Los Angeles Mirror.*

WEDNESDAY, APRIL 5, 1961

A small group of photographers were comparing strategies on how to cover the Finch verdict and the arraignment of Spade Cooley in Bakersfield. Cooley, a country western singer who had had his own national television show, was the famous "Western King of Swing." He had been charged with murdering his wife. Initial reports were sketchy, but it appeared that someone had witnessed part of the incident; Cooley had been seen with a shotgun. He was charged with beating his wife to death.

Alice Mishikawa was again clearing her throat. As she shuffled the papers, only the ticking of the wall clock could be heard; it was 4:39 P.M. The clerk's tiny voice delivered.

"Carole Anne Tregoff: We, the jury, having found her guilty of conspiracy to commit murder, sentence her to life imprisonment." Carole leaned into Bringgold, Mishikawa kept reading. "Raymond Bernard Finch: We, the jury, having found him guilty of conspiracy to commit murder sentence him to life imprisonment. Having found him guilty of first-degree murder, life imprisonment."

Silence. Then a loud, cracking sound exploded through the courtroom. Finch, had been thrown forward, turned, startled and in apparent pain. He looked. It was Maxwell Keith. The broadly smiling attorney had slapped him on the back, knocking him almost flat onto the table.

"Thank God." Keith was excited. "We finally got a break."

Carole turned to Bringgold. "No, no, no!" She was shaking her head. "I'll be an old woman when I get out."

427

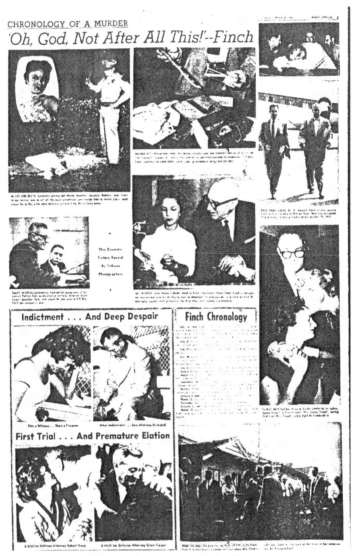

Tribune chronology. *Valley Tribune.*

three
Chino, California

IT WAS 41 degrees; the sun would rise in a few minutes. Unusually cold air had spilled down onto the desert town from the higher plateau to the north, bringing with it chilling gusts of wind that kicked up dust, carrying it away in white coils.

A thin, hunched-over man in his late eighties had just parked his 1964 green Buick two-door sedan. He was walking slowly to a tall chain link fence topped with swirls of sharp "razor wire." He was wearing a light green sweater, holding it closed at the top. Stopping at the fence, he tilted his head up, looking first to the left, then to the right, where he saw a sign. Unable to see well in the dim light, he moved closer.

"'California Institution for Men.'" he was reading. "Okay, well then, where is everybody?" Then down lower he read: "'Deliveries Only.'"

It was quickly getting lighter. He looked to his right and saw another gate, about two hundred yards away. This one had a small booth next to it. There were about twenty people next to the booth, most wearing overcoats and hats. Many were blowing into their hands and shifting their weight from one foot to the other. A few had cameras strapped to their necks.

The old man drove to the gate. In the booth was a guard who was expecting him.

"They've been waiting for you, Mr. Finch," the guard greeted him.

"I got lost," the old man said. "I was at the wrong gate. Do I go in?"

"Yes, sir. You go right on in; they're waiting for you inside." The guard got out of the booth and opened the gate.

At 8:27 A.M. the car arrived at the gate once again, this time to leave. The older man was in the back seat now. Driving was a younger, fifty-three-year-old man, with short, gray hair. He wore sunglasses, a golf cap, and an old striped suit coat. The guard in the booth had been on the phone. He hung up and opened the gate, waving at the car to come through. The driver did not see him. He watched the small crowd moving toward the car.

In the passenger seat was an obviously happy woman in her late forties.

"Who's the woman, Dr. Finch?" One of the group asked. The driver said nothing. His pale face was void of any emotion. The car was not moving. He looked at the guard.

"Who's the mystery woman?" someone else yelled, thinking of a headline.

"You can go now, Doctor." The guard said. Still the car stayed. The guard walked closer and leaned down, speaking louder. "I said you can go now, Doctor."

The car passed through, reached the main road, turned left, kicking up loose gravel, and was gone.

"Hey," one of the group asked the others. "How can he drive? How do you get a driver's license in prison?"

Dr. Raymond Bernard Finch had been paroled.

RELEASED—Dr. R. Bernard Finch is shown with "mystery woman" as he was released from Chino prison today after serving 12 years for the murder of his wife, Barbara, in West Covina.

AP Wirephoto

MYSTERY WOMAN
Dr. Finch Freed

Finch driving out of prison with his social worker.
Valley Tribune.

four

Long Beach, California

It was a small meeting room, one of the many in the Superior Court building. Sitting behind a large oblong table were eight people. Near the center was Marguerite C. Geftakys, the presiding administrative law judge; to either side were representatives of the State Medical Quality Review Committee.

A few feet away, seated at a smaller table, were R. Bernard Finch, two of his attorneys, Donald Goldman and Kathleen Allyn, and a representative of the Attorney General's Office, Barry Ladendorf.

Between the two, at a small desk, was the clerk-stenographer for the hearing.

Geftakys declared the hearing was in session for this matter. She looked at some papers in front of her.

"Matter number L-30353. Raymond Bernard Finch. You may proceed, Mr. Goldman."

"Thank you, Your Honor. This hearing is in regards to case number D-173, that was effective July 6, 1964, wherein the certificate issued to petitioner to practice as a physician and surgeon was revoked. Said revocation was pursuant to the respondent's conviction in March of 1961 in a proceeding before the Superior Court of the State of California, in and for the County of Los Angeles, for violating Penal Code Section 187, murder, on July 18, 1959, and of violating Penal Code Section 182, conspiracy to commit murder. As the result of said conviction, respondent was sentenced to state prison for the term of his natural life.

"While he was incarcerated in the California Institution for Men in Chino, California, a citizens' group from Missouri visited petitioner to interview him and subsequently extended an invitation to him to come and practice medicine in Missouri. In October of 1971, petitioner's request to be paroled to the State of Missouri was granted. Pending petitioner's application to practice medicine in the State of Missouri, he worked as an x-ray technician. The Missouri Board of Medical Examiners denied him the opportunity to take the examination for licensure based upon his California conviction. The petitioner appealed that decision and two years later his license to practice medicine was granted pursuant to an Administrative Hearing Commission Order. Petitioner took the examination and passed.

"In 1974, petitioner and his wife were married. He first met her when she was serving a student internship in the California Correctional System in connection with her training in social work. Mrs. Finch has a Master's Degree in social work from San Diego State University and was graduated from the Menninger School of Psychiatry in Topeka, Kansas. She is a licensed specialist clinical social worker.

"Petitioner and his wife opened the Finch Medical Clinic in Bolivar, Missouri, in 1974. He was one of three physicians that served the rural community of 5,000 people and has earned the respect and gratitude of the community he serves.

"He has been active in civic organizations. He served as president of the Southwest Citizens' Advisory Board, composed of judges, attorneys, ministers, and businessmen.

433

The board serves to help convicted offenders on probation and parole in their efforts to reintegrate into society. He also was active in the construction of the new Bolivar Community Hospital, which was completed in 1982.

"Petitioner has continued his medical education, particularly in regard to emergency medicine, and has been offered a position as an emergency room physician with a hospital owned by a major chain of hospitals in southern California.

"We offer these written reports from an examining psychologist. In 1973 petitioner was diagnosed as having a passive-aggressive personality. This personality has paled and does not seem to be a part of him now. Petitioner was re-examined by the same psychologist in 1983. The examiner found petitioner and Mrs. Finch close and mutually dependent upon one another. The psychological report indicates that over the last decade petitioner has become more mellow, more emotionally responsive, and is able to recognize his emotional needs for affection and companionship that he receives from his wife. The report further states that petitioner has been diagnosed as psychologically normal, with clear thought processes, a youthful attitude, and a psychological perspective younger than his stated age. And that petitioner was only a danger in the past, in a unique and unrepeatable situation.

"Petitioner seeks reinstatement of his revoked certificate, as he and his wife want to return to California to be with and get to know their children and grandchildren who reside in the state. Moreover, Mrs. Finch suffers severely from arthritis during the harsh winters in Missouri."

On November 3, 1983, the board quietly mailed its decision to the attorneys.

"The petitioner has established he is presently rehabilitated to the point that it would not be contrary to the public interest to reinstate petitioner's medical license on a probationary basis and subject to certain terms and conditions.

"The Physician and Surgeon Certificate number previously issued to respondent Raymond Bernard Finch, M.D., is hereby reinstated on a probationary basis and respondent is placed on probation for a period of two years.

"Petitioner will obey all state, federal, and local laws and submit quarterly declarations stating whether he has complied with the conditions of the probation. He will participate in the probation surveillance program and appear for interviews when requested. He will notify the board if he moves..."

five

Carl's, Jr., and Other Places

MARCH 14, 1992
HOME OF EVA REED

"THERE WERE SO many people hurt by this tragedy. And their agony was so public. Lyle was a victim; so was Frances, Bernard's first wife. And the children suffered so. Those poor little children."

Eva was looking at her *Cardinal*. Frequently she was silent, her fingers nimbly darting about the pages, stopping often at a picture or handwritten note.

APRIL 13, 1992
CARL'S, Jr.

I was at the local quick diner, interviewing Dan Martin, the officer who had once stopped Bernard Finch for driving erratically. He was telling me, as most people did, where he was when he heard the news of the Finch murder.

"It was about midnight, the night of the murder." Dan told me. "You know, I would have been the lead investigator on that case, except I was in the hospital. They were getting me ready to have a hernia fixed the next day. First news of the murder for me was over the radio that night."

Sitting next to him in the small booth: Don Goddard, who had joined us, offering to talk of his finding the first car Finch stole in his escape. Don finished his coffee and started making some sort of pattern in the top rim of the styrofoam cup with his right thumbnail. He was in his early seventies; Dan, in his late sixties.

"It didn't come as a big shock," Dan continued. There had been trouble in the house. We all were aware of that. And a lot of us figured something like this would happen."

It was 10:30 A.M., about the time that many officers from West Covina P. D., retired and otherwise, would meet at this particular Carl's, Junior. Jimmy Keith came in through the back door and greeted us. He spread onto one of the helpless stools, testing the stainless steel bolts anchoring it to the floor.

I asked if there might be anyone else with whom I should talk.

"Most of the guys around now," Jimmy said, "Why they wasn't even born then, or else they was babies, just babies. Now there was Schneider, he might have been there. Last I heard, he run a gym somewhere up in Azusa."

"I remember when I found that car he stole from the golf course." Don Goddard was waiting no longer. "It was down in La Puente."

"You didn't find no car." Jimmy was leaning forward, speaking loudly. He seemed irritated; his face pulled into its center. "We got a call that it had been found by that L.A.P.D. officer, *then* you went over there."

"Well, whatever it was. I remember it was a Cadillac." Don continued. "Over in La Puente."

"It wasn't no Cadillac, either," Jimmy's face was more contorted and red. "It was a Ford."

"Well, whatever it was, it was down in La Puente."

Jimmy turned to me. "You know, Doc, I think this whole thing happened because she had him by the throat, every which way. She had control of all his money and his business, too. He was just desperate."

Dan Martin, the veteran detective and investigator of scores of murders, watched Jimmy closely, waiting untill he finished. "People are capable of anything, if pushed far enough. Just about anything you can think of. He was just under a lot of pressure and got pushed over the edge. That's the way I figure it. Plus he was a spoiled brat, always had everything he wanted, the way I hear it. And here was this woman, his wife, taking it all away from him."

"Well, let me ask you something, guys." I was getting to the question that closed most of my interviews. "Suppose I told you Dr. Finch had his money back, and his license to practice medicine. Suppose I said he was living in a large, white-stucco mansion back toward the mountains. What would you say?"

"What's right? What's fair?" Dan asked. "If he paid the price the justice system asked of him, then it's right."

"Sure." Jimmy chimed. "He paid his price. He deserves a second chance now."

Then talk turned to the "old days," and my interview with Dan Martin was over.

"Some of our cars didn't even have radios in 'em, Doc." Jimmy was telling me. "And all we had was our service revolvers, no shotguns."

"We had that old 'Tommy gun' at the station," Dan remembered. "Remember that thing?" He was looking at Jimmy. "We used to take it out back and shoot it. You couldn't keep it held down. It kept rising up when you'd shoot it."

And the banter continued. It was after this I decided to interview policemen one on one.

"Remember those two drunks we found sleeping in the car? You know, they was about ten feet from the county line."

"Yeah, we were going to breakfast, so we pushed them into the county and called the sheriffs out to come get 'em." All laughed.

They were celebrating, as they always did when they met, the fact they were able to meet. And that by virtue of chance, circumstance, or wit they had survived the shootings, fights, and high-speed chases.

They seemed still to have the irrational certainty, the delusion of youth: Could death be cheated with anticipation, skill, or luck, so would be mortality.

"You know, Doc," Jimmy said, "There was a lot of people who could have told you about this, but they're deceased." He was looking at Dan.

Dan turned to Jimmy. "I guess that's right. Ryan passed away a couple of years ago; he had lung cancer, I think."

"And 'Pappy' Rund, he done passed away," Jimmy continued.

"How about that attorney, Cooper?" Don asked the group. "I saw him on TV just a few months ago. They were interviewing him about a big case somewhere, or something."

"I talked to his widow on the phone a few days ago," I informed him. "He passed away in 1990."

"Fred Whichello still around? I remember being impressed with him." Dan added. "Always seemed like a gentleman."

"I talked to his widow, too, a few days ago." I delivered the news. "In 1977."

"Well, I know Carole Tregoff's still around. I'd like to see her again. She was something else to look at, Doc." Jimmy was smiling slightly. The he looked down and rubbed his chin with his right hand. "Of course, it's hard to imagine that she's fifty-something now."

Then Jimmy looked up. He and Dan locked eyes for a few seconds. No one spoke. Only the clatter of the fast food restaurant rattled about us, punctuated with the sizzle of raw potatoes meeting hot grease. Don finished torturing his cup and tossed it into a trash container.

I watched the men for a moment. The celebration had stopped. Jimmy looked away.

He looked through the glazed front window of the restaurant. A marked police car was heading north, toward the freeway. It was one of the city's new cruisers, a shiny black Caprice. I studied the antennas on the car; there were six–four, at each corner of the roof, were a foot high. A slightly larger antenna was at the center. The trunk lid anchored the largest of all the antennas, about four feet tall.

It was ninety degrees outside. The car's windows were closed. The short sleeves of the man inside were blown gently by the air-conditioner. The officer appeared to be in his early twenties and was wearing aviator-style sunglasses; he had a neatly trimmed mustache. The sun visor was down just enough to cast a dark shadow across his face, ending just below his eyes.

"You know, they think they got it made." Jimmy's eyes followed the unit slowly go by. His voice had lowered. He turned to me. "But you know what, Doc? These young guys don't know nothing." He leaned closer, jabbing the table with his index finger.

Two furrows settled between his eyes as he glanced back at the shiny cruiser. "They just don't know nothing." All others nodded in agreement.

**CONVERSATION WITH
MR. ROBERT ADAM NEEB, JR.
JUNE 7, 1993**

He was still defending his client.

"She was innocent *and* not guilty. What happened to her could have happened to anybody in this country in those days. There was a pattern with police and prosecutors."

Now eighty-five, Mr. Neeb walked slowly, using a round, wooden cane, topped with a polished brass hand grip. He settled into a well-padded chair. In front of him: Notes from one of his more memorable cases. His mind was quick; he spoke in clear and concise sentences, never missing an opportunity to joke, often about himself. When talking about the Finch-Tregoff case, the still-bushy eyebrows drew together and he leaned forward, balancing his weight on the cane, and his voice lowered to a near-growl.

"It goes back before the Constitution–before the Fifth Amendment–to the Magna Carta. Everyone is entitled to a legal trial and cannot be compelled to testify against himself. That girl's trial was invalid; as soon as I asked Whichello, 'You mean you asked her questions *after* you decided she was a suspect?' and he said 'Yes'—that's when her trial was illegal. They knowingly allowed her to incriminate herself. Prosecutors in those days didn't want to get at the truth; they just wanted to *win*, and would do anything to win.

"Before I started to argue this point of law in the Finch-Tregoff trial, I had already filed a Writ of Certiorari with the Supreme Court of the United States to test this view and I knew the Supreme Court agreed because I talked with the Clerk of the Supreme Court, whom I knew at the time. I suspected that the Supreme Court was looking into this matter because the Justices may have been concerned about a pattern of behavior by government officials; people all over the country were being tricked or coerced into confessions or statements.

"One of my more memorable events of this case was presenting the matter to the Supreme Court; the writ was pending when I argued the point of law with the trial judge; he ruled in my client's favor that Exhibit 60 was inadmissable."

The Supreme Court petition was then withdrawn.

"My arguments were what they used later to set up the Miranda case. After the first trial, I wasn't as involved, but I always had an interest in it."

I wondered why this was the only interview he had ever granted regarding any of his famous cases.

He delivered another lawyer joke, laughed, then looked away. Looking back at me, his face darkened; his eyes narrowed. He lifted his cane, planting it nearer to me by a few inches, then leaned forward. Robert Neeb was still angry.

"That girl was *framed*," he growled, slowly tapping the floor with his cane. His voice lowered even more. "She was innocent and the authorities *used* her to win, not to seek the truth."

SOUTH HILLS COUNTRY CLUB
MAY 25, 1992, 11:30 A.M.

"You know, Jones, I fought every liquor license applied for in this town. I spoke out against it. I knew if they got a liquor license, well, then there'd be dancing, and when there was dancing you'd have women. Then there'd be fights. I fought every liquor license. I told them not to be giving them out."

I was walking with Allen Sill in the parking lot of the club; our interview had concluded, so I thought.

"You told me it's going to take you two years to finish this book. What's going to take so long?" He looked angry. I felt intimidated by the man who had been West Covina's Police Chief during three decades.

"Chief," impulse framed a question, "what would you do if Dr. Finch were here, right now, and I introduced you to him?"

"Why, I'd shake his hand." Sill's stride was regular, never missing a beat. "Then I'd tell him he ought to be dead. Her too. Tregoff ought to be dead, too. That's how I was brought up: If you take another person's life, you pay for it with your own."

LARKHILL DRIVE
WEST COVINA, CALIFORNIA
APRIL 15, 1992, 10:30 A.M.

"Choc-o-mints?" I asked. Dan Leonard and I were at the Larkhill address to take some photographs of him where his adolescent world had been excited by the prospect of becoming a policeman if he could just "find that gun." I had asked him to wear his captain's uniform. We had been talking of his plans for retirement, in two years.

"Yeah, choc-o-mints." He was holding a brown cylinder, three inches long, three quarters of an inch in diameter. As he shoved it closer to me, I noticed the ends were capped with rough silver disks.

"They were a chocolate-flavored Life-Saver. They don't make them anymore. I've saved these for, well, almost thirty-five years now. Can you believe some idiot at the station today asked me if he could eat one?" His head shook slowly from side to side.

"Well, I guess I do sort of remember them, Dan. And they were good as I recall." I humored him as I matched my camera's dust cap to the lens.

"You asked me to think about how such a thing as the Finch murder could happen. My personal opinion, and I think I've seen it all in thirty years of police work, is that people are capable of almost anything if they are under enough pressure. Greed is the great motivator. Barbara Jean had all of his assets tied up. He had to go to her every month to get his paycheck. There he was with a beautiful girl friend he wanted to take care of. He was desperate."

443

We were walking back to our cars, on a walkway lined by some of the area's many eucalyptus trees; now thirty years taller, their leaves whispered in the slightest of breezes.

Dan looked at the cylinder, now held close to his face. A smile eased to the sides of his mouth.

"These are no ordinary choc-o-mints." He was singing his words, teasing, sounding like a teenager.

"Okay, Dan. What is so special about them."

"I stole them from Dr. Finch's clinic when I was about, oh, twelve years old, I guess. They used to have mints and gum for sale in a little rack in the reception room. I didn't have much money in those days."

I looked: Dan's face showed no guilt. His voice hinted no remorse. He waited, then glanced at my camera.

"What do you say we get a picture of them." I snapped a photo and memorialized his prize as he smiled broadly, holding the cylinder close to his cheek. We started walking again.

"If Dr. Finch does allow you to interview him, Jim, let me know and I'll give you these to give back to him. I don't know why I never ate them.

"And maybe you could ask him," he continued, "you know, see if he'll tell you, well, where anybody might... Oh, never mind, I guess."

I told him Finch had not responded to three of my requests for interviews. Dan was quiet. As we walked, I thought of something. "Dan, why did you save those choc-o-mints for all these years?" I looked back; he hadn't heard.

He was behind me, walking slower, looking to the left of the walkway, into the thick Boston Ivy. He seemed to study every leaf and stem, and every space between.

Dan Leonard with his Choc-o-mints and Jimmy Keith.
Finch driveway in back.

**NEAR THE FORMER HOME OF
STEVE AND NADINE HAYS
COVINA, CALIFORNIA
APRIL 17, 1992
9:30 A.M.**

"She loved him. That's how she got involved." Nadine was giving me the verdict of the neighborhood.

"Ask anybody who was around. Carole was just eighteen years old when she got mixed up with Finch. What does an eighteen-year-old girl know about such things?"

"That's right," Steve echoed. "You know something else—"

"Plus a couple of other things. He was a spoiled brat. He'd always gotten things his way, always," Nadine continued, "and I think everybody got a little greedy. Even Barbara Jean may have been lured away from Lyle by all the money.

445

And then there was the big houses with the swimming pools and all. Yep, greed played a part in it, too. That's what we women of the neighborhood thought."

Steve nodded.

six

Phone Calls from Sweden

THURSDAY, AUGUST 6, 1992
WEST COVINA, CALIFORNIA
5:00 A.M.

"YOU KNOW, MY ten years there were like ten years that were lost out of my life." I had telephoned Marie Anne in Sweden. We had talked almost four hours by now. "It has been hard for me to share my experiences with my friends here. It was all so long ago and so far away." She was finishing telling how the marriage to her first husband, an American, had ended in divorce in the mid-sixties. "I worked at Lincoln National in Torrance," she told me, "until about 1968. Then I returned to Sweden."

We talked about her job. She worked in the International Department of one of Europe's largest banks.

Her second marriage, to a Swede, also ended in divorce. It produced a daughter, now 18. "It was my daughter's birthday when you called the other day," Marie said. "And I remember thinking that I was her age when all this happened. After you called, she asked me to tell her about it. I don't know if this 'talking about things' is such a good idea. It doesn't make any difference." She sounded sad, hopeless.

"Marie." I was surprised at her answer. "You mean to tell me you've never talked to your daughter about this?"

447

"Well," she said, "I told her I was over there once, and that there was some trouble, you know."

"Have you ever talked to anyone about what you went through? Your mother or father, your brother or sister?"

"I didn't want to bother anybody with it. I was the oldest, you know. After my parents were divorced in 1954, I had to help quite a bit with the household. My Mother didn't have it so good. The family had enough problems."

"You must have a best friend," I tried again. Had this experience been locked in the Swedish girl all this time?

"Oh yes, it is the same person I came to America with in 1958. She was getting married to a man in Pasadena. Stewart was his name. I was to go along so she wouldn't feel alone. She has ended up back in Sweden, too."

"Well, have you ever talked to her about what happened?" I persisted.

"Well no. She was too busy with her own life at the time, and I only see her about once a year now. We have other things to talk about. I guess you are the first person I have ever talked to about this, you know, as far as my feelings are concerned."

She kept talking.

"I found the letter Barbara Jean wrote to me in 1958. It is the one outlining my duties and how much they were to pay me.

"You know, I have dreams about living back there in that house with Mrs. Finch. Dr. Finch is not in the picture for some reason. It's just the two of us, Barbara Jean and me, taking care of the little boy and Patti. They were such lovely children, and they were all just taken away from me so abruptly that night. I barely got to say good-bye to either of them. The last I remember of Raymie was that he was giving me his cat, so I could protect it. And I dream about the day I got her letter, saying they wanted to hire me for the job.

"Sometimes I still have nightmares about what happened. I wake scared. Or I'll see something that reminds me of that night. I think that if I could go back and talk to everyone, to the children, to the grandparents next door—they loved those children so much—if I could just talk to the people. Of course, it's hard to realize that many of them are dead, and the others are so old."

"What happened with your lawsuit, the one against Dr. Finch?"

"I think it was two hundred dollars, or so, that I got. That was all. Just what was owed me for my wages."

She took an uncustomary pause.

"What's Dr. Finch doing now? Is he out of prison?"

"He was paroled in 1971. He does not want to be interviewed." Dr. Finch had been at San Quentin, then was transferred to Tehachapi in March of 1967. In July of 1968 he was sent to the minimum security prison in Chino. His parole of 1971 lasted for six years. His sentence was discharged on September 28, 1977. He stayed in Missouri until 1983.

"I was afraid of him from the start. He gave me goose bumps. He never looked at me, even when he was speaking to me. I always thought he had the coldest eyes." Her voice lowered.

There was another pause. I waited.

"And the girl, his girl friend?" she asked.

"She was paroled in May of 1969, soon after she was eligible," I told her. "She doesn't want to talk to me, either."

"I can understand that. Sometimes you just want to leave things in the past."

There was a pause, then Marie spoke again.

"You know, I guess I thought that if I didn't talk about it, it would just go away. Somebody told me that 'time heals all.' But I don't think it does. I still feel guilty about what happened to Barbara Jean. I feel like it was my fault, that I could have done something different to prevent it.

"She was so certain that she was going to die. She told me she knew for sure that she wasn't going to live until

Christmas. She was so sure, so sure. And she knew it would be on a weekend, also. She was never there on the weekends. She would always make sure we had enough groceries, make sure I knew where she would be, then she would leave. Why she was home that weekend I don't know.

"It will be good to see how you summarize everything that happened. It was all such a blur, being there at the time. I had no conception of what was going on around me. Nobody thought of me. I had no money; I had to support myself by working. I was all alone. And then I would have to tell my story over and over again to these lawyers, and they were good lawyers who tried to confuse me."

Marie Anne had a crystal clear memory of most events, but curiously had none of some critical moments of the night of July 18, 1959. She did not, for instance, remember if Patti had been with her when she walked back outside to look for Barbara Jean.

"Barbara Jean was more than just an employer to me. She would confide in me often, about her problems. I trusted her. It is hard for me to trust people now. I'd rather keep my problems to myself, take care of things myself, you know. It is good to be self-sufficient, you know, not to have to rely on others for things."

Marie had most of the elements of post traumatic stress syndrome—after thirty-three years. We were to talk for hours and hours; she eventually began to incorporate her experience into her present life.

"Why was this such a big deal?" she asked me.

"I used to think that most of the attention was generated by the fact that Finch was a doctor. You know, Marie Anne, any time a doctor kills anybody, especially his wife, it's big news."

"Was that all?" she asked.

"I'm not sure. It seems that about this time many were starting to have doubts about some of our institutions. You know, the placid secure years of the Eisenhower administration ended with headlines like 'Ike Lied About Gary Powers.' Russia had launched the first satellite. And there were seeds of unrest in the youth, in their music, and in their dress. Conformity was being challenged. And the world was starting to hate America for the first time. There had been demonstrations against Eisenhower and Nixon during their world tours. And as the Finch-Tregoff trials ended, Kennedy was beginning to grapple with the Communist threats in Laos, Berlin, and Cuba."

"But, why so much press? Why were people from all over the world writing stories about us?" she asked.

"Who knows for sure?" I answered. "Maybe people wished for at least a couple of institutions to stay safe.

Maybe they were hoping families couldn't be tempted apart, and doctors could be trusted, even in the worst of times.

"You know, *Life* magazine, in its February '60 story, had an interesting subheading." I was sitting next to a stack of periodicals I'd gathered. "Here it is. The Fascinating Finch Affair Absorbs the Nation.' There's a picture of some of the spectators. You remember. You must have seen all the people who would mass outside the courthouse, just hoping for a look at Dr. Finch and Carole Tregoff."

"Yes, there were so many reporters and so many curious people."

"Well, to me anyway, this picture doesn't show just curious people." It was the picture of four women and one man that spread across pages twenty-two and twenty-three of the issue. "To me, they look worried, as though wondering what was happening to their reliable, predictable world."

"What do you mean?" she asked.

"Let me explain this way. I had some friends over recently. They brought their children, about four and five years old, who began to look at some old photo scrapbooks I have.

After looking at all the black and white pictures of the '50s, then the color ones from the '60s, when I was in college, they asked, 'Hey, when did the world change from black and white to color?' I explained, of course, that it was just the photographs that were black and white—not the world.

"But, you know, in a way I wonder if they were right. Maybe the world, in the '50s, was black and white. People trusted their doctors and stayed married. Moms were there when kids came home from school, and Dads came home from offices to catch up on family news over dinner, when the TV was off. The world was safe and predictable. You know, people felt safe if things were black and white. Maybe it was easier to trust that way.

"I'll send you a copy of this picture. These people—well, they just look worried to me."

"And I'll send you a copy of the letter Mrs. Finch wrote to me before I was hired. There I was, a seventeen-year-old girl about to come to America—California no less. I felt like I was getting a fresh start, you know, a second chance to make up for the sad times of my parents' divorce. I was so excited. The dream I still have about that day is so clear. Our mailbox was next to the street—"

EARLY AUGUST, 1958
LIDHOLM RESIDENCE
GOTENBURG, SWEDEN

A seventeen-year-old Swedish girl is running back from the household's mail box. A long-anticipated letter has arrived; she holds it high, hoping those inside might see. Finding her mother in the kitchen, she waves the still-sealed parcel and explains; the doctor's wife has finally written. The girl hugs her mother, then bolts excitedly to her room. She is certain the American family will hire her as governess for their children; it has to be the start of a new life, a happier life, in America.

She dives onto her small bed, tearing into the envelope:

July 22, 1958

Dear Marie Anne:

Thank you for writing to us to let us know a little about you. We are pleased you are able to read, write and speak English so well.

Hugh probably told you a lot about us, but I do want to let you know a little further of your duties here before you decide definitely to come. We have two children, a boy who is five years old and a girl almost eleven. My husband and I are frequently away from home and we especially want a reliable girl here to look after the children when we are not here. I also would want you go help with the house-work. We live very informally, but the house is rather large and it does require a lot of work keeping it clean and in order. There is also a moderate amount of ironing. When we are not at home, you would be required to prepare simple meals for the children and yourself. Do you think you will be able to do these things?

We have a swimming pool, but the children swim so that would be no worry to you. It would be an advantage if you can swim. My daughter has been taking ballet lessons for two years now and loves it so you and she would have a lot of fun together with your dancing. She also loves any phase of art.

Have you learned to drive a car yet? It would help if you could as there would be times when I would want you to pick up my boy at school for me. Also it would be easier for you on your days off to get around. Perhaps Hugh could later help you find a not too expensive car.

We would want you here five days a week, taking Monday and Tuesday off (or possibly Monday and Thursday). We would pay you $100.00 per month.

Enclosed are the certificates for the American Consulate General as you requested. I do hope these are satisfactory. If there is anything further you require, please let us know.

Very truly yours,

Barbara Finch

Marie-Anne Lidholm
c. 1960. *Getty.*

CPSIA information can be obtained
at www.ICGtesting.com
Printed in the USA
BVHW071224050121
596834BV00001B/53

9 780615 481005